D1418152

Between Qur'an and Crown

.

Between Qur'an and Crown

•

The Challenge of Political Legitimacy in the Arab World

•

Tamara Sonn

Westview Press

Boulder • San Francisco • Oxford

For John

Copyright © 1990 by Westview Press, Inc.

Published in 1990 in the United States of America by Westview Press, Inc., 5500 Central Avenue, Boulder, Colorado 80301, and in the United Kingdom by Westview Press, Inc., 36 Lonsdale Road, Summertown, Oxford OX2 7EW

Library of Congress Cataloging-in-Publication Data
Sonn, Tamara.
    Between Qur'an and crown: the challenge of political legitimacy in the Arab world / Tamara Sonn.
        p.   cm.
    Includes bibliographical references.
    ISBN 0-8133-7579-7
    1. Arab countries—Politics and government.   2. Islam and politics—Arab countries.   I. Title.   II. Series.
DS38.9.S58   1990
320.956—dc20
                                                                                    90-12048
                                                                                    CIP

Printed and bound in the United States of America

The paper used in this publication meets the requirements of the American National Standard for Permanence of Paper for Printed Library Materials Z39.48-1984.

10   9   8   7   6   5   4   3   2   1

Contents

Preface

The purpose of this book is to give some perspective on the apparently radical changes that have taken place in the Arab world over the past century. In particular, its goal is to explain the current disarray in which Arab states find themselves, to suggest a reason for the Arab states' inability to work together to solve regional problems such as underdevelopment and Palestinian homelessness, and to show some hopeful directions for the future.

The book begins by recounting how the Arab world got into its current condition. Much of this story has been told before. I owe a great debt to historians Philip Hitti, Marshall Hodgson, Albert Hourani, Halil Inalcik, Richard Mitchell, and George Antonius, on whose works the historical account is largely based. I have recounted the tales here for readers who may not be familiar with the overall development of modern Arab history as well as for those who are already initiated into Arab studies but who might appreciate a ready reference to the broad outlines of the story. The historical account is designed not for detailed analysis but to highlight those salient developments that gave form to the contemporary Arab milieu.

The roots of the modern Arab states, like those of modern Europe, go back to the transition from a centrally organized and religiously legitimated imperial structure to a decentralized system of autonomous regional units, that is, to the rise of states and the concomitant separation of religious from political authority. For that reason, the historical account begins with the demise of central caliphal authority in the medieval Islamic world.

The contemporary Islamic world is characterized by a rejection of political forms that it considers at once Western, secular, atheistic, and immoral. That rejection is not so much a reasoned response to the real problems at hand or a practical program for the solution of those problems as it is a reaction against the machinations of European nations that are responsible for so many of the problems facing the Third World in general and the Arab world in particular. What is more, separation of religious from political authority—the root of secular political forms—

is neither atheistic, immoral, nor intrinsically Western or Christian. Indeed, the Arab world is undergoing the same processes that produced the political forms assumed in Europe. I have therefore introduced this book with an account of the development of secularism in the Western world.

The Introduction has a dual purpose. It is by no means meant to compare Arab history with European history, and it is certainly not intended to set out the latter as a model for the former. Rather, it is to remind Western readers of the relative novelty of nationalism in their own heritage and of the extreme difficulty their forebears had in establishing suitable political forms for geopolitically limited states. For Western readers the Introduction is a pedagogical device—to provide a basis of familiar things from which to delve into the unfamiliar. More importantly, for both Western and non-Western readers, it is meant to explicate the nature of the developments both regions have experienced and continue to struggle with.

In the European experience, modern forms of political authority evolved in two stages: first, from the centrally governed Holy Roman Empire to the political disunity of the early Protestant Reformation and, second, from that disunity to sovereign nation-states. The central authority of the Holy Roman Empire had been legitimated by the church's claim to ultimate authority through universal religious validity. But as the economic and political unity of the empire dissipated, that legitimacy was questioned. Protestant leaders criticized the church's failure to maintain political and economic stability. They proposed alternative interpretations of religious truth that served to legitimate new, regionally autonomous political formations. Then, as these new formations themselves evolved into sovereign states based on geographic, linguistic, and ethnic affinities, their claims to legitimacy also evolved. The new national entities no longer required the sort of universal legitimacy accorded by religious truth. Instead, the right to authorize government was claimed by the governed people. In this way claims to political authority automatically became geographically limited, political sovereignty lost its autocracy, and the nature of citizenship rights became a major issue.

The overall development, then, was from an empire based on universally valid religio-political claims, through an intermediary stage of religious factionalism and political disunity, to geographically limited nation-states with correspondingly limited claims to political legitimacy. The same process is being followed in the modern Middle East, but with at least one major difference. Instead of evolving into independent nation-states, the Middle East's period of political disunity led to a protracted stage of foreign intervention and imperial domination. This has resulted in a strong tendency to revert to the first stage of religio-political organization. After an initial period of experimentation with modern political forms, reassertion of the unity and primacy of Islam as the basis of political legitimacy has become the order of the day.

Unfortunately, this view represents a misunderstanding of the nature of modern political organization and certainly of the separation of religious from political authority. That distinction was essential for the development of stability among the geographically limited states that characterize modern political order. Religiously legitimated government, barring any sort of built-in limiting factor such as ethnic or tribal affiliation, is suitable for a potentially universal political entity, that is, an empire. When the religion on which the legitimacy is based claims universal applicability, it is by nature expansive, rejecting the inviolability of geographic borders on which national stability is based. The return to Islam as the legitimating basis of government therefore has serious repercussions for Middle Eastern states seeking political stability. Leaders who base their leadership on Islamic authenticity—as well as the popular movements such leaders inspire—understandably appear threatening to other leaders in the Arab world. Thus the conflict between universal religious claims of political legitimacy and the limited nature of political legitimacy required by modern states creates a constant state of insecurity among Middle Eastern leaders and, I believe, characterizes their current instability.

On the brighter side, there are significant movements in the Arab and Islamic world that recognize the need to develop Islamic political forms to suit the contemporary geopolitical context. The book therefore closes with a chapter outlining some of those formulations. As noted in Chapter Nine, it is too early to determine just how much influence such attempts will have. Nonetheless, their very existence indicates positive direction to the search for political stability in the Arab world.

Tamara Sonn

Note: Standard transliteration has been used for Arabic terms except in cases in which a term or name has acquired a common transliteration in English, as in the names Hussein (Husayn), Qadhafi (Qadhdhafi), Nasser (Gamal 'Abd al-Nasir), Alawite ('Alawi), al-Banna (al-Banna'), etc. The apostrophe (') is used to indicate both the 'ain and the hamza.

Acknowledgments

I thank the many people who made this book possible, including Nancy Martin, of St. John Fisher College Library, and the St. John Fisher College Presidential Research Award Committee, whose support made this project possible; Dr. George Irani, who supplied the title for the work; professors John Esposito and John Morreall, and Victoria Varga, who furnished valuable criticisms; and Frank Mullaney of Harvard University for his careful proofreading and helpful suggestions.

In particular, I acknowledge the inspiration of my mentor, Professor Fazlur Rahman, to whom the final chapter is dedicated.

T. S.

CHAPTER ONE

Introduction:
The Development
of Secularism

*W*hen interminable and ferocious religious wars threatened to destroy human happiness and civilization, the movement of Enlightenment, the wave of rationalism which started about 1680 and dominated the eighteenth century, led to the depolitization of religion. In this process, religion did not lose its true dignity; it remained one of the great spiritual forces, comforting and exalting the human soul. But it lost the element of coercion which had been so "natural" to it for many centuries.
—Hans Kohn[1]

Sayyid Qutb, ideological successor to the founder of the Muslim Brotherhood and a leading exponent of Islamic antisecularism, has called for the establishment of Islamic government. He says it is necessary in order to carry on Islam's "total revolution" against exclusive domination of the earth by humans. Laws devised by human beings, he thinks, are inevitably idolatrous.[2] Ayatollah Khomeini claims that secularism "means the abandonment of Islam; it means burying Islam in our cells in the madrasa!"[3] Even the late Fazlur Rahman, known as the most moderate of Islamic modernists, said, "[S]ecularism destroys the sanctity and universality (transcendence) of all moral values. . . . Secularism is necessarily atheistic."[4] These and other antisecularist opinions typical among modern Islamic thinkers are based on the assumption that secularism is an ideology, complete with metaphysical presumptions, rather than simply a political form. These Islamic thinkers

1

impute ontological conviction to those who enjoin the separation of religious from political authority, and they think the decision to remove institutionalized religion from the political arena implies the condemnation of religious pursuits in any sphere, a complete denial of religious values. Secularism, they believe, is antireligious and therefore immoral and atheistic.

Historian of ethics Max L. Stackhouse criticizes those who hold such opinions for having "ignored the ways in which key *theological* and *religious* movements provided the decisive impetus for the desanctification of these areas of life, not to diminish the role of religion, but to establish it more firmly at its proper level" (emphasis in the original).[5] Stackhouse is referring to the historical development of European secularism, in which religious reformers reacted against the increasingly secular concerns of the papacy. The Holy Roman Empire had been established as a sort of compromise in the struggle between kings and popes to fill the vacuum of power left by the decline of the Roman Empire. The Roman popes were themselves involved in conflict with the Byzantine authorities over supremacy within the church at the time. When Rome sought the assistance of European tribal chieftains in that dispute, a symbiotic relationship was born, in which the expansionist aspirations of the tribal leaders were supported by the universalist claims of papal leadership. But as universalism lost ground to regionalism—i.e., as the feudal economic basis of the Holy Roman Empire was replaced by the growing mercantile and capitalist economy of the later Middle Ages—both emperor and pope struggled to maintain the power they had achieved. Reformation leaders criticized the popes for such worldly concerns and, in their effort to resanctify the papacy, called for the separation of religious from political power. This was the original impulse of secularism.

The European Experience: From Empire to Nation-States

Strains Between Religious and Political Authorities. Feudal Europe was actually a transition between the potentially universal Roman Empire and the system of independent states of modern Europe.[6] It was the origin of the economic localism that led to the political localism called nationalism. But the transition was long and slow. Feudalism was a delicately balanced system of power and loyalties. Originally, someone would promise loyalty to a master in return for the right to earn a living from the master's land. (In feudal language, he pronounced himself the master's vassal in return for a benefice or fief.) Eventually, the vassal assumed greater responsibility for the administration and defense of the fief, freeing his lord (or suzerain) for other affairs. Every task that passed from lord to vassal was called an immunity. The lord's ability to maintain control over his vassals required a balance of immunities; if the vassal assumed too many immunities, he would become independent of his lord. Before feudalism could recede into history, therefore, economic circumstances had to tip in favor of the local vassals. But at least as important, political theory had to develop that would justify such limited, local authority. The longevity of feudal Rome and its universalist pretensions were largely due to the collusion of the church in supporting its political claim. As a result, before the localist or regionalist economy that supplanted the Holy Roman imperial economy could achieve political legitimacy, the universalist claims of Roman religio-politics had also to be replaced.

Christianity was established as the basis of political legitimacy in the fourth century. That was when Constantine, one of several heirs to the Roman imperial title, recognized that by championing the cause of the suffering Christians he could garner sufficient support to outdo his competitors. He could also make use of the Christian hierarchical system already in place throughout the Mediterranean lands to rebuild a basis of unity for Rome. Christian Rome was divided into four prefectures, each subdivided into twelve dioceses that were administered by vicars who looked to the bishop of Rome for guidance.[7] These positions were civilian, carefully separated from the military to avoid possible rebellion. Constantine could simply incorporate the vicars and the bishop of Rome into his administration and thus reunify Rome on an entirely new basis.[8] The only institution that transcended the localism of classical Rome's agricultural economy was the church. Thus, in the vacuum of power left by the crumbling classical empire, representatives of the church became the most respected local authorities.

There was another reason for the success of Constantine's strategy. The decline of ancient Rome had resulted in utter misery for its citizens. Historian Robert Lopez describes the fall of Rome as "an unexpected, almost unbelievable nightmare" for the majority of Roman citizens. Lopez cites Pope Gregory I, for instance, who testified that in Corsica people were forced to sell their children to meet the mounting tax burdens. Lopez also recounts church historian Bede the Venerable's (d. 735) tales of mass suicide: "After three years of drought, a terrible famine spread among the people and destroyed them. It is said that often forty or fifty people, exhausted by hunger, went together to a cliff top or to the sea and flung themselves over, holding hands."[9]

In the face of such terror, it is not surprising to find the populace seeking spiritual solace. There was as yet no split between religious and political authority in Roman history. The Roman emperor had been the *pontifex maximus*—the bridge between the gods and the people. Now the pope became the "pontiff." But there was a widening gap between heavenly and earthly things. When Saint Augustine provided the theological explanation for the terror of the times in his *De Civitate Dei* (428 C.E.), he established the basis for distinguishing between things of this world and things divine. Trying to console a populace bewildered by the fall of the empire, Augustine explained that the Roman Empire belonged to the *civitas terrena,* the kingdom of the earth. The church, by contrast, belonged to the *civitas dei,* the city of God. Ultimate human goals of perfect peace and justice were only to be found in the latter; what happened on earth really was not all that important. Augustine's explanation suited the times. It minimalized the significance of the radically changing political order and suggested that the changes were too overwhelming for the people to comprehend; better just to follow the church's teaching and hope for better times in the city of God. Thus were laid the foundations of Christian Rome's authoritarian control.

The church also played an essential political role in consolidating and expanding Roman sovereignty. Conversion to Christianity became an integral part of the successful annexation of conquered lands and subjugation of their inhabitants to a unified legal system. Many a Christian saint earned his title by contributing to these efforts. What was more, Christian clergy became trusted vassals. By the twelfth century the majority of important administrative positions and many local government positions were held by royally appointed clergy. The ubiquity of clergy in feudal government was such that they gave the English language its word for administrator: *clerk.* Even those clergy who were not actually royal agents were still considered the social elite. Monasteries were the centers of intellectual and cultural activity well into the thirteenth century.

And finally, the church played a pivotal role in providing land to be granted as benefices for the expanding feudal empire. Since the fourth century, the church had enjoyed special privileges. Constantine and his successors had given Christians favored status, and Theodosius I (r. ca. 379–395) had made Christianity the official religion of the empire. Therefore, although in the early fourth century Christians composed only about one-fifth of the population, the church was in control of the choicest lands. The Carolingians (Charlemagne's family) expropriated these lands to grant as benefices to vassals who would pledge their fidelity to the Carolingian empire.

In Christian Rome, therefore, political legitimacy was integrally related to spiritual authority. Just as in classical Rome, religious and political power were united. But it was no longer a simple identity, as it had been in the time of the caesars and, indeed, as it remained until Saint Augustine's revolutionary text. Now there were two separate sources of power—the king and the pope. Yet there was only one sphere in which both operated together. Sovereignty was shared or, more precisely, mutually supported. There were two sources of power but only one authority: the king as legitimated by the church. There was still no separation of spheres of authority as yet in the Christian church.

This is contrary to the belief that there is an inherent separation of church and state in Christianity that Saint Augustine merely made explicit.[10] Granted, Christianity had a heritage on which Augustine's separation of heaven and earth was based. Jesus had said his kingdom was not of this earth; he had also advocated rendering to Caesar the things that are Caesar's and to God the things that are God's. But that was not a political theory; it was simply a reflection of the Christians' *outré* status. They were outside the political order and did not appear to have hope of gaining political ascendancy. It was also a reflection of the Christian perception of God as a transcendent God of love who could not be identified with war-mongering power politics. Thus, when Christians did assume political power, they were heir to political practice as it existed at the time. And that was the religio-political model of classical Rome. As Hans Kohn says:

> State and church, empire and Christianity were indissolubly linked. There was an all-dominating recognition of the necessity of a universal empire, and this empire was by necessity Christian and Roman at the same time. In no walk of life was there any separation of the secular and temporal from the eternal, which at the same time was ecclesiastical.[11]

Nevertheless, now there were two persons wielding the universal religio-political claim; the dual-edged sword was no longer in the hands of one person—the emperor or the pharaoh or the *pontifex maximus.* The pope and the emperor each had a universal claim. Theoretically, they were neither separate nor equal. Of Saint Augustine's two cities, the divine one was given clear priority. The cooperation that bound the mundane and the spiritual in the early Christian empire, therefore, was bound to feel the strain of competition.

Initially the church's role in strengthening the Carolingian empire had been voluntary. But the church had never accepted state rule, as such. It had always resented any meddling in its affairs, such as in the church councils. The councils had been instituted by the emperor in order to maintain uniformity of doctrine in his realm. The emperor nominated the committees in charge, frequently presided over their proceedings, and maintained the right to accept or reject the councils' decisions. The bishops of Rome, therefore, tried to assert their supremacy by declaring that the Roman pontiff had the ultimate voice in defining church doctrine. They developed the doctrine of papal primacy, initially in response to the patriarchs of the eastern church, who considered themselves equal to the Roman authorities. The Roman popes, by contrast, claimed they not only were supreme in the Western church, but also were in fact the only true successors to Peter. The emperor was willing to support Pope Leo I's claim to the title of supreme priest with exclusive jurisdiction over the Western church (455 C.E.). But when, at the end of the fifth century, Pope Gelasius I claimed the bishops' power was "more weighty" even than that of kings, competition for universal control in Christian Rome was under way. The papal coronation of Charlemagne in 800 was actually both the high point of the papal-imperial cooperation and the beginning of the rivalry that would undo it. For Charlemagne, the coronation spectacle represented the height of his imperial pretensions. He was no longer content to be the leader in Europe; he chose to become "Emperor of the Romans," in conscious imitation of ancient Rome. For him the church was an aid to social stability within his Holy Roman Empire. For Pope Leo III (r. 795–816), however, the coronation was an effort to gain leverage over the king and become the arbiter of imperial authority, but the effort was unsuccessful. Charlemagne's fame spread far and wide as the emperor who controlled the papacy. His son Louis the Pious went so far as to abandon his title of king of the Franks and the Lombards; he called himself simply "emperor" and in 824 ordered that no pope should be consecrated before taking an oath of fidelity to the emperor. The popes would have to await the weakening of the emperors for their chance to reassert papal primacy.

The Emergence of Localism. The root of the weakening of the emperors lay in the incongruity of the kings' imperial claims and the administrative devices at hand. The emperors aspired to the power of ancient Rome, but they failed to implement Roman administrative methods. Doing so would have meant setting up a system of taxation and using the proceeds to employ a staff whose loyalty could be ensured through the threat of being fired. As well, the emperors needed a manipulable source of wealth that could be withdrawn when vassals' loyalty waned. But money was not the primary legal tender of medieval Europe. Instead, like the Merovingians before them, the Carolingians ended up spending their royal estates in return for loyalty. Once the lands had been granted they were essentially out of the emperor's control. As relatively self-sustaining agricultural units, many fiefs developed their own local governments congruent with their independent local economies and consequently felt no need for the imperial apparatus. Therefore, despite oaths of loyalty to the emperor—even witnessed by God under the threat of eternal perdition—there was little to keep these local units under any real central control.

Historical events further strained the Carolingian system. In the ninth and tenth centuries Europe was subjected to a wave of invasions. Scandinavians, Hungarians, Slavs, and even some renegades from the declining 'Abbasid Islamic empire descended upon the splintered feudal system. This resulted in accelerated decentralization as holders of benefices sold their loyalty to the highest bidder. Because the feudal lords' military services were at a premium under these circumstances, they could demand larger and larger grants in return for fewer services. Naturally, the central government receded farther into obscurity. The local vassals became paramount in their regions and came to rule with scarcely any reference to the interests of the sovereign.

Among the initial manifestations that localism was outstripping imperial centralism was the appearance of local languages. Latin remained the official language of the realm, but in the early ninth century, the church recommended that sermons be translated into local tongues so people could understand them. When the empire was split among Charlemagne's heirs in the mid-ninth century, the division was along linguistic protonational lines. The Treaty of Verdun assigned the French provinces to Charles the Bald and those entirely German to Louis the German.[12]

Perhaps of greatest significance to the decline of central authority and the emergence of localism was the evolution of mercantile capitalism. Since ancient Roman times, there had been some trade, although it was generally carried on as a sideline rather than a full-time occupation.[13] But significant mercantile activity appeared in the autonomous ports of Italy, such as Venice, Amalfi, Naples, and Gaeta, whose pivotal positions between the Byzantines (Eastern Rome), the Arabs, and Europe (Western Rome) gave them an unusual advantage, particularly during the crusades.

The crusades had begun in the late eleventh century during a spurt of religious zeal. A perfect example of the universalism of the Holy Roman Empire, the early crusades sought to conquer Jesus' homeland from the "infidel" Muslims. Participants were offered complete remission of punishment due in the afterlife for sins committed here and now, provided they died in battle. Eventually, however, the pious motivation of the crusades was overcome by the lucrative business opportunities they offered. Their spiritual benefit was institutionalized as a "plenary indulgence" and, in fact, became available on the open market for a price, to accommodate those whose domestic responsibilities prevented foreign adventure. The church ultimately banned the selling of indulgences, but the crusades continued, with manifestly commercial motives. The Fourth Crusade, for instance, was initiated by the Venetians, who recruited pious Christians to conquer Egypt. But when some thirty thousand volunteers answered the call, the Venetians were unable to afford sufficient transportation. Instead, they arranged to conquer Zara, just across the Adriatic. This worked out well for the Venetian merchants, because Zara was a serious commercial competitor. However, it was also Christian. The original goal of the crusades having been completely forgotten, the mercenaries then went on to conquer Christian Constantinople at the bequest of the dethroned Greek prince Alexis.[14]

In any event, the crusades unintentionally opened up vast new worlds to the emerging merchant economy. Eventually, in fact, mercantilism was to become the dominant economic feature of Europe. By the fourteenth century, it would reach the very center of everyday life, for it fostered the major sociopolitical development of medieval Europe: the growth of towns.

The Development of Towns. Towns began to emerge in the eleventh and twelfth centuries. It was then that merchants became recognizable as a new social class, an addition to the traditional tripartite social division of noble, cleric, and serf. The term *bourgeois* appeared to describe the new communities of merchants who used the old Roman towns, *bourgs,* as bases of operation. At that time strains had already begun to appear within the feudal manor populations. Their numbers had nearly doubled as the various foreign invaders mentioned above eventually settled and became attached to the land. As vassals achieved virtual independence from the emperor, they had tended to reassess the system of taxation. In the days of strong central leadership, taxes (in the form of goods and services) were required of the manor as a whole. But the newly autonomous lords began to assess individual fields and households within the manor. The net effect of this development was that the communal mentality, with its emphasis on survival of the individual clan or extended family, was replaced by a greater concern with the nuclear family as the basic unit of society. Furthermore, under the new system it became customary for a family's land to remain under its control from one generation to the next, heightening the sense of proprietorship at the expense of communal, manorial identity. Therefore, when the lords did attempt to exercise their right of prior ownership, for instance, in times of war, the peasantry tended to resist with growing ferocity.

The introduction of money as legal tender for the payment of feudal dues in the twelfth and thirteenth centuries further increased the peasants' sense of independence. It allowed them to behave as voluntary renters rather than indentured serfs and gave them the incentive to rebel when they disapproved of the lord's policies. In fact, by the thirteenth century the feudal manor was irrevocably fragmented, and peasant rebellions were commonplace.

To the former serfs, then, the newly forming cities proved a powerful draw. *Stadtluft macht frei*—"City air makes one free"—became a popular maxim. In cities the peasants found opportunities for freedom and for learning new skills that gave them an alternative to serfdom. What was more, cities—the creation of merchants—developed a very different ethos from that of the feudal manor. Feudal knights achieved their social and political status by conquering land. Chivalry was the order of their day—the arts of warfare. Merchants, by contrast, needed peaceful relations among population centers. They needed safe roads and good communications. Therefore, they worked to create governments that would enhance the flow of trade and the development of industry. By the eleventh century merchants had begun to form their own social orders, and craftsmen followed suit in the thirteenth century. These groups began to demand the repeal of arbitrary tolls and tariffs, which they felt impeded economic development. They insisted on a voice in shaping their own government. When the lords, who technically still controlled the towns, balked, revolts in the cities became common as well.

The feudal system was thus beset from the countryside and in the towns, and the emerging urban powers would eventually bring the old system down. Towns and local kings, whose power had been eclipsed by their wayward feudal vassals, tended to work together. The kings made use of the townspeoples' newly developed administrative skills as well as their liquid wealth, replacing the nobles and the clergy in key positions and hiring mercenary armies to replace the feudal cavalry. Clearly, this was the beginning of territorial consolidation. Regions sharing economic, linguistic, and now political affinities began to take precedence over the archaic universalist claims of the Holy Roman Empire.

Pope and Emperor Compete for Universal Control. The feudal economic system had been transitional; it had been effective in rebuilding the Western Roman empire but had outlived its usefulness. Yet neither the popes nor the emperors seemed to grasp that reality. Instead, each attempted to consolidate his universal claim at the expense of the other. As noted above, the popes chafed under the control of the emperors and awaited the chance to reclaim the "plenitude of power." A period of papal weakness had allowed the emperors to appoint and depose popes. But a reform movement in the late ninth and early tenth centuries culminated in the creation of the College of Cardinals (1059). With that, the papacy—in a decisive step in the separation of religion from politics—declared its independence from the emperor and claimed that only church officials could elect a pope.

But the papacy's independence was challenged when Pope Gregory VII tried to extend his power to the appointment of bishops. Because bishops were traditionally among the emperors' most loyal vassals, the reigning Emperor Henry IV not only saw Gregory's move as a direct challenge to his power but also accused him of trying to secularize the empire. When Henry therefore refused to comply with the order, Gregory promptly excommunicated the emperor and absolved all his subjects from loyalty to him. Because the feudal lords—delighting in their own independence—sided with the pope, Henry had no choice but to beg the pope for forgiveness.

The papacy appeared to be at its height. Pope Gregory IX (r. 1227–1241) reasserted the "Donation of Constantine," in which Constantine was said to have granted Pope Sylvester and all the pope's successors spiritual authority throughout Christianity, as well as complete dominion over Rome, Italy, and the Western part of the empire. Pope Boniface VIII (r. 1294–1303) issued the papal bull *Unam Sanctam,* in which he claimed, "This one and unique church has one body, one head—not two heads, like a monster—namely, Christ, and Christ's vicar Peter, and Peter's successor, as the Lord Himself has said to Peter: Feed my sheep." The bull cited Saint Paul: "There is no power but of God: the powers that be are ordained of God" (Romans 13:1); and Jeremiah: "I have this day set thee over the nations and over the kingdoms" (Jeremiah 1:10).[15] But the major issue of the age had not been addressed. The question was not whether the pope or the emperor was to retain ultimate control; in fact, universalism was giving way to localism and neither official was destined to complete dominance. The regional alliances of townspeople and kings continued to gain ground against both imperial and papal claims. In England, Henry II placed limits on judicial appeals to Rome with the Constitutions of Clarendon (1164) and reclaimed control over the election of bishops. In France, Philip Augustus defeated the Holy Roman Emperor Otto IV (r. 1198–1215) to establish the basis for the independent French monarchy. Meanwhile, Pope Innocent III (r. 1198–1216) centralized and expanded church taxes on both clergy and laity, charged fees for holding church office, and assumed exclusive right to absolve sins—i.e., spiritual as opposed to civil crimes—and to issue dispensations. Thus everyone had to deal directly with Rome for pardons or exemptions. And to make sure his financial matters were handled efficiently, Innocent III employed Lombard merchants and bankers. In support of this powerful structure, he elaborated on the doctrine of papal plenitude of power, canonized those whose virtues seemed supportive of ecclesiastical power, and established a system of his own benefices and loyal servants. Pope Urban IV (r. 1261–1264) went even farther, creating for the church its own law court, the Rota Romana, and institutionalizing clerical taxation.

But with these actions the church placed itself squarely in competition with other political powers and opened itself up to criticism for corruption and impiety. Such criticism became apparent as early as the tenth-century reform movement, when pious churchmen attempted to resanctify the clergy. Some believers, however, were not satisfied with these efforts and established their own religious communities. The Albigensians or Cathars ("pure ones") of southern France, for instance, called for a simple and pure religious life on the ascetic model of Jesus and his apostles. They believed the church had deviated from true Christianity in teaching the incarnation of God, among other things, and called for a return to true belief. Naturally, they were condemned as heretics. So intent was Innocent III on church unity that he declared a crusade—technically designed to combat non-Christians—against the Albigensians in 1209. The sect was finally eradicated as a political entity following a series of massacres that ended in 1226. Pope Gregory IX (r. 1227–1241) continued Innocent's policies. He introduced the use of the Inquisition (originally a formal tribunal used by bishops to maintain discipline within their dioceses) as a means not only to detect and punish heresy, but also to suppress dissent within the church.

Soon other reform movements began to appear. The Waldensians, the Beguines, and the Beghards, for instance, like the Albigensians, called for a return to the simple, Christian life of poverty in imitation of the example of Jesus. Pope Innocent III recognized the expediency of channeling such sentiments and sanctioned two official mendicant organizations, the Franciscans and the Dominicans. In dramatic contrast to the splendor of the regular clergy, these "friars" and "monks" lived in poverty. They dressed in humble robes and went about preaching ecclesiastical rectitude, supporting themselves by working or begging. The creation of these orders has been called "a response to heterodox piety as well as an answer to lay criticism of the worldliness of the papal monarchy," especially that of Pope Innocent III.[16] The new orders were answerable solely to the pope, so much so that soon after the death of Saint Francis—whose immense popularity Innocent acknowledged by declaring him a saint just two years after he died—the pope abandoned the founder's own rules and replaced them with guidelines he considered more practical for spreading church policy. Eventually, those among Saint Francis's followers who refused the new rules were condemned, and the previous Franciscan ideal of absolute poverty was declared un-Christian. The Dominicans fared somewhat better, concerning themselves only with correcting doctrinal error in the community. In fact, they were instrumental in combating dissent in southern France and served the staff of the Inquisition.

Criticism of the Imperial Church. The church, however, could not stem the tide of criticism begun in the pietist movements. The fourteenth and fifteenth centuries were pivotal. As economic decentralization continued, local and regional authorities continued to consolidate their power and to develop the administrative infrastructure to wield it. Social upheaval attendant upon the breakup of feudalism was exacerbated by almost constant warfare as regional powers sought to define their respective territories. The Hundred Years' War (1337–1453) is perhaps the best example. The British king held several French territories as fiefs from the French king, and the English monarchy claimed hereditary right to the French throne. The century-long dispute over British and French claims and counterclaims makes the recent Iran-Iraq war seem petty. The war was brutal, especially in its later years, when gunpowder and artillery were introduced; it was convoluted—among other subplots, France tried to subvert British power by supporting revolts against English control in Scotland; and it was ultimately futile. There was no way either country could exercise the sovereignty it claimed over territory whose economy it did not control. Yet even war's terror paled next to the bubonic plague—the Black Death—that struck Europe in the mid-fourteenth century. In a population already weakened by famines during the early fourteenth century and unhygienically overcrowded in the new urban centers, as many as one out of three lost their lives in a two-year span.

It is no wonder the population believed it was being punished by God—and thus criticized the church for failing to provide proper leadership. Despite the overall economic, social, and political changes that were occurring, the populace at large was still, above all, Christian. There were still no officially recognized national states, and there was still no institution claiming priority over the church. Historian Robert Lopez summarizes:

> God was called to witness in every agreement; a blessing was asked on every enterprise; a pious pretext was sought for every amusement; time was measured in canonical hours. There was an exorcism for every illness, a formula to excommunicate the insects which devoured the harvest.

God was invoked to establish the truth in legal proceedings, by means of the duel for nobles and by the ordeal of red-hot iron, fire or water for the commoners; or if these methods were discarded so as "not to tempt the Lord," by the sacred oath of the interested parties on the Gospels or on a relic.[17]

Two common reactions to the plague, for instance, were self-flagellation and condemnation of Jews. The self-flagellants would parade through the town, beating their bodies until they bled, hoping to atone for whatever sins they may have committed. Surely they had erred somehow, for their religion did not allow them to believe the omnipotent God would allow this scourge for no reason, and medical knowledge had not advanced far enough to convince them there may have been another cause of their problems. The only really obvious offense they could think of was allowing non-Christians to live peacefully—if unequally—among them. The Jews, after all, had killed Jesus, the Christians reminded themselves, and refused to submit to the authority of the pope; perhaps God was punishing Europe for not avenging these "infidels." Anti-Jewish riots, often incited by the flagellants, occurred in several cities.

Fortunately, there were more intellectual responses to those troubled times, most of which took into consideration the political entanglements of the church. Innocent III's insistence on central papal control and the rising tide of localism inevitably clashed in Italy. When the popes were defending themselves against the emperors, they found many supporters in their native Italy. But when the emperors faded into emerging German politics and the popes continued to assert their dominance in Italy, they found themselves in political competition with their former allies. Pope Boniface VIII (r. 1294–1303), for instance, was a member of a noble family, the Gaetani. Their strongest rivals, the Colonnas, were followers of the Spiritual Franciscans and, in an effort to weaken the Gaetani position, accused Boniface of heresy, simony, and even the murder of his predecessor, the pious Pope Celestine V. Boniface's *Unam Sanctam,* claiming there is only one sovereign and that is the church, only further infuriated papal critics. The Colonnas joined forces with the French king, who was already annoyed with the pope's attempts to control his clergy, and totally routed the pope's forces in 1303. Boniface's successors were thus forced to come to terms with the French monarchy and to try to avoid entanglements in Italy. To this end, they established the papal court at Avignon in southeastern France.

The "Avignon papacy" lasted from 1309 to 1377, initiating a period of French domination of the College of Cardinals. If a pope challenged the French king, the king simply deposed him and set up his own pope. At one point there were three different popes contending for authority, marking one of the lowest points in the history of the papacy. But the weakened papacy did force the church to seriously scrutinize its organization in light of sociopolitical reality, and that effort produced some of the most important thinkers of the age.

For example, William of Ockham (d. 1349), an English Franciscan, defended the rights of royalty vis-à-vis the pope. For this he earned excommunication but also a lasting place in the history of philosophy. Ockham supported his convictions with a theory of knowledge that denied the extra-mental reality of universal concepts. Universals are only mental constructs that stand for a whole class of things by convention, he said; there is nothing in real life that corresponds to a notion such as universal power.[18] Marsilius of Padua was also declared a heretic for teaching the independent origins of secular government. He accepted the universality of Christian doctrine and upheld the highest ideals for the clergy. But, he said, papal jurisdiction was concerned with divine law, and divine retribution was a matter for the afterlife. Therefore, in the most direct attack against papal claims to political jurisdiction up to that time, Marsilius confined religious power to spiritual functions and advocated the separation of religious and secular power.[19]

Criticism of the medieval church gained widespread popular support in the movement begun by John Wycliffe (d. 1384) in England. An Oxford theologian and philosopher, Wycliffe, like Ockham, criticized papal secularism and materialism. He upheld Franciscan ideals of clerical poverty and therefore justified the English government's control of local church property. Although condemned by the pope, Wycliffe gained many followers. Known as the Lollards, they expressed their growing independence from Rome by teaching in the vernacular language, rather than the church's universal language, Latin. The egalitarian nature of Lollardy made it very popular among English peasants, so much so that it was blamed for the English Peasants' Revolt of 1381. As a result, despite its support for local autonomy from Rome, the movement was made illegal in England by the turn of the fifteenth century.

After the mid-fifteenth century there was no denying the sovereignty of national monarchs in Britain, France, and Spain. Even the Holy Roman emperor, though retaining that title, became in reality the king of the Germanic regions. Yet religious and political theory had not caught up with these developments. The popes continued to exercise what was left of their power and became progressively embroiled in the emerging Italian national politics.

Italy at the time enjoyed a unique position in European society. Its great trading cities had maintained their thriving international commerce and attendant urban prosperity throughout the feudal period. As mercantile economy became increasingly important in thirteenth- and fourteenth-century Europe and the popes and emperors continued to preoccupy one another, the Italian trade cities became virtually autonomous, dominating political and economic life in their respective regions. Their most demanding challenge was commercial competition. The newly rich merchant classes and the increasingly important professionals vied with the old nobility for dominance. The situation bred despotism, the cleverest and richest securing control through intrigue and mercenary bartering. This environment did not inspire confidence in the traditional political order, as evidenced in the searing indictment by Dante Alighieri (d. 1321). Dante's work—defiantly written in Italian rather than Latin—still envisioned no alternative to a universal empire. But he claimed that the justly ordered world monarchy, to be created by the Roman people, must be ruled by an emperor who derived his authority directly from God, not from the pope. The source and nature of power remained undivided and divine; political philosophy itself was not altered. But its execution was reevaluated. The pope had shown himself unworthy of his weighty task and therefore was expendable. The system could function without him.

Dante represented a new breed of Italian thinker. Called humanists, these scholars exercised a growing intellectual independence, especially among the laity. Lorenzo Valla (d. 1457) was another humanist. Valla, a renowned scholar of Latin philology, exposed the "Donation of Constantine" as a fraud. The document supposedly recorded Constantine's gift of vast territories to the papacy in the fourth century, which were the source of the church's worldly power. But Valla showed that it used anachronistic terminology and made references that were meaningless until the eighth century. Unlike Wycliffe and Huss, however, Dante and Valla were considered loyal Christians. Criticism of the church was becoming more acceptable, and the events of the next generation only heightened the church's vulnerability.

The Search for a New Order. The end of the fifteenth and beginning of the sixteenth centuries witnessed the collapse of the delicate balance that had been achieved by the competing Italian city-states, and the popes were as much involved in the scramble for power as anyone else. This was the era of the infamous Borgia popes, who contrived to consolidate their power—and that of their children. Through duplicitous agreements they succeeded in luring the French into Italian politics. The Italian cities ultimately had to reunite and ask the help of Spain to oust the French, which then led to some sixty years of conflict between France and Spain.[20]

As the papacy descended farther into political intrigues, it inspired new heights of criticism. Niccolò Machiavelli (d. 1527) became famous for his complete abandonment of morality in politics. "Where it is an absolute question of the welfare of our country," he wrote, "we must admit of no considerations of justice or injustice, of mercy or cruelty, of praise or ignominy, but putting all else aside must adopt whatever course will serve its existence and preserve its liberty."[21]

Machiavelli's attitude was indicative of the utter degradation achieved by the archaic system. Like the U.S. antiwar movement in the 1960s, it was symptomatic of disgust with an institution previously trusted as the custodian of social morality. Despair in the face of degraded values is not an uncommon reaction. To the populace at large, the turmoil of fourteenth- and fifteenth-century Europe indicated above all that God was no longer pleased with humanity. As people had been taught—often the *only* thing they had been taught—God punishes those who worship the golden calf. The intensity of the search for the proper relationship to the divine is evidenced in the popularity of lay religious movements, such as the Brothers of the Common Life (commonly known as the Modern Devotion). The Modern Devotion movement was founded by Gerard Groote (d. 1384) in the Netherlands, and "brother" and "sister" houses quickly appeared throughout northern Europe. The houses were centers of simple, common lives of individual piety. Even the lower clergy were attracted to the life, which required no religious vows or special dress. Members could pursue their regular jobs or participate in any of the programs sponsored by the brotherhood: religious education, publications, hospices for the poor. The *Imitation of Christ* by Thomas à Kempis (d. 1471) summarized the teachings of the brotherhood and became one of the most widely read books of the period.

It was the Brothers of the Common Life who originally inspired the work of the famous humanist Erasmus (d. 1536).[22] His satires of the papacy became immensely popular, but his dialogues on proper behavior proved even more influential. The dialogues were eloquent expressions of the classical ideals of humanity and civic virtue and the Christian ideals of love and piety. Like earlier reformers, Erasmus preached following the pious life in imitation of Jesus. He sharply criticized the overly dogmatic, disputatious, and ceremonial medieval church and demanded the reevaluation of classical learning:

> The Stoics understood that no one was wise unless he was good. . . .
> According to Plato, Socrates teaches . . . that a wrong must not be repaid

with a wrong, and also that since the soul is immortal, those should not be lamented who depart this life for a happier one with the assurance of having led an upright life. . . . And Aristotle has written in the *Politics* that nothing can be a delight to us . . . except virtue alone. . . . If there are things that belong particularly to Christianity in these ancient writers, let us follow them.[23]

This was the clarion call for the Reformation. Not only had the papacy lost its political control through the decline of feudalism and the rise of national monarchies, and in the process lost its spiritual prestige, but also Europe had entered yet another stage of economic development and concomitant social challenge. In the late fifteenth and sixteenth centuries, Europe's Age of Exploration led to the establishment of colonial empires whose exploitation provided a seemingly endless supply of natural resources. The newly found wealth supported scientific invention and industrial development on an unprecedented scale. But it also produced a dizzying inflationary spiral. It is estimated that prices in Spain doubled between the end of the fifteenth and the middle of the sixteenth centuries and doubled again by 1600. Records indicate that in Luther's Wittenberg the cost of basic food and clothing doubled in the first half of the sixteenth century, while wages remained almost fixed.[24] The mercantile economy was still in its developing stages; no legal limits had evolved, for instance, to control monopolies or interest rates. To the traditional divisions—between the clergy and the laity and between the landed nobility and the peasantry (who, despite the growth of mercantilism and industry remained the majority of the population)—was added the division between the owners of the means of production and the laborers. Gaps between those in control of wealth and those at their mercy became ever more pronounced. It was in this context that the Christian world's period of self-scrutiny reached its climax.

Complaints about clerical misbehavior such as simony, nepotism, and selling indulgences had been circulating for years. Efforts to resanctify Christian life and leadership had become common. Martin Luther (d. 1546), another product of the Brothers of Common Life and heavily influenced by William of Ockham, became a symbol of the entire movement. His doctrine of justification by faith alone was the ultimate rejection of ecclesiastical manipulation of indulgences. The last straw had come when a heavily indebted local archbishop, Albrecht of Mainz, formed a joint venture with his bankers and the pope and enlisted a seasoned indulgence salesman to raise money for all three.[25] When Luther posted his Ninety-five Theses on the door of Castle Church in Wittenberg in 1517, most of his complaints were against such manipulation of indulgences.

Luther's theses quickly became a *cause célèbre*. The ground had been well prepared for popular acceptance of his criticisms, and news of them spread quickly with the aid of the newly invented printing press. The church finally realized it had to deal with its people's discontent. Luther was therefore summoned to answer to Dominican and papal authorities. Initially, he was given official sanction. It was not until he directly challenged papal authority, the inerrancy of church councils, and the traditional seven sacraments—all on the basis of Christian scripture—that he earned excommunication. He was declared no longer a member of the Catholic Church and had to seek "community" elsewhere. Not surprisingly, he found it among the Germanic princes, who were experiencing their own troubles with the tenacious Holy Roman emperor.

Religious Protest Becomes Political Protest. When Emperor Maximilian I died (1519), there were two claimants for his position: the French Valois King Francis I (Maximilian's grandson) and the Hapsburg Charles I of Spain. Despite papal support for Francis, Charles claimed the throne (becoming Charles V). But to achieve his goal, Charles had had to bribe several imperial electors, who happened to be German princes. He also needed their support in his wars with France and with the Ottoman Turks. It was under these conditions that Charles granted the ultimate concession to the German princes. In 1526 German princes were given religious autonomy within their territories—where Luther had sought refuge. They were allowed to enforce or not, at their own discretion, the Edict of Worms (1521) against Luther. This revolutionary sanctioning of territorial autonomy became the basis of the Peace of Augsburg (1555), which declared *cujus regio, ejus religio:* The ruler of the land gets to determine the religion of the land.

Nothing could have been more significant in the developing history of regional autonomy. The Peace of Augsburg became the model for other regions as well, such as Switzerland. Switzerland was at this time a loose confederation of autonomous cantons, some of which had accepted Protestant teachings. Those who remained loyal to Roman Christianity clashed with the Protestants until 1531, when a treaty confirmed the right of each canton to determine its own religion. Thus *Protest*ant Christianity, i.e., religious protest, became the vehicle of political protest. It removed from Rome the last possible claim to universal authority—the authority to judge spiritual rectitude. As in England, where Henry VIII had broken with Rome (1534) by declaring himself head of the Church of England, political and religious authority were still one. But authority was no longer "catholic" in the literal sense of the term: universal. It was geographically limited, at least in principle.

Yet there remained other obstacles to the establishment of peace within and among European regional powers. Even though regional religio-political autonomy had been officially sanctioned by Rome, the Holy Roman Empire still officially existed; there was still an emperor with universalist claims based on Catholicism. What was more, because religious and political authority remained united, both at the imperial level and on the limited regional level, claims could be made and rights could be denied on the basis of religious affiliation. The foundation had been laid for geographical limitation of power. But the logical counterpart to that limitation—the redefinition of citizenship—had not been addressed. In the obsolescent imperial form, citizenship was a matter of ideological affiliation, so that one could be a citizen no matter where one was. Citizenship had no inherent geographic implications. In the emerging state structure, wherein sovereignty was geographically limited, some adjustment to the notion of citizenship was required to reflect that development. As well, there were no clear-cut boundaries to distinguish any given leader's *regio/religio* from another's. The old form of sovereignty and citizenship based on ideology recognized only fluid boundaries. Wherever the dominant ideology was accepted, there also extended the regime. The concept of inviolable, fixed borders simply had not been established yet. These issues were at the root of what is called Europe's Age of Religious Warfare.

Even when local leaders' de facto autonomy was finally officially recognized, many rulers still feared each other's aggression, and others sought to gain power that had eluded them. It was as if each had been given carte blanche to grab as much power as possible. Emperor Charles V started the scramble when he realized the impact of the concessions he had made in Germany. Throughout the mid-sixteenth century he tried to bring the Germanic princes to heel, but the leash had been cut. Even the church's effort to reform itself—the Council of Trent (1545–1563), called at the insistence of Emperor Charles V— was too little too late. In fact, many rulers initially resisted Trent's reform decrees, assuming they were just another of the popes' attempts to reestablish political power within their territories. Clearly, the issue had passed beyond religious orthodoxy. The centrality of political rule, despite its religious justifications, was anachronistic and actually had been so since early feudal days. But theory takes time to catch up with reality. The fragmentation of formerly unified religio-political power came well before political theory reflected the separation of religious from political power previewed by Saint Augustine in the fourth century.

Now, some thousand years later, political fragmentation was solidifying into autonomous nation-states.

Nation or State?

The distinction between *nation* and *state* is key to understanding the process Europe underwent as the Holy Roman Empire disintegrated, which is also the process that the Middle East is currently undergoing. A nation—from the Latin *nasci, natus,* "to be born"—is a sociopolitical configuration based on common birth or something analogous to common birth. Its distinguishing characteristic is that membership in the nation is based on something that transcends territory: common ancestry, common religion, etc. As a result, the boundaries of the nation are fluid. They ebb and flow with the inclusion or exclusion of peoples participating in the national identity (by converting to the legitimating religion, for instance, or confederating with the legitimating tribe). A state, on the other hand—from the Latin *status,* "position"—has geographically fixed boundaries. It is defined first and foremost by territory. Theoretically, at least, anyone born within a given set of territorial boundaries is a member of that state. A nation-state is a combination of these two concepts: It is a nation or group of people with a common identity who accept territorial limitations, or it is a geographically limited territory whose inhabitants have developed some sense of common identity.

The basis of the claims for new autonomy in Europe were religious; religious claims remained the political language of the realm. But these claims were not univocal. There were many formulations of protest, and each identified itself as a mini-nation. Germany became Lutheran, Switzerland was Calvinist, England was Anglican, France was Catholic, and Spain was Catholic. Before the fighting within and among these new entities could stop, their internal order had to be altered to accommodate somehow the claims of all within the territory, and the geographic boundaries of the new autonomous groupings had to be determined. In short, the new nations had to become states.

Europe's Age of Religious Warfare

Europe's Age of Religious Warfare is a fascinating laboratory of the dynamics of emerging nationalism. The almost continuous conflict was both internal, within the regions trying to maintain their independence from imperial or papal authority, and external, among the powers attempting to establish the extent of their regional control. There were many levels of conflict. The popes and the emperors were attempting to maintain an outmoded form of central religio-political control and repeatedly fought with each other to determine which of them was to maintain it. But the constituent regions of the former religio-political Holy Roman Empire had already established economic autonomy. They were therefore working to break the political bonds that held them to the empire. On the regional level, the various leaders clashed among themselves in their attempts to determine the boundaries of the autonomous units, the emerging nation-states. And last, but far from least, various factions within the emerging nation-states were contending for leadership of the new political entities.

The Peace of Augsburg (1555) had made Lutheranism legal within the Holy Roman Empire. But Luther's was not the only form Christian reformation took. His contemporary John Calvin (1509–1564), working in France and Switzerland, had devised another version. By the second half of the sixteenth century, having devised a kind of egalitarian organization based on regional and local religious authority, Calvinism reached a face-off with Catholicism in France. Boards of presbyters represented the various congregations of Calvinists so that all felt they had a say in the shaping of church policy. Furthermore, although Calvin condemned outright rebellion against lawful government, he did justify resistance to tyrannical authority by teaching that lower clergy had the moral responsibility to resist unjust orders. Catholicism, on the other hand, maintained its highly centralized organization of hierarchical power, from pope to parish priest, stressing absolute obedience to one's superior. Not surprisingly, then, Calvinism became the language of opposition to totalitarian government, while Catholicism often remained attractive to proponents of the status quo.

In France, Calvinism became popular under the leadership of Besançon Hugues. During the ill-fated reign of Valois King Francis I, the government was controlled by the Catholics. Spain was under Hapsburg control at the time, still trying to hang on to the Holy Roman Empire and therefore championing its religious basis, Catholicism. Francis I had lost the emperorship to Hapsburg Spain, but he wanted them to at least let him keep his position in France. So to placate the Spanish, he severely oppressed the Huguenots (French Calvinists). But when a weak Valois (Francis II) ascended the French throne, a struggle ensued among the leading aristocratic families to gain dominance. When Francis II came under the control of the Catholic Guise family, the other two strongest families in France, the Montmorency-Chatillons and the Bourbons, became leading Huguenots. The struggle for control of the French throne culminated in the massacre of thousands of Huguenots on Saint Bartholomew's Day, 1572.

It was only when Henry III (r. 1574–1589) ascended the French throne that any sort of equilibrium was regained. Henry is credited with realizing that religious disputes were destroying France. Adopting a compromise position between the two factions, he gained support from both sides. The principle of national unity was finally taking precedence over religious factional loyalty. Thus Huguenots were granted religious freedom and civil rights with the Peace of Beaulieu (1576). This horrified the Spanish King Henry II, as well as Pope Sixtus V, both fearing the rise of a Protestant France. So they sent in troops to help the Catholics continue their fight against the Huguenots. But by 1598 the French people recognized the foreign interventions as a threat to national independence. In the ultimate settlement, the Edict of Nantes (promulgated by Henry IV, "Henry of Navarre") recognized France as officially Catholic, but reaffirmed the rights of religious minorities.

Meanwhile, Spain remained officially Catholic, having rid the country of Muslims and Jews by means of the Inquisition at the end of the fifteenth century. Spain's strategic location had allowed it, more than any of its competitors, to profit from global exploration. The wealth pouring in from New World colonies achieved for Spain the competitive edge in the growing mercantile economies of Europe. The imperial title had passed to the Austrian branch of the Hapsburg family, but Spain's Philip II, aware of the power his wealth afforded, decided to try to reclaim the Holy Roman Empire. In so doing, he inaugurated what would be Europe's last, convulsive phase of universalism.

The Netherlands was part of the Hapsburg empire. But unfortunately for Philip, it was a region of independently wealthy merchant towns, among the richest of all Europe, and these towns had no intention of submitting to Philip's imperial designs. Under the leadership of William of Orange (d. 1584), the Netherlands fiercely opposed Spain's attempt to reimpose imperial rule. Like France's Henry III, William of Orange seemed to place national autonomy above the religiously based claim Philip was making for unity. When Spain insisted the Netherlands conform to the decrees of the Council of Trent, the people of the Netherlands joined in resistance under a covenant called the Compromise and invited assistance from the French Huguenots and the German Lutherans. Spain responded by sending in troops and establishing a reign of terror during which several thousand alleged heretics were publicly executed. So insistent were the Dutch on maintaining autonomy that they opened the dikes and flooded their own country in order to repulse the Spaniards. When the remnants of the Spanish mercenary army massacred seven thousand in the streets of Antwerp, the ten largely Catholic provinces of the south (modern Belgium) joined with the seven mainly Protestant northern provinces (modern Netherlands) in the pacification of Ghent (1576). According to their agreement—again, like the Peace of Augsburg—regional leaders were sovereign in matters of religion. They then went a step farther and declared that there would be cooperation even among territories of differing religious conviction. Although the southern provinces later broke with the north, it was this Union of Utrecht (completed in 1579) that finally declared complete independence from Spain's imperial claims (1581). Peace was not achieved with Spain, however, for another dozen years. Philip II continued to press his claims throughout the former empire. But he only succeeded in so enraging the French and the English with his meddling that they both helped the Dutch continue resistance to Spanish rule. By the time Britain defeated Philip's Armada in 1588, Spain was so overextended that the Dutch were finally able to evict Spanish soldiers. France and England formally recognized Dutch independence in 1596. Spain granted it in 1609, and the Treaty of Westphalia made the Netherlands' independence official in 1648.

Philip even caused trouble in England, which had sorted out its territorial disputes with France in the Hundred Years' War and had declared its independence from the pope in 1534. When Catholic Mary Tudor assumed the English throne in 1553, it was over the protests of Anglican leaders. She immediately sought to strengthen her base of legitimacy by marrying militantly Catholic Philip of Spain (1554). Her Parliament repealed statutes previously enacted to accommodate Protestant religious practices, and virtually all the great English Protestant leaders of the age were executed for heresy. Hundreds of others were either burned at the stake or exiled. It was not until Mary was succeeded by Elizabeth I (r. 1558–1603) that England's Act of Supremacy was restored. Elizabeth's Parliament repealed Mary's anti-Protestant legislation and reorganized the religious system. As it had been in France and the Netherlands, national unity was placed above religious unity.[26]

But there was to be one final paroxysm throughout the European continent before its territorial and power conflicts were settled. The Thirty Years' War (1618–1648) really represents the culmination of the struggles to carve nation-states out of the Holy Roman Empire and in many ways prefigures the current war in Lebanon. The Peace of Augsburg had established the principle of *cujus regio, ejus religio* for Catholics and Lutherans, but it had ignored Calvinists. Yet Calvinism continued to spread. Palatine (one of the some 360 autonomous entities of which Germany was composed at the time) became a center for Calvinists, who were spurned elsewhere, to develop their ideas and send out missionaries. The Lutherans still had some grievances against the Catholics, because the latter were somewhat more rigid about religious concessions within their territories, and the Catholics were annoyed that the Lutherans had not given up the positions they had gained through the Catholic Church. But both feared the Calvinists' expansion. The war broke out when a staunchly Catholic Hapsburg (Ferdinand) ascended the throne in Bohemia and revoked religious freedom there. When Ferdinand became Holy Roman Emperor Ferdinand II in 1619, the Bohemians defied him and declared their sole loyalty to a Calvinist, Frederick V. Before the war was over, virtually every major power in Europe was involved. Spain sent troops to support Ferdinand, who was thus able to rout Frederick's troops, reimpose Catholicism in Bohemia, and extend his power over Palatine. Next Denmark came in, encouraged by England, France, and the Netherlands, to try to prevent reestablishment of Catholic Hapsburg domination. Ferdinand tried to reassert control through the Edict of Restitution (1629), reasserting the legitimacy of Catholicism and Lutheranism, but again ignoring the Calvinists, and calling for the return of all church lands acquired by Protestants since 1552. As such lands involved at least sixteen bishoprics and twenty-eight cities then under Lutheran control, it clearly was not the way to end the war. That was when the Lutheran Swedish king entered the fray—with the support of the Netherlands and France. One historian's summary of the final years of the Thirty Years' War could—with only a few changes—easily apply to present-day Lebanon:

> After [France's] entrance the war dragged on for thirteen years, with French, Swedish, and Spanish soldiers looting the length and breadth of Germany—warring, it seemed, simply for the sake of warfare itself. The Germans, long weary of the devastation, were too disunited to repulse the foreign armies; they simply watched and suffered. By the time peace talks began in the Westphalian cities of Münster and Osnabruck in 1644, an estimated one third of the German population had died as a direct result of the war. It was the worst European catastrophe since the Black Death of the fourteenth century.[27]

Separating Religious from Political Authority

The Treaty of Westphalia finally ended the war in 1648. It would take over two centuries for Germany to transcend the fractured religio-political condition ratified by the treaty, and France and Spain would remain at war over their borders until 1659. But the agreement did mark the end of the Holy Roman Empire. It also officially denied governments the right to indefinitely expand their borders with religion as their only justification. The treaty ratified the principle of geopolitically limited states and, in so doing, liberated political from religious thought.

It raised the question: What is it that gives all Christian communities in Europe the right to autonomy, regardless of sectarian orientation?

This question, more than any other, characterized Europe's Age of Enlightenment. Finally released from the conflicts that had drained their resources for so long, Europeans could assess their progress, consolidate their gains, and develop the theoretical or philosophical apparatus to explain the new reality. It was never a question of jettisoning the values that had shaped the archaic structures; indeed, the structures had to be altered to preserve the values. The process required distinguishing the essential from the accidental: Europe's intellectuals had to figure out which aspects of the defunct Holy Roman imperial order were necessary for Christian life and which were simply a function of the changing socioeconomic context. The challenge was to determine what were truly Christian values and how best to preserve them in the new socioeconomic milieu.

Since the Reformation, intellectuals had been trying to break free of the church's grasp. Philip Melanchthon, for example, Luther's collaborator in revising the curriculum of the University of Wittenberg, had condemned the prevailing intellectual elite. The scholastics, he said, whose methods amounted to little more than logical arguments over the relative merits of classical authorities, were "barbarians who practice barbarous arts."[28] Their control of the universities, he believed, had mitigated the individual's responsibility for personal piety. It placed metaphysics (the attempt to put into rational terms the nature of God and "being as such") at the pinnacle of religious learning. So long as that remained the highest intellectual pursuit, clearly the practical sciences, including politics, would suffer.

In the next generation this line of thinking would bear fruit in the empiricism of Francis Bacon (d. 1626). Bacon encouraged confidence in the ability of the human intellect to produce useful results. Like Melanchthon—and very similar to some current Islamic reformists, as we will see—he criticized scholasticism for its dogmatism and impracticality: "The [scholastic] logic now in use serves more to fix and give stability to the errors which have their foundation in commonly received notions than to help the search after truth."[29] Bacon was quite conscious of the revolutionary nature of his thought. He compared himself to Columbus as a seeker of new discoveries. Humanity simply must be capable of something beyond the accomplishments of the ancients; clearly there was room for improvement of the human condition. Thus, Bacon encouraged people to go beyond traditional sources and methods, to experiment, with a view toward progress.

Religio-political control, however, continued to exert itself well into the seventeenth century. England experienced a century of Puritan resistance to Queen Elizabeth's religious compromise; the rise of Oliver Cromwell's "godly men"; the restoration of a religiously tolerant Anglican monarch, Charles II (r. 1660–1685) (to whom Louis XIV of France offered a monetary bribe if he would declare his conversion to Catholicism); and the Titus Oates affair, which inspired terror of a "popish plot" to regain control of England through a Catholic king and culminated in the Glorious Revolution, in which a benevolent Protestant (William of Orange, of the Netherlands) assumed the English throne. France witnessed the rise of absolute monarchy through the devices of Cardinal Richelieu (d. 1642), who was Catholic but also so fiercely French that he supported Protestants in Germany against any gains the equally Catholic Hapsburgs might make. A series of revolts culminated in the absolute monarchy of Louis XIV (d. 1715), which was enshrined by Bishop Jacques-Benigne Bossuet in the theory he called the "divine right of kings." Citing biblical sources, the bishop claimed that the French king was answerable only to God.[30] This attempt at ultimate reassertion of the unity of religious and political power, of course, paved the way for the abuses that led to the French Revolution.

But by this time theory had finally begun to catch up with reality. The new rationalism heralded by such thinkers as Melanchthon and Bacon was not without its critics. Blaise Pascal (d. 1662), for instance, heavily influenced by Saint Augustine's belief in the utter degradation of the earthly world, taught that reason and science were of no value in religion. Even if one had doubts, it was better to believe in God just in case the whole thing was true. Despite such reactionary responses, the works of more progressive thinkers clearly pointed the direction of the future.

Thomas Hobbes (d. 1679) is probably the most important of this group. Hobbes was heavily influenced by Calvinist views on social order. Calvin had taught that individual piety lay in the common effort to transform society morally. In a growing recognition of the nature of religious commitment, Calvin asserted that Christians simply do not have the leisure to sit idly by while society is directed in an ungodly way. He described the ideal human society as a commonwealth, based on a covenant among the populace to obey a ruler elected from among those best suited to rule. He also taught that, ideally, religious and political control should be separated. The church and state are two kinds of society, distinguished by their tasks. The former is supposed to guide the latter, for the goal of the state should be to ensure civil and economic justice, i.e., to prevent gross social inequality. The role of the church is to guide the consciences of citizens and leaders, to make sure the laws they devise are in accordance with the laws of God.

Hobbes can therefore be called the first political philosopher of the Christian world, because he definitively extricated political thought from theology. He taught that all actions have political consequences, even the actions of people oblivious to politics. Therefore, human beings must be properly trained to work in concert for the betterment of society. The greatest human power lay in the collective or the commonwealth, in "which people are united by their consent in one all-powerful person." Such a commonwealth was to be the source of political authority, he said, not the church.[31]

Hobbes' articulation of the separation of religious from political authority is what allowed the development of the more advanced work of John Locke, Jean-Jacques Rousseau, and Montesquieu. Locke (d. 1704) opposed the belief in absolute authority. He held that all people are equal and independent and that no one had the right to harm another "in his life, health, liberty, or possessions."[32] Accordingly, in Locke's view, whenever the preservation of people's life, health, liberty, or possessions is threatened the government automatically forfeits its position. "The trust must necessarily be forfeited and the power devolve into the hands of those that gave it, who may place it anew where they think best for their safety and security."[33] This was, in effect, a theory of just revolution, a provision for orderly change of government over which people had conscious control. Montesquieu (d. 1755) went even further. He taught that freedom from despotism can only be assured by a balance of power among a monarch, an aristocracy, and commoners and by constitutional limits to the power of the state overall. In biting satire on the triviality of religious warfare, he claimed that societies' strength lay in solidarity of common interests, not religion. But whereas Locke had emphasized separation of church and state, Montesquieu emphasized their cooperation. In his view, the people must be well imbued with religiously inspired principles of justice and equality to truly ensure good political order. Rousseau's (d. 1778) major concern was freedom. There is true freedom only in democracy; the only legitimate political order is that formed deliberately by thinking people. As it had in the work of his predecessors, religion played an important role in Rousseau's theories. But he rejected the standard Christian hierarchy that placed intermediaries—earthly or otherwise—between the individual and God. He taught, instead, that individuals achieve salvation by fully participating in a moral society. Indeed, the strength of the state depends on the morality of its citizens, rather than on sheer force.

The Reality of Secularism

The significance of the theoretical separation of church and state in this context and of granting individuals the right to ratify the state is that both concepts automatically limit the extent of governmental control. In proposing a "social contract" (Rousseau's formulation) or constitutional form of government, these theories not only limit the *kinds* of power governments may exercise over people, but they also provide a *geographical limitation* to the legitimation. If the community's consent—democracy—is necesssary to legitimate political authority, that authority can only extend to the areas where the consenting populace lives.

This is the reality of secularism. It is clearly not something endemic to Christianity or to any other religion, for that matter. It is not an ideology, as such, or a claim that the separation of the two orders—religious and political—is based on a metaphysical division or compromise of divine unity or sovereignty. It is, rather, a practical response to the socioeconomic reality of geographically limited states. Secularism developed out of a need to find political legitimacy consistent with limited geographic claims, unlike the claims of the church. Once the separation had been articulated, a democratic and therefore limited political legitimacy was substituted for religious, potentially unlimited political legitimacy. And in the exposition of democracy came the development of secularism. In a pluralistic society divided into geopolitically limited democratic states, secularism developed from the beliefs that all members of the community share responsibility for directing society and that no human being should be denied either responsibilities or rights on the basis of religious affiliation. The development of secularism had nothing to do with denigration of religion or religious values, as such. On the contrary, it was to preserve the values of social justice and equality and of religious piety that the basis of secularism—separation of religious from political authority—developed.

It took centuries for the theories justifying the separation of church and state to develop: for political theory to catch up with reality. But when the potentially universal extent of a government legitimated religiously was superseded, those with the will to expand politically finally lost their theoretical mandate to do so. Historian Joseph Strayer says it was this—the recasting of people's primary duty from obedience to the church to the implementation of its teachings within a geopolitically limited state—that more than anything else marks the beginning of modern Europe.[34]

The term *secularism* itself is actually of very recent origin. It was coined in 1854 to express "a certain positive and ethical element, which the terms 'infidel,' 'skeptic,' [and] 'atheist' do not express."[35] Later, concerning the issue of state-provided education, the term was used to describe the exclusion of sectarian considerations from policy decisions. But the basis of the concept was laid with the separation of religious from political sovereignty, which brought stability to Europe. To summarize: In developing theories of democracy and the "social contract" of political legitimation, European thinkers provided the essential elements of modern statecraft. A political leader was authorized by the people she/he ruled. Therefore, her/his authority was limited to the geographic area inhabited by the legitimating populace. And the contract was conditional: If both sides did not meet their obligations the contract was null and void; if the authorized political power failed to fulfill its obligations, it forfeited its legitimacy.

These two elements—geographic limitation of sovereignty and a mechanism for orderly change of government—most significantly characterize modern European states. They were what allowed the cessation of the almost constant warfare that marked the birth of modern Europe. That warfare was the combined death throes of religiously legitimated and therefore potentially universal sovereignty, under which political protest was indistinguishable from heresy, and the birth pangs of democratically legitimated and therefore geographically limited sovereignty, under which universal religious authority was separated from any given political application. This is what Strayer means by "modern" Western states: When he says that popular allegiance to the state replaced primary allegiance to the church, he does not mean that allegiance to the church was negated but that the separation of religious from political authority allowed the allocation of loyalty on different levels. In the political sphere there is only the state, to which people must pay taxes and whose direction they must guide through the exercise of democratic responsibility. The moral principles that inform that guidance are still the province of religion. In that sense, religion is prior to the church. Political loyalty has been devalued, as it were. Primary political loyalty is to the state, but religious loyalty may remain primary on a level made more significant by the separation of the two spheres.

The Islamic Middle East is currently involved in a struggle similar to that undergone in the evolution from the Holy Roman Empire to modern European states. It is moving from a system of theoretically unlimited religio-political sovereignty to one of geopolitically limited states. As expressed in the antisecularist sentiments quoted in the opening paragraph of this chapter, the concern is clearly how to maintain the universal applicability of religious values in the context of a changing political atmosphere. Just as it was in the European experience, the process of transition in the Middle East has been long and arduous. But the milestones have been very different from those that marked Europe's progress. To understand the intensity of the current struggle, then, and the significance of the present antisecularist movements in the Islamic world, we must examine the history of the Arab transition.

CHAPTER TWO

Islamic Decentralization and Initial Responses

*T*here is visible, in fact, a widespread trend, of which Ibn
Taymiyya's is the most forceful example, which
ultimately resulted in those reform movements of
various shades that characterized Islam immediately before the
impingement upon it of modern western influences.

—Fazlur Rahman[1]

The Medieval Islamic World

The decentralization of the Islamic empire began as early as the tenth
century. The economic basis of the Islamic empire was, of course, quite
different from that of Christian Rome. For one thing, the Muslims had
taken over former Byzantine (Eastern Roman) and Sasanid (Persian)
provinces. These were largely agricultural regions in which the Muslims
often left intact the administrative systems established by the Romans
or the Persians.[2] As a result, the Islamic administrative system was
characterized from the outset by a lack of uniformity. This was compounded by the fact that the Byzantine and Persian practices themselves
varied widely from region to region. The general pattern was for the
Islamic conquerors to exact some sort of tribute to reflect their sovereignty, leaving it to the local authorities to collect the taxes according
to established customs. The degree of autonomy of the local officials
was frequently affected by the nature of the conquest. When the lands
were acquired by military victory (*'anwatan*), the system established
generally reflected more the conqueror's discretion than did the systems
in lands acquired by a treaty of capitulation (*sulhan*). At times, however,
a system of taxation was simply imposed regardless of means of conquest,

or the amount of tribute expected was fixed in advance of conquest and only the means of collection was left to local officials.

Iraq, for instance, was acquired by military victory over the drained Sasanid forces. Native Arab subordinates left in control of the system of taxation followed the Persian tradition of exacting both poll and property taxes. In the Persian system, only the aristocracy were exempt from the poll tax. To maintain this exemption under the Arabs, the Persian aristocracy tended to convert to Islam. In Syria, on the other hand, where Islamic dominance was achieved largely by treaty, the tax collection and tribute were left to the discretion of native administrators. The Syrian administrators followed, in general outline, the fiscal system of their former overlords, the Byzantines. More complex than the Persian system, the Byzantine model included a personal tax only on colonists and non-Christians and a property tax that varied with the size of the estate. In Iran and Central Asia, the Sasanid system of land tax and poll tax, regardless of conversion to Islam, seems to have remained intact. A tribute was simply fixed by the conquerors and the local chieftains were left to administer taxation as they saw fit.

Another significant difference between the medieval Europeans and the Islamic Arab world is that the economy of the central Arab lands was largely commercial. By the seventh century, Mecca, the birthplace of Islam, was a rich commercial city.[3] It was strategically located at the junction of two major trade routes through the Arabian peninsula: the "incense route," connecting India and the Yemen with Syria and the Mediterranean, and the east-west route, linking the Central Asian lands with eastern Africa via the Red Sea. Watered only by its central well, the fabled Zamzam, Mecca was unsuited for agriculture. The annual caravans, which included food staples for Arabia, were therefore essential. The Meccans gained a reputation as expert traders. The scant historical records of the day reveal sophisticated fiscal practices, such as silent partnerships (*mudarabat*), whereby anyone could invest in a caravan and share proportionately in the profits. Records also indicate that the Quraysh, the leading family of Mecca, controlled the lucrative caravan trade, a source of massive wealth. A typical caravan reportedly consisted of one thousand camels, and larger caravans were more than twice that size. The Quraysh held monopolies on the camel and caravan provisions and were overseers of a complex system of free passage treaties with the desert nomads through whose territory the caravans had to pass. Besides that, the Quraysh controlled Mecca itself, the location of annual trade fairs and pilgrimages to the Ka'bah, the sanctuary containing fetishes for the religions of the tribes in the surrounding desert. The Quraysh were therefore the major employers in Mecca.

It would be anachronistic to describe Mecca as a capitalist economy. It was a pre-industrial society in which private ownership of property was not a major economic concern. However, slave labor was widespread, and that effectively put ownership of animals in the category of private property: Those who owned animals were able to use slave or near-slave labor to produce wealth. Animal husbandry therefore became like a means of production, rather than a form of subsistence. Animal ownership allowed the development of a great distinction between the poor and the wealthy, a characteristic of capitalist economies.

In fact, the few records available describing pre-Islamic Mecca have this distinction as their primary observation. The ten major clans of the Quraysh tribe occupied the center of the town, near the Ka'bah and the well of Zamzam, while clans with more distant ties were relegated to the dry hills and rain-gouged ravines surrounding Mecca. Clearly, the inhabitants of these quarters, described as suffocatingly hot and plagued with swarms of flies, were the underprivileged classes, those who lived by selling their labor to the owners of the caravans and the proprietors of the pilgrimage concessions. They lacked the means to profit from the enormous gains being made in trade and its accoutrements and lived instead at subsistence level. The Prophet Muhammad was himself a product of this poor class of Quraysh, a fact that no doubt contributed to his overriding sympathy with the oppressed.

The other major cities the Islamic polity would incorporate were more complex in organization. Damascus, for instance, which welcomed Muslim troops in 635, was a prosperous urban center when it first appeared in historical records. By the time it was mentioned in the Bible (Genesis 10:22 and 11:15, for example), it was a well-developed city built on a grid pattern and served by a system of canals, with residential areas, markets, temples, and palaces. Successive waves of conquest—by King David, the Assyrians, the Babylonians, the Achaemenids, the Greeks, the Romans, and the Persians—confirm that the city had earned the envy of its neighbors in the first millenium. Under Roman rule in the early second century, Damascus was officially ranked a metropolis, and records reveal a prosperous and growing population. The Romans therefore had to provide additional canals and an aqueduct and build walls to protect their treasure. The population was diverse, occupied in various aspects of trade and light industry; the hinterland was agricultural. Jerusalem was likewise well known as a complex urban center, as were the Persian cities of Iraq and Khurasan. Arab chronicles of the conquest of the Persian capital of Ctesiphon (637) concentrate on descriptions of its lavish treasures and wealth. The southern reaches of the Arabian peninsula—the Yemen—were ancient homes of prosperous agricultural and trading kingdoms.

Therefore, the economic structure of the early Islamic empire, unlike that of the Holy Roman Empire, was a delicate balance of a complex urban culture and a highly developed agrarian sector. Nevertheless, the religio-political structure of the Islamic empire was strikingly similar to that of Rome. The raison d'être of the Islamic entity was Muhammad's prophecy. The Qur'anic command to spread the Islamic message, to issue the call to Islam (in Arabic, *al-da'wa*), was the sole justification for establishing the empire. Just as the Romans felt they had a mission to civilize the world, the Muslims claimed a divine mandate to correct the scriptural misinterpretations of the other monotheists—the Jews and the Christians—and to implement the final installment of the prophetic saga. The Jews had mistakenly assumed the prophetic message applied only to them, and the Christians—having corrected that error—had fallen into their own. They had deified a prophet, thus compromising the very basis of monotheism. Muhammad and his followers felt compelled to point out the error of making any but *the* God (in Arabic *al-ilah* or Allah) God.

The Prophet of Islam also had to expand Jesus' teaching. Jesus had correctly portrayed the universality of God's plan, but he had not specified the nature of the planned kingdom of God. In fact, his allusions to the extraterrestrial nature of God's kingdom had allowed Christians to place far too much emphasis on the afterlife, in the Muslim view. Muhammad had to impress upon believers that the just and egalitarian society God had enjoined human society to create was to be established on earth. Human salvation could not be accomplished by the sacrificial, symbolic death of one individual; it was the responsibility of each individual to contribute to social justice. That, in the Muslim perspective, was the route to salvation.

That is why the most important date in Islamic history, the date from which the Islamic calendar begins, is 622 C.E. That is when Muhammad realized that the best way to demonstrate God's command was to actually create a political entity based on God's will for social justice. He began with a small band of followers that year and from their base in Medina set about subjugating the Arabian peninsula, Syria, North Africa—theoretically there were no limits. Subjugation meant either accepting the message ("There is no god but *the* God, and Muhammad is the prophet of God") or, if one was already a monotheist, accepting the status of *dhimmi* (protected person) and paying a tax (*jizya* or *kharaj*) in place of the alms (*zakat*) Muslims were required to give. In either case, the issue was accepting Muhammad as supreme arbitrator and commander. Political authority was inseparable from religious authority. Submission to the leadership of Muhammad was based solely on his religious mission. The supreme purpose of Islamic society was moral. The Qur'anic injunction to do good and prevent evil (3:110), a simple aphoristic summary of Islamic teaching, has been called the most important verse of the Holy Book. It does not deny that practical concerns may differ from moral concerns, but it places the moral order irrevocably at center stage. Politics and religion are not considered separate moral spheres.

On the strength of this message, Muhammad's followers were able to create the most widely spread and influential society on earth at the time. But religio-political unity did not mean the empire was geographically unified. The complexity represented in the system of taxation had never been overcome. It is easy to see the wisdom of maintaining a continuity of administrative practices in the conquered territories: The conquered peoples' lives were scarcely disrupted and the flow of tribute remained constant. However, the administrative divisions militated against homogenization of the various distinct regions into a single Islamic social entity.

In fact, the regional divisions were further intensified by the caliphal policy of keeping the Arabs separate from the populations they conquered. From earliest times Arabian Muslims were forbidden to own land outside the peninsula. Members of the first Muslim community and their families were to receive a portion of the income from conquered lands, but the original ownership and cultivation of those lands were to be left intact.[4] Arabs who went to regions outside the peninsula were required to live in exclusively Arab towns. Thus al-Fustat, which was to become Cairo, the center of Islamic Egypt, was built to garrison the conquering Islamic troops in 643. Kufah and Basra were established by and for those Arabs who drove the Persians out of Iraq.

Even the tribal differences among Arabs continued to play a role in Islamic politics. The caliph 'Abd al-Malik (r. 685–705) initiated reforms designed to unify and consolidate the Islamic realm. Among other things, he gathered and converted the various land registry methods into a single unified system in the Arabic language. But that deprived the local landowners of the autonomy many had enjoyed under previous systems. Especially under the forceful implementation by 'Abd al-Malik's lieutenant in Iraq, al-Hajjaj, these reform measures led to conflict with local tribes. Attempts to reassert the dominance of the central authority in the garrison towns interfered with the dominance local tribes sought to maintain over one another. This was the perennial problem of Arab politics: The decentralizing force of tribal chauvinism and its resulting feuds challenged the Islamic spirit of equality and brotherhood.

Decentralizing Pressures in the Arab World

One of the most persistent examples of this type of dispute was that between the northern and southern Arab tribes. The former comprised the tribes of Rabi'ah and Mudar, along with their leading Qays clan, and lived along the Tigris and Euphrates (present-day Iraq), having immigrated in pre-Islamic times. The tribes that had settled in Syria, on the other hand, were called Yemeni, supposedly having immigrated from southern Arabia, and were led by the Kalb clan. The northern Arabians (often called Qaysites, but also including other tribes) trace their heritage to Ishmael, son of Abraham. The southern Arabians, tracing their descent to Joktan (in Arabic, Qahtan) in the book of Genesis (10:25ff), consider themselves somehow of an older and nobler line than the northerners.

The dispute between the two groups first came into play in Islamic politics with the accession of the Umayyads to the caliphate. The Umayyads were a leading Syrian branch of the Quraysh family. They were represented in Mecca at the time of the Prophet by Abu Sufyan, a strong opponent of the Prophet during his early career. Abu Sufyan's son, Mu'awiyyah, founded the Umayyad dynasty (661–750), whose claim was based on Yemeni legitimacy. The first three caliphs (successors to the Prophet)—Abu Bakr (632–634), 'Umar b. al-Khattab (634–644), and 'Uthman b. 'Affan (644–656)—had all been chosen on the Arabian model of bay'a (literally, commercial transaction or agreement), whereby the elders elect from among themselves the one considered most capable of ruling and the rest of the tribe agrees to abide by his decisions. But since the death of the Prophet in 632 C.E., there had been partisans (in Arabic, shi'a) of hereditary legitimacy pushing the candidacy of the Prophet's closest male heir, his cousin and son-in-law, 'Ali b. Abi Talib. The third caliph, 'Uthman, was a pious but weak old man who allowed his administration to be run by less than scrupulous relatives. When he was murdered in an uprising that included 'Ali's supporters in Kufah, 'Ali became the fourth caliph—but not without a fight with 'Uthman's kinfolk, the Umayyads. 'Ali moved his headquarters to Kufah, which was Qays territory, while the Syrian Umayyads prepared their Yemeni/Kalbite revenge. Their work was done for them four years later, when 'Ali was murdered by a member of an extremist group who considered both the Umayyads and 'Ali heretics. Then Mu'awiyya was able to assert his claim to leadership of the Muslim world, and he moved the capital to Damascus.

This victory for the "southerners" never sat well with the Qaysite ("northerner") Iraqis. Kufah became a hotbed of discontent against Syrian rule. Although 'Ali's hereditary legitimacy became the rallying cry for opposition to the Umayyads, at the root were far more practical disputes. 'Ali quickly became the great martyr (*shahid*) of Shi'i Islam, and his tomb became the popular pilgrimage site it remains today. (The same is true of his sons Hasan and Hussein, each of whom was murdered in turn—Hasan in his home in Medina and Hussein on the battlefield against the Umayyads at Karabala.) But resentment of Umayyad, Syrian, or Yemeni/Kalbi superiority grew as inequities in the administrative system surfaced.

In Khurasan (in northeast Persia) the Arab colonists were divided into the Tamim tribe of northern Arabians and the Azdites, southern Arabians. The two factions alternately held positions of power throughout the Umayyad period. In the dispute to determine the successor of Yazid (Mu'awiyya's son and successor, r. 680–683), who was married to a Kalbite woman, the Qays refused to recognize Yazid's son, Mu'awiyya II (r. 683–684) and supported Ibn al-Zubair instead. The Qays were ultimately defeated by the Kalbites at Marj Rahit in 684; however, the feud still smoldered and was fanned at the time of Caliph 'Abd al-Malik (r. 685–705). Not only was 'Abd al-Malik's lieutenant al-Hajjaj a Qaysite, but so were Muhammad, al-Hajjaj's cousin and conqueror of India, as well as Qutaybah, the conqueror of Central Asia. Rebellion finally burst forth in the Iraqi army, led by a Yemeni (Kalbite) chief, and both Basra and Kufah joined in the uprising. The Yemeni rebellion was put down, but it marked the end of any expectations of loyalty to Damascus on the part of the Iraqis of Basra and Kufah.

Thus Qaysite Iraq became a center of Shi'i opposition to Umayyad rule. But Shi'i opposition soon spread to Persia (Iran), where another kind of national sentiment bred considerable discontent. The Persians, of course, were non-Arab. They had a long history of high civilization, stretching back to Cyrus the Great, Darius, and Xerxes. They had become Muslim early on and had every expectation of being treated on a par with Arab Muslims. But the administrative policy of Arab separateness resulted in Persians being treated as Arab subjects. Persian resentment of Arab claims to superiority surfaced in what is known as the Shu'ubiyya ("people's" or popular, i.e., non-Arab) movement. The Persians made common cause with another group, the descendants of the Prophet through his uncle al-'Abbas b. 'Abd al-Muttalib b. Hashim— the 'Abbasids—who also opposed their kinsmen's rule in Damascus. The 'Abbasids were not Shi'is, who claim leadership of the Muslim community belongs to the Prophet's descendants through his daughter Fatimah, but they were opposed to the Umayyads.

The revolution that led to the Umayyads' ultimate downfall began in 747, when a former Persian slave led a contingent consisting of Yemeni tribesmen and Iranian peasants, all under the 'Abbasid banner, against the Umayyad governor of Khurasan. The reigning Umayyad, Marwan II (r. 744–750) was already occupied with a series of uprisings, including a conflict between the Qays and the Yemeni in Syria. This allowed the 'Abbasids' supporters to take over city by city: the Khurasani capital (Marw), Basra, Kufah, and Harran. In 750 Damascus surrendered, and the 'Abbasids claimed the caliphate.

But the Islamic empire was never to regain even the nominal unity it had achieved under the Umayyads. The meteoric rise of Islamic power is a popular theme among Muslim historians. It is true the realm spread from a small Arabian town to the Pyrenees in the West and China and India in the east, including all the Middle East and North Africa on the way, within the brief span of one hundred years. But its unity faded just as fast. By the mid-tenth century Islamic society was still, as Islamic historian Marshall Hodgson put it, "a single historical whole."[5] But it was no longer a single political entity. With the ascent of the 'Abbasids to the caliphate came the first major split in the empire. The 'Abbasids established their capital at Baghdad and from there ruled the eastern portions, while their predecessors, the Umayyads, maintained control of Andalusia (southern Spain) and portions of West Africa. This initial fragmentation was followed eventually by the rise of many independent principalities. The period between the mid-tenth century and the early thirteenth century saw the rise of the Daylamis, the Ziyarids, and the Seljuq Turks in the sub-Caspian regions; the Fatimid caliphate in Egypt; the Bedouin Hamdanis in Syria; the Samanids in northeastern Iran and the Syr-Oxus basin; the Buyyids (Buwayhis) and the Khawarizmis in Mesopotamia (Iraq); and a host of other virtually autonomous local leaders who only nominally acknowledged the 'Abbasid caliphs.

Sources of Islamic Political Fragmentation

The decline of 'Abbasid authority came as a result of several factors. The Islamic empire at its height, in the early tenth century, was a well-developed combination of the commercial and agrarian economies from which it was composed. Lying at the crossroads of the world's overland trade routes, the region's cities were extensive and prosperous and, therefore, like cities in later medieval Europe, virtually independent. But the economic basis of the 'Abbasid central bureaucracy was agrarian, specifically the rich Mesopotamian agricultural region known as the Sawad. The Sawad had been developed by the Sasanid Persians before Islamic conquest for the same purpose: support of the state bureaucracy. The system of taxation, again little changed from that of the previous rulers, was the basis of imperial budgets and expenditures. Thus the caliphal leadership drew its aristocracy largely from the agrarian gentry. Responsible for maintaining the productivity of their respective regions and delivering the taxes, the agrarian aristocracy was the support on which the caliphal bureaucracy dependend.

However, this placed the aristocracy in a precarious position, for the economic structure of the empire was in a state of transition. Whenever different sources of wealth are combined into a single system, new alignments among those sources tend to shift the existing balance of power, and that is exactly what was happening. There were really three bases of economic power in the Islamic world: the traditional agrarian aristocracy, the urban notables whose wealth was often a combination of mercantile and agrarian sources, and the nomadic or pastoralist tribal groupings. This last group often lacked the raw wealth of the former two elites, but it did have social cohesion provided by the tribal hierarchy, which its urban competitors frequently lacked. Accordingly, the tribes could muster manpower; they had in effect a standing military force that could be brought to bear in cases of local power struggles. As a result, these tribal groupings were often courted for their potential role as power brokers. Economic power, and its attendant sociopolitical and military power, were therefore fluid at the time. The fortunes of all three elites were in transition; none of them could be said to hold undisputed—and therefore enforceable—dominance.

In this context, the agrarian aristocracy of the 'Abbasids seemed to command more political power than their relative wealth would merit. In fact, the vagaries of agriculturally based production made their hold quite tenuous. For one thing, agrarian resources are not mobile. To base a far-flung political system on agrarian resources means to base it on widely scattered real estate. This was indeed the dominant characteristic of the 'Abbasid aristocracy's resources. Their estates were frequently separated from one another by stretches of nonagricultural or uncultivated land, which militated against efficient management. More significantly, it made raising armies from among their peasants in time of local disputes very difficult. Even when contingents could be summoned from the various estates, they often lacked the solidarity of tribal armies. The cities were in a somewhat better position in this context. The peasants and former pastoralists who had been attracted to the cities often retained a certain tribal organization, at least in the early generations. There was also frequently a strong social solidarity among urban artisan classes. Even among separate cities there was frequent contact, which was lacking among various rural groupings.

Even worse for the agrarian elite were the inevitable vicissitudes of agricultural production. Overirrigation without adequate drainage often led to salinization of the water table. As a result, of course, the land became less productive, which meant peasants had to work harder to meet tax demands. Frequently, they would be left with no surplus whatsoever to live on. Peasants under those circumstances typically moved to other fields. Efforts to force peasants to remain on the land were largely ineffective, especially in times of famine or epidemic disease. This lack of a permanent peasantry increased the instability of the agrarian aristocracy.

As the aristocracy's position weakened, those of the cities and pastoralists were strengthened. Often the peasants abandoned agriculture altogether and went to the cities. Others reverted to pastoralism.[6] Obviously, in a region where the major source of water was a marginal rainfall, nomadic pastoralists were a constant threat to agriculture. The competition between the two is a common theme in Middle Eastern society, as in other societies with a mixed agrarian and pastoralist economy. But it was not the peasants themselves who felt threatened by the pastoralists. For many of them, pastoralism was a viable option in bad farming years. Instead, it was the landowners who felt the tension. The loss of their laborers or land to pastoralism weakened their position of dominance in the government.

This was especially threatening as the pastoralists developed their relations with the cities. Though European cities generally depended on an agrarian hinterland, Middle Eastern cities could do just as well depending on pastoralists. Both cities and pastoralists needed some agricultural products for survival, but both could get such products through trade. And trade in pastoralist products (textiles, such as the precious carpets woven by pastoralist women, and animal products such as skins, meat, milk, and cheese) was just as lucrative as trade in agricultural products. Pastoralists were harder to control and tax than peasants, of course. Nevertheless, where cities wanted to exercise autonomy from the central agrarian-based bureaucracy, reliance on pastoralist power was a viable alternative.

Accordingly, in both potential military manpower as well as mercantile wealth, the pastoralists were a decisive factor during 'Abbasid times. The fact that they were so difficult for a central bureaucracy to control made them natural enemies of the imperial establishment. This was compounded by the fact that they held the balance of power between the agrarian elite and the increasingly powerful cities. Simply by throwing their support behind the local urban elite, they could effectively ensure its autonomy and thus fragment the central government. This is, in fact, exactly how the Seljuqs and the Hamdanis, for example, asserted their regional independence.

Caliphal Attempts to Consolidate Central Control

The potential weaknesses of this precariously based central bureaucracy became actual in the second half of the ninth and the tenth centuries. The Sawad's productivity depended upon its massive irrigation system, which demanded central control. But by the ninth century, even under efficient 'Abbasid management, its revenues were diminishing. The Diyalah River, which waters the region, seems to have begun flowing faster and carving a deeper bed for itself. This produced higher banks, which required significant changes in the canal system that was the lifeblood of the 'Abbasid agrarian aristocracy. The caliphal engineers even tried paving the riverbed to stabilize it. Such projects eventually proved prohibitively expensive, compounded as they were by diminishing returns due to overirrigation and its attendant salinization of groundwater.

The 'Abbasids had already been experiencing sporadic rebellions throughout the empire, even in the early ninth century. Most were suppressed by local governors, such as the Aghlabids in the Maghrib (northwest Africa) and the Tahirids in Khurasan. But with the weakening of the central 'Abbasid power, these local governors became virtually autonomous. With their own territorial bases and their own armies, they were often able to found hereditary dynasties. The caliph was being overlooked in his own administration.

The rebellions always took religio-political form, as had the very revolution that brought the 'Abbasids to the caliphate. Following the 'Abbasid triumph the Shi'i continued to fight for control well into the early ninth century. At one point the 'Abbasid Caliph al-Ma'mun (r. 813–833) tried to pacify the Shi'i by naming 'Ali al-Rida, one of its most popular leaders, as his heir. But the attempt failed. 'Ali died before the move could be effective, and al-Ma'mun had other problems to face.

Among the most vocal opponents of the Umayyad dynasty had been a group of religious scholars (*'ulama'*) who opposed innovation (*bid'a*, considered deviation from orthodoxy in Islam), creative interpretation of texts (*ijtihad*), and rationalism. They believed literal interpretation of the Qur'an and reports about the Prophet (*hadith*) were the most important sources of religious authority. They became popular enough after the 'Abbasid revolution to strongly influence the development of at least two of the four major schools of Islamic law (*shari'a*). Calling for strong Islamic leadership and opposing revolutionary activity, they supported early 'Abbasid suppression of dissident movements. Unlike the Shi'i, who developed a well-earned persecution complex, these so-called Hadithi exuded a sense of confidence in the Muslim community's ability to emerge victorious, provided it followed the respected examples of simple piety conveyed explicitly in the Qur'an. Not surprisingly, therefore, the Hadithi *'ulama'* found official support in the 'Abbasid administration.

However, certain elements of Hadithi thought were not so popular with the caliph. Al-Ma'mun recognized that their condemnation of non-Hadithi religious factions was a destabilizing factor in his administration. He therefore required that all Islamic scholars and judges (*qadis*) reject those Hadithi doctrines most offensive to other Islamic groups, such as the more rationalist Mu'tazili. For instance, the Hadithi believed so intensely in the Qur'an that they actually identified it with God. The Qur'an was uncreated, they said, the divine word itself, co-eternal with God, and available to inspire anyone who reads it. To the Mu'tazili *'ulama'*, this position not only fostered factionalism, by allowing uncontrolled independence of scriptural interpretation, but it also bordered on blasphemy. To reduce factionalism among the *'ulama'*, then, al-Ma'mun decreed that anyone who held the doctrine that the Qur'an was uncreated was not a true Muslim.[7]

This attempt at institutionalizing Islamic belief and creating an official Islamic doctrine, however successful it was on the ideological level, could not salvage the 'Abbasid regime. Caliphal power continued to wane. And as opposition grew the caliph was less and less capable of countering it. Al-Ma'mun's successor, al-Mu'tasim (r. 833–842), tried another strategy to enhance the caliph's independence: a basis of military strength independent of his local governors. It had already become customary to include slaves in the caliph's personal guard. But al-Mu'tasim instituted the practice of putting his personal-slave guards in control of military units, displacing the traditional elite from those positions. In that way he hoped to rise above factional quarrels and, at the same time, create a weapon to use against those local generals who turned the caliph's reliance on them to their own advantage. The slaves were purposely taken from among Turks who would have no allegiance to either Arabs or Persians. Al-Mu'tasim also built an entirely new city, Samarra, fortified and far enough from Baghdad to avoid its quarrels.

But again, in the absence of a unified economic base, the caliph effectively created just one more power he could not control. As the Sawad deteriorated, investment in its maintenance proved futile. When one of its main canals was damaged in factional fighting in 937, little effort was made to restore it. Eventually, the government lost control of its best agricultural land. As Marshall Hodgson observes, this land fell to the control of autonomous cities or pastoralists, "who alone had the tribal social structure and the nomadic alternative resource which would enable them to hold out against pressure from the cities. In the following centuries, the Sawad was eliminated as a primary source of centralized revenues in the region."[8] And with the Sawad went the government's resources to maintain its centralized bureaucratic empire.

Succeeding 'Abbasid caliphs came to rely more and more on their Turkic slave guards, eventually becoming little more than the guards' mascots. The former slaves had become a virtually independent military force in themselves. Having been drawn from outside of mainstream Islamic lands, they felt no social allegiance or responsibility beyond their own internal loyalties. Nominally legitimated by the caliph, they were able to vie successfully with local competitors and gained significant power. The classic example of 'Abbasid submission to the slave guards ("mamluks") came during al-Mutawakkil's reign (847–861). Originally put on the throne by the mamluks, he left governing to them and occupied himself with fabled extravagances. Perhaps best known is the story of a theme party at which everything had to be his favorite color, yellow. The guests had to wear yellow clothes, only blondes were invited, and only yellow food was served on golden dishes. The party was held in a garden whose stream was dyed yellow with saffron. But the servants had forgotten that water in streams moves; soon the yellow color was gone. So the servants collected all the precious fabrics that had been dyed yellow and soaked them in the stream to keep it yellow until the caliph "became too drunk to notice."[9]

The Hadithi, who had managed to survive various attempts to neutralize criticism and factionalism, remained in control of the institutionalized religious framework. Without strong central authority to limit their power, they tended to entrench their antirationalism at the expense of the Mu'tazili and other more philosophic scholars. Under Hadithi guidance, Shi'i and non-Muslims suffered severe oppression. Shi'i shrines and many churches and synagogues were destroyed. Imperial policy was ignored as the Turkic slave guards pursued consolidation of their own power. Ultimately, the mamluks murdered al-Mutawakkil and placed his son on the throne.

With few exceptions the remaining 'Abbasid caliphs at Samarra served only at the will of the royal guard. By the early tenth century the state finances were largely under the control of wealthy entrepreneurs. Gone was even the semblance of an independent aristocracy. Gone also was a bureaucratic class that had some vested interest in government stability. The former Sasanid bureaucrats originally recruited by the 'Abbasid administration had largely gravitated toward the more efficient local governors. Financial mismanagement was chronic, leading to discontent in the military when wages were late. By 932, the end of al-Muqtadir's reign, the state was utterly bankrupt. In 945 Baghdad itself was occupied by one of the Buyyid chiefs. Within thirty years the caliph was a virtual pawn, the Buyyid chief even demanding to be crowned by the caliph as king in an official Persian ceremony. It was under these conditions that the Muslim empire disintegrated into regionally autonomous units.

The First Foreign Invasions

Despite the loss of central caliphal control, the Islamic empire continued to grow. The period from 945, when Baghdad was taken over by the regional Buyyid power, to 1258, when Baghdad was burned to the ground by Mongol invaders, saw the spread of Islam farther north into the Balkans, farther west into Africa, and farther east into India and beyond. It also saw the integration of many influences from these regions into an Islamic idiom. Islamic mystical thought (Sufism), Islamic philosophy, and Islamic theology (*kalam*) continued to develop de-spite—and sometimes because of—the lack of a strong caliph, and Islamic legalism became further entrenched. Nevertheless, the Islamic empire's world dominance was being challenged. The global balance of power was shifting in ways that would affect the Islamic world both directly and indirectly. The direct results were the first to be felt, in the form of foreign invasions by the crusaders from Europe and, later, by the Mongols from Central Asia.

The crusades effectively reversed the phenomenal spread that took place during Islam's first one hundred years. During that time Muslims from North Africa and Spain had made their presence felt in all the northern ports of the Mediterranean, through raids and, occasionally, occupation. By the turn of the eleventh century Christian Europe was sufficiently organized to fight back. The Europeans drove the Muslims out of Sicily and northern Spain and launched periodic raids on the North African shore. This movement gained strength throughout the eleventh century, and by the end of the century the caliph had almost totally lost control of Syria. Most of the significant towns were auton-omous, many under nominal control of the Seljuq dynasty in Aleppo (in Syria). When the Europeans began their surprise invasions, therefore, it was virtually impossible to plan a unified defense. Each amir (prince) could only try to hold his own city and hope the plague would be over as quickly as it had come. But that was not to be.

To the Europeans, the loss of what had been part of the Christian (Byzantine) empire to the Muslims was still relatively recent. As discussed in Chapter One, the ostensible goal of the crusades was to retake Christian heartlands from the "infidels." Taking advantage of the burst of religious enthusiasm that marked the era, the crusaders were able to return large parts of Anatolia to Christian rule. But they also conquered portions of Syria that had never been under Byzantine rule; these were often awarded to them in perpetuity as income-producing fiefs, nominally under Byzantine sovereignty. Yet it was no easier for the Byzantine government to control these European vassals than it had been for the caliph to control his. The European conquerors frequently maintained their domains for their own enrichment. Following their notorious plundering of the eastern Mediterranean coast, which culminated in the massacre of Jerusalem's population in 1099, many former crusaders settled into relatively stable, autonomous principalities throughout the Syrian countryside. They formed their own local alliances, such as those with Christian Armenian groups who felt closer to the Europeans than to the Byzantines or their Muslim countrymen. Supported by Italian navies, the crusaders were for a time impregnable to the feuding local amirs (leaders).

Fortunately for the Muslims, however, the crusaders (called Franks by the Muslims) were just as petty as the local rulers. Jealous of each other's domains, they preferred a delicate balance of contending powers to a strong central government. Therefore, when in the twelfth century the Muslims overcame their own conflicts long enough to form a unified force against the Europeans, it was the Franks who were at a disadvantage.

The originator of the unified Muslim command was the amir of Mosul, Zengi, son of a Turkic slave officer of the Seljuqs. He extended his power to Edessa (Ruha) in 1144 and, upon his death in 1146, was succeeded by an equally capable son, Nur al-Din. Nur al-Din, a Sunni, was intent on consolidating his control, as much against the Christian invaders as the ubiquitous Shi'i competition from the east. He therefore championed institutionalized Islamic law—the Sunni-formulated Shari'a—winning the strong support of the *'ulama'* and recreating an Islamic identity among his troops. As a result he was able to assert his dominance in Damascus, the only major city in the area not controlled by the crusaders. From Damascus he launched his attacks on Christian Jerusalem. But the crusaders' hold on Jerusalem was still too strong for the local powers. And Nur al-Din could count on no help from Egypt at this point, whose Fatimid Shi'i leadership was itself in disarray. Therefore, turning his attentions first toward Egypt, he took effective control of the country in 1169, under nominal loyalty to the 'Abbasid caliph. Joining his forces with Egypt's, he finally formed a Muslim force stronger than the crusaders'.

When Nur al-Din died in 1174, his able lieutenant in Egypt, Salah al-Din (Saladin) managed to take control—despite initial resistance based on the fact that he was an ethnic Kurd, rather than a Turk. Egypt became his base of operations. By fostering relations with other

Muslim rulers, including the caliph, as well as with Greek and Armenian Christian powers, Salah al-Din was able to restore Egyptian power. He became an inspiring and respected leader and was able to retake Jerusalem in 1187. After that the crusaders were confined to their seaport towns, and eventually the crusading spirit faded from Europe. Future crusades, even those led by the kings of France and England and supported by the power of the Italian cities, were deprived of significant success. Their most enduring effect was probably the discredit earned by the Europeans in the Muslim world. (Muslim records of the crusades reveal a horror at the barbarity of the Christians. While Salah al-Din was respected even by the Europeans for his fairness and equanimity, the crusaders gained their reputation in such exploits as the massacre of Acre: When the crusaders captured the town, they reneged on their pledge to allow the residents to be ransomed, instead massacring the entire population, including women and children.)[10]

The reappearance of Muslim unity, however, was brief, and it faded again upon the withdrawal of the foreign enemy. Salah al-Din's successors were unable to hold Ayyubid power for long. In 1250, the slave soldiers regained dominance and, in fact, created their own joint Egyptian-Syrian dynasty, the Mamluks. But soon another power was to make itself felt in the Islamic world: the Mongols.

The Mongols were a group of nomadic pastoralist tribes from the northern reaches of the Eurasian steppe. Heavily involved in trade from the Black Sea to northern China, they were more dependent on agrarian and commercial centers than were the pastoralists of Arabia. It was therefore in the Mongols' interest to form tribal confederacies under a single leader. They then could control the towns along the trade routes passing through their territories. The Mongols formed such a confederacy in the early thirteenth century and, in the absence of a strong power in both China and the Islamic world, were able to extend their power virtually unchecked.

The charismatic leader of the Mongols was Chingiz (Genghis) Khan. After consolidating his power in the East, he turned his attention westward toward the Oxus basin. He defeated the dominant Khawarizmis and spread his control well into Iran. Under the leadership of Chingiz's successors, Mongol expansion continued in northern China and throughout eastern Europe as far as Germany. In 1279 Qubilay (Kublai) Khan overcame what was left of Chinese resistance.

The Mongol conquest of the central Muslim lands was facilitated by the infighting of the Sunni and Shi'i leaders. The Iranian amirs had already been subdued, and the ferocity of early Mongol military conquests inspired them to step obligingly aside. In fact, Islamic leaders sometimes encouraged the Mongols to enter their territory and destroy competitive Muslim powers. Such was the case, for instance, with the Sunnis' erstwhile enemy, the (Shi'i) Nizari Isma'ilis of Alamut. Although by the mid-thirteenth century the Nizaris ceased to be the threat they once had been, still they were independent and—worse yet—fostered an intellectual ethic of rationalism and free thinking.

The story of the Isma'ilis themselves is an interesting reflection of the decrepitude of the 'Abbasid regime. The historians of the age, for the most part, were 'Abbasid partisans and therefore roundly condemned the Isma'ilis, who were critical of the 'Abbasid regime. In his *History of Intellectual Movements in Islam,* Bandali al-Jawzi (d. 1942) dismisses as mere propaganda the aspersions cast upon the Isma'ilis by such chroniclers as Abu Mansur al-Baghdadi (d. 1037)—that they were immoral profligates, atheists, Iranian subversives, etc.[11] In truth, al-Jawzi claims, the Isma'ilis were a pious lot devoted to intellectual and moral perfection: "The means of achieving this goal was, in their view, the development of intellectual power. Then proper conduct and moral life will follow, in accordance with the demands of sound reason."[12] They therefore scorned the excessive legalism of institutionalized Islam as prohibitive of intellectual development. They believed people should be encouraged to question all beliefs in order to clarify and confirm their own. They also criticized the exclusivity of institutionalized Islam, with its strict distinction between believers and nonbelievers. The Isma'ilis believed instead that the principles of true religion were universal. They therefore minimized the external trappings of institutionalized religion—which was blasphemy, no doubt, to the established hierarchy—and concentrated instead on the social message of Islam. As such, according to al-Jawzi, they were authentic continuators of the original Islamic impulse to social justice. As al-Jawzi puts it, "[T]he Isma'ilis were truly the first in Islam to rise above the nationalist zeal against which both the Umayyads and 'Abbasids had been powerless."[13] It was only under the caliphal dynasties that Islam had deviated from the Prophet's message and, in the process of institutionalizing a power structure, become an intolerant religion virtually devoid—on its official level—of the driving, living spirit of Islam's call to universal social justice. The popularity of the Isma'ilis and other groups like them reflect the widespread discontent with the caliphal version of Islam.

The betrayal of the Isma'ili group at Alamut by Nasr al-Din Tusi provides another interesting comment on the times—this one on the intellectual temperament. Nasr al-Din Tusi (d. 1273) was a Shi'i philosopher of some note. Like all intellectuals of the time, however, he was at the mercy of the religio-political regime. As with the Isma'ilis and other groups representing the discontent of the populace, criticism of the institutionalized religio-political structure brought condemnation.

In true Machiavellian fashion, Tusi thus manipulated the various power centers to ensure his own survival. He began his career under the protection of the Isma'ilis, while they still held some power in the northern highlands. When the Mongols destroyed the remnants of that Shi'i power (with encouragement from the caliph's ambassadors), he praised the Sunni regime's decisiveness. When it became obvious the Mongols were the power to deal with, he encouraged them to destroy Baghdad, became counsellor to the Mongol court, and was able to use his position to the benefit of the Iraqi Shi'is.

In any event, Hulegu Khan (d. 1265), successor to Chingiz's line in Iran and Iraq, captured most of the Isma'ili towns and in 1256 massacred the remnants of the regime in Alamut. The Mongols then moved on to Baghdad and Syria. In a single battle in 1258 the Mongols destroyed the caliphal army and ravaged the city. Once they had defeated the Seljuqs in Anatolia, their control of Muslim lands (with the exception of the sultanate of Delhi and the Mamluk Baybars in Syria) was complete.

This was the final blow to Islamic centralization. No longer was there even nominal unity. As contemporary historian Ibn al-Athir (1160–1234) described it:

> Islam and Muslims have during that period been afflicted by such disasters that no other nation had experienced. One such affliction was the invasion by the Tatar [Mongols]. They came from the East and inflicted overwhelming damages. Another was the onset of the Frankish people (God's curse be upon them) from the West to Mesopotamia and Egypt, and the occupation of its port, that is Damietta, which nearly subjected all of Egypt to their rule, had it not been for God's mercy and victory over them. But another affliction was that the Muslims themselves had been divided, and their swords lifted up against their fellows.[14]

Intellectual Responses to Caliphal Decentralization

This was the situation that faced Muslim intellectuals of the day. The decline of caliphal authority and foreign invasions presented challenges to traditional Islamic society's self-understanding. As had the medieval Christians at the time of the Black Death and the Hundred Years' War, the Muslims tried to figure out how they had displeased God and what they could do to correct their errors. Reflecting the fragmentation of Islamic society, the intellectual formulations of the time are widely varied. Shi'i thinkers intellectualized the validity of supreme loyalty to the family of 'Ali. They attested to God's leadership through the hereditary imam (leader), and when there were no descendants of 'Ali available for the imamate, they rationalized such absence. Those thinkers influenced by Hellenic intellectualism—the *falasifi* (philosophers)—formulated metaphysical systems for Islam on Platonic, Neoplatonic, and/or Aristotelian models. These were countered by religious thinkers who attempted to use philosophical methods to dispute the philosophers' claims; the result was *kalam* (literally, "disputation"; often translated as "theology"). Meanwhile, the mystical strain of Islam—Sufism—was attracting more and more followers as the orthodox elite became so embroiled in erudition that they failed to meet the common believers' daily needs for spiritual leadership.

Often these formulations proved unacceptable to the state intellectual hierarchy, the Sunni *'ulama'*, and were condemned. Meanwhile the most influential of the *'ulama'*, the legal scholars or *fuqaha'* (from *fiqh*, jurisprudence) attempted to systematize their analytic principles. They wanted to instill rigor in the legal process to transcend accusations of arbitrariness and withstand the divisive pressures of rationalism, Shi'ism, and Sufism—considered the state's three greatest challenges. Although the caliphate was losing ground economically and politically, it was still in control of the state intellectual apparatus.

By the tenth century, Islamic legal thought had evolved into four official schools (*madhhab*, pl. *madhahib*). Each had grown up around a leading jurisprudent in various regional centers of the empire and only really differed from the others in details of methodology and degree of flexibility. All agreed that the sources of Islamic law were the Qur'an, the hadith reports of the Prophet's behavior (the Sunna), and what could be inferred from the Qur'an and Sunna by personal judgment (*ra'y*) or through analogical reasoning (*qiyas*). In Iraq, Abu Hanifa (d. 767) rose to dominate the field of legal thought. Stressing the exercise of individual intellectual effort with regard to the traditional sources of religious knowledge, this early approach to Shari'a (Islamic law) became known as Hanafi. In Medina, Malik ibn Anas (d. 795) laid greater stress on the Sunna as well as on the authority of religious scholars' interpretation of it. His followers are called Malikis. Another leader of Medinan legal thought (as well as of that of Cairo, where he spent his later years) was Malik's student, Muhammad ibn Idris al-Shafi'i (d. 819). Al-Shafi'i pushed the reliance on hadith even further. Although he was himself a keen legal thinker, his rejection of arbitrary legal thought and insistence on strict analogical reasoning tended to denigrate the validity of *ijtihad* (the creative interpretation of texts). His followers, the Shafi'i *madhhab*, are frequently characterized as reactionary, stressing conformity with precedent rather than progressive or creative thinking. The views of Ahmad Ibn Hanbal (d. 855), founder of the Hanbali school, reflect not only the influence of al-Shafi'i but also the growing perception of the threat to Islamic unity posed by the Sufi and Shi'i thinkers. A native of Baghdad, Ibn Hanbal was a supporter of those *'ulama'* who sought to limit this dangerous "rational-ist" trend, the so-called Hadithis or Traditionists, and placed ultimate emphasis on following the Sunna. Each of these schools, as well as the Shi'i Ja'fari *madhhab*, was and remains to this day mutually acceptable, although Muslims of various regions traditionally follow one school of law or another.

With the establishment of the four schools of law, the institution-alization of Islamic thought was complete, for the *fuqaha'* added to the three traditional sources of Islamic law—the Qur'an, the Sunna, and what could be derived from them—a fourth: *ijma'*, which was effectively an agreement among the *fuqaha'* to agree on exactly what were the implications of what could be derived from the Qur'an and the Sunna. According to this principle, the consensus of legal scholars on any point was infallible. *Ijma'* had always been included among the sources of Islamic law, but it gradually gained greater and greater prominence and at the same time narrowed in scope. Only the *fuqaha'* could practice interpretative thinking—*ijtihad*—and only their consen-sus made *ijtihad* authoritative. The only accepted doctrine or practice was what was promulgated under the consensus of the four recognized *madhahib*.

Thus the earlier openness with which scholars had expressed legal opinions gradually was replaced with a closed "door of creative rea-soning" (*bab al-ijtihad*). By the turn of the tenth century, as scholar of Islamic law Joseph Schacht puts it:

> [T]he point had been reached when the scholars of all schools felt that all essential questions had been thoroughly discussed and finally settled, and a consensus gradually established itself to the effect that from that time onwards no one might be deemed to have the necessary qualifications for independent reasoning in law, and that all future activity would have to be confined to the explanation, application, and, at the most, inter-pretation of the doctrine as it had been laid down once and for all.[15]

As historian Ibn Khaldun (1332–1406) described the situation:

> The study of hadith was limited in all regions to the *taqlid* [indiscriminate imitation] of the four *madhahib*. The *fuqaha'* investigated no further, but closed the door to further investigation by others . . . to the extent that no options were left other than merely copying what had been done before. . . . There was, therefore, no new *fiqh* [legal thinking], and anyone who claimed he was capable of *ijtihad* was excluded and discriminated against. All of Islamic law now consisted of these four.[16]

Thus the only acceptable teaching became that promulgated by the four official schools of Islamic jurisprudence. Because the supreme political ruler was also the supreme religious official, this amounted, of course, to state censorship. The *fuqaha'*—whose positions depended on the caliphal bureaucracy—had the right to condemn anyone who criticized the caliphate, and that became the state's most potent weapon.

This sort of intransigence extended to philosophy, as well. Studying the works of Ibn Sina ("Avicenna," d. 1037), the most famous Aristotelian philosopher produced by the Islamic world, was outlawed in 1245 by the *fuqaha'*. The only legal doctrinal system was that of Abu'l Hassan al-Ash'ari (d. 935?), who had devised an interpretation of revelation that denied the doctrine of free will and causality. Though philosophers argued that there could be neither merit nor guilt in acts not freely chosen, al-Ash'ari felt it was more important to defend the omnipotence of God than the responsibility of human beings. He therefore concluded that all acts are created by God and simply attach themselves to the human will. Historian al-Maqrizi (d. 1442) confirmed the official nature of the doctrine in those regions still loyal to the caliph and reported that in the Egyptian government established by Salah al-Din, for instance, anyone who publicly challenged Ash'ari views was executed.[17]

A Reformulation of Islamic Thought

The weakened caliphate no longer had the resources to enforce its central tributary system. When local leaders became economically and therefore militarily independent, it was possible for them to declare their political independence. As noted above, some local leaders maintained a nominal relationship with the caliphate as the basis of their political legitimacy. Many, however, declared a decisive break with the caliphal authorities. In a world where political legitimation depended on religion, just as it had in medieval Europe, virtually every revolution of the age was justified religiously. The justification for non-cooperation with the caliphate was given in Islamic terms; invariably the caliphate was criticized as deviating from true Islamic practice.[18] Accordingly, as we saw, the attempts of the *fuqaha'* to counter such criticisms and uphold the central authority they represented generally tended toward intransigence.

However, this was not always the case. Taqiyy al-Din Ahmad Ibn Taymiyya (d. 1328) is among the most famous of the Muslim legists precisely because, instead of ignoring or simply condemning the forces splintering the Islamic body politic, he faced them head on. In doing so he set an example for modern Islamic attempts to deal with changing geopolitical reality—an example that would not come to fruition for some six hundred years.

Ibn Taymiyya was a jurist of the Hanbali school who operated in primarily Hanafi Damascus. He gained fame for his utter rejection of *taqlid,* the ethic of indiscriminate imitation of precedents established by the *fuqaha'*.[19] He in no way rejected the authority of the four schools of Shari'a. In fact, he wrote a treatise entitled *Raf' al-Malam 'an al-A'immah al-A'lam* ("In Defense of the Four Imams") in which he said it is incumbent on all Muslims to obey God, his Prophet, and the *'ulama'* "who are heirs of the prophets, and whom God gave the status of stars for guidance in the darkness of land and sea."[20] But he went on to explain how, this being the case, there could be discord among their learned opinions and interpretations of the sacred sources of law. The possible reasons for such discord included ignorance of pertinent hadiths or doubt of their authenticity or applicability. Divergence of opinion among the *fuqaha',* he said, is not a defect. It only points to the scholars' human fallibility. And in the exercise of *ijtihad,* the creative interpretation of the texts, they are to be applauded.

On the other hand, reliance on *ijma'* (consensus among the juris-prudents) was not so commendable, according to Ibn Taymiyya. In the first place, as a Hanbali, he believed that *ijma'* really applied only to the first generation of Muslims, the Prophet and his companions. After the dispersal of Muslims far and wide, there was no way to determine whether there was unanimous agreement among the scholars of a given age. The interpretation that *ijma'* refers only to consensus among the leaders of the four *madhahib* was not a suitable substitute, he said.[21]

Instead, Ibn Taymiyya expanded on the Hanbali notion of *istislah,* having regard for *maslaha,* "social well-being" or "public interest." The Malikis and Shafi'is also use the principle of *istislah,* whereas the Hanafis prefer a similar principle, *istihsan,* "approval" or "preference." In either case, the principle is a mechanism whereby strict adherence to the accepted sources of Islamic law can be bypassed in certain cases determined by public well-being. Exercise of this option—i.e., the use of informed personal opinion to solve complex social problems in keeping with Islamic principles—is how Ibn Taymiyya described *ijtihad.* And it was the tool he used to address the pressing question of disintegrating Islamic unity.

Ibn Taymiyya accepted the standard interpretation of *istislah* but expanded it subtly and significantly. He said that *istislah* is to be practiced not only to derive benefit for society, but also to protect it from harm.[22] And to determine what was beneficial or harmful, he considered it necessary to articulate a standard of *maslaha:* The well-being of the Islamic community lay in its unity. Ibn Taymiyya used the word *ta'awun,* "solidarity," to describe that force that binds together all Muslims throughout history, from the Prophet and his companions to the Final Judgment. *Ta'awun* is primarily a unity of doctrine, he said, a unity of belief and purpose, not necessarily of politics. Just as he had explained the existence of several schools of law, he accepted a certain amount of variety in religious practice. In the treatise *Ikhtilaf al-Ummah fi al-'Ibadat* ("Diversity of Religious Observances in the Islamic Community"), he explained that diversity in itself is not due to any defect in the sources of Islamic doctrine, but only to the fallibility of human interpreters. Nor need such differences concern believers, he said. The interpretations devised by the *fuqaha'* are all interrelated; discrepancies on individual points do not mitigate agreement on the overall corpus, again, the basis of Islamic unity.[23]

This did not translate into religious tolerance for Ibn Taymiyya. In fact, he believed the participation of non-Muslims—especially Christians—in Islamic political life had weakened Islamic resolve. He accepted Christians and Jews religiously, viewing them, as does the Qur'an, as an integral part of the prophetic tradition. He even negotiated with the Mongols on their behalf at one point.[24] But he believed the high positions non-Muslims had attained in the Islamic political structure had weakened the solidarity of the Islamic community (*umma*). He blamed the Fatimids of Egypt in particular for putting Jews and Christians above Islamic unity. From the time of Caliph al-Mu'izz (r. 953–975), Christians had finagled their way into the administration, relying on their crafty amiability, in Ibn Taymiyya's view. This led to a dilution of the Islamic spirit, for the Christians did not uphold Islamic principles. They were exempt from even the basic Islamic duties of prayer and almsgiving. And they were known for even worse behavior, such as gambling in their own churches and drinking wine. The same applied to the Jews, who went so far as to sell wine to Muslims.[25] The Christians had proven they were a threat to Islam by their collusion with the sectarian Shi'i. And both Christians and Jews had collaborated with the crusaders and the Mongols at the expense of the Sunni Muslim community. Besides that, he said, the Christians had introduced their idolatrous saint-worship and ineffectual asceticism into the Islamic community, misleading the already confused Sufis.

Therefore, Ibn Taymiyya's acceptance of diversity was reserved for the Muslim community. But within that context, he worked assiduously to establish the acceptable limits of diversity while preserving the essential unity of Islam. Islamic unity was a moral unity, unanimous in encouraging goodness and denouncing inequity. The ideal Muslim community is mutually supportive in just behavior and in offering corrective advice when necessary, in word and by example always issuing the invitation (*da'wa*) to follow the law of God. This call, he said—the call to make the Islamic community God's witnesses on earth—is at the very heart of the unity of the Islamic community. Provided this type of unity exists, variations on detail are acceptable.

This was how Ibn Taymiyya broke the mold of the official *fuqaha'* and justified the undeniable political diversity that characterized the age. Instead of condemning all those who failed to submit to caliphal authority, however effete that authority might be, Ibn Taymiyya boldly accepted the fragmented political reality. Like many philosophers before him, he recognized the necessity of some political hierarchy.[26] Indeed, he accepted Ibn Hanbal's belief that sixty years under a tyrant is better than one night of anarchy.[27] But this did not imply to Ibn Taymiyya that all Muslims must be under the same political authority.

Distinguishing Religious from Political Unity

In fact, Ibn Taymiyya believed that excessive insistence on political unity can be harmful to the Islamic community. The kind of exclusivism that keeps people tied to an original tribal or ritual group (be it Qays or Kalb/Yemeni, Umayyad or 'Abbasid, Sunni or Shi'i) actually militates against Islamic unity. If, for instance, one tribal faction attains power and then chooses its agents and ministers from among only its own members, the result is discontent among other, equally qualified members of the community. Islam was supposed to supersede such tribally based solidarity and replace it with moral solidarity. Islamic solidarity is based on shared standards of piety, he said, on shared goals, and on agreement concerning human destiny. Ibn Taymiyya scholar Henri Laoust summarizes this view on the subject of Islamic solidarity:

> The community thus forms a great being, each party in solidarity with the whole, each generation in close moral continuity, responsible to those preceding it and bearing a legacy to transmit to those following, in which each ethnic or racial grouping is legally acceptable to the extent that it contributes to the unity of the whole.[28]

Again, this unity consists of submission to the will of God as revealed through Prophet Muhammad and interpreted in the corpus of Islamic doctrine. That, in fact, is the merit of Sunni Islam, as opposed to Shi'i, according to Ibn Taymiyya. Sunni Muslims—*ahl al-sunna wa'l-jama'a*, "the people of the Sunna and the community," as Ibn Taymiyya calls them—place Islamic unity above personal, tribal, or national concerns. By implication, the failure of the Shi'i is not so much in the way they interpret Islamic theories of leadership as in their insistence on the correctness of their own theories to the detriment of Islamic unity. The same criticism is leveled at the philosophers: Regardless of the nature or content of their conclusions, it is their insistence on those conclusions despite the consensus of the Muslim community that earned Ibn Taymiyya's scorn.

Perhaps most importantly, Ibn Taymiyya believed this unity is to be achieved through the contribution of every member of the Islamic community. As noted above, each member of the community is charged with the responsibility not only to do good, but also to offer corrective counsel when she/he sees others deviating from the righteous path and to call all those within earshot to submit to the will of God. That is the basis of Islamic moral solidarity: each member of the community actively participating in the creation of a just society, the establishment of God's kingdom on earth. Ibn Taymiyya cited a hadith in which the Prophet is reported to have said, "The believers, through their mutual affection, their reciprocal compassion, their common sympathy, resemble a single body, so that if one complains, the others get a fever and insomnia."[29] God has ordered Muslims, Ibn Taymiyya concluded, to cling to one another in this sense, to support and sustain the moral bond of the community, and has forbidden divisiveness on matters of belief.

But to interpret that as a requirement for political unity would be to ignore the Qur'an itself, which recognizes and even sanctions as God's will the variety among nations. The Qur'an readily accepts the diversity among peoples, claiming to have sent revelation in various forms to all nations: "There is no nation to which a warner has not come" (35:24) and "For every people a guide has been provided" (13:7). Both the Torah and the Christian Gospel are accepted as valid revelation, as are other forms sent to other peoples (42:15). In that sense—the oneness of true revelation—all peoples are united. But there is no denying sociopolitical diversity: "If your Lord had willed it, he would have made mankind one community, but they remain divided" (11:118; cf. 10:19). Thus the responsibility for social diversity is with God. All revelation is valid and no community has exclusive claim on it. The responsibility for Islamic unity is with each individual Muslim; it is a moral affair, not a political one.

The result of this revolutionary approach to Islamic unity was a reorientation of the nature of politics. It turned the tables on the central administration. The leadership was no longer the headquarters and arbiters of Muslim unity; the people were. Members of the Muslim family are called to support and sustain one another—socially, spiritually, and even physically. In the face of poverty and destitution, mere faith is a phantom, Ibn Taymiyya felt. Islam is an active faith and the kind of activity it demands requires at least minimal physical amenities. Therefore, if someone in the community falls on hard times it is the responsibility of the others to furnish whatever is necessary to restore her/him to a life of meaningful faith. The community is obligated to ensure that each of its members is strong enough to serve God. Accordingly, each member of the Muslim community serves politically. The difference between the humble and the elite is only one of degree. All contribute in the service of God.

Again, this relegates political unity as such to secondary importance. Ibn Taymiyya strengthens this argument in his discussion of the unity that prevailed in the early Muslim commmunity. That was the unity of true and practical *tawhid,* he said: the socioreligious unity reflective of the unicity of God.[30] It was a spontaneous and automatic unity, emanating from rather than forced upon the community. The community was powerful because of its moral cohesion, not cohesive because of its power or force. From these observations Ibn Taymiyya concluded that a community held together only through political or military force is not truly united. And political force had been necessary to hold the Muslim community together since the earliest days of the caliphate. Thus, for Ibn Taymiyya political unity is not an essential characteristic of Islamic unity. It is secondary and therefore may be dispensed with. And, he reiterated, if the community is expending its efforts to maintain political unity through force, it may well be doing so at the expense of true Islamic endeavor. It is to the realization of God's will, the creation of a just society, that Muslims should devote their energies. This unity of endeavor is true Islamic solidarity in Ibn Taymiyya's view.

Conditional Political Authority

If all Muslims are in this sense political agents, how are political leaders to be characterized? What is the nature of political authority if it is not, as had been previously assumed, the basis of Muslim unity? In Ibn Taymiyya's decisive treatise on political theory, he compared political authority (*wilaya*) to the responsibility of a shepherd. Citing a hadith wherein the Prophet is supposed to have said, "All of you are shepherds; and every shepherd is responsible for his flock," Ibn Taymiyya said that political authority is "a trust [*wakala*], for rulers are trustees of the souls of believers as in a partnership."[31] In addition, he said, "Treasurers have not the power to apportion the funds as an owner may divide his property; rather they are custodians, representatives, stewards, not owners."[32] Political leadership is therefore a responsibility, not a right. It is based on the leader's ability to execute God's law; if he fails to do so, he forfeits his trust—shades of Rousseau's "social contract."

What was more, though political hierarchy is necessary, no given individual is indispensable to the community. This argument is given in opposition to the Shi'i notion of an infallible imam, especially as articulated by Ibn Taymiyya's contemporary al-Muhaqqiq al-Hilli (d. 1277). Al-Hilli claimed that once the line of prophecy ended, as it had with the death of Muhammad, God had provided infallible leadership for the community through the imam. Even certain Sunni thinkers claimed a single spiritual and political leader of the Muslim community was necessary, despite the absence of Qur'anic texts on this point.[33] Ibn Taymiyya rejected these arguments and said that only the leadership of the Prophet was divinely instituted. Even the leadership of the esteemed Rashidun, the first four "rightly guided" caliphs, was only relatively or conditionally perfect.[34] They were close enough to the Prophet himself that they were able to lead the community properly. But following that period, the caliphate gradually evolved into a simple kingship (*muluk*), temporal and no more than a matter of expedience.[35] The Qur'an never dictated a particular form of government for the Islamic community, he said, nor did it address the problem of successorship to the Prophet. And it never limited the number of imams (as the Shi'i claimed). It only said to obey God, the Prophet, and those in authority within the community.[36]

Thus Ibn Taymiyya described political leadership of the Islamic community as a temporal and practical matter, rather than a sacred or doctrinal issue. On the question of how that leadership should be chosen, Ibn Taymiyya again took issue with al-Hilli, who said leadership of the Islamic state is a matter of divine designation. Ibn Taymiyya said instead that leadership is to be decided by consensus or near-consensus of an electoral body—*ahl al-hall wa 'l-'aqd,* "those empowered to bind and loose."[37] This is a republican principle of election: Choice is not by direct plebiscite but by representatives of the constituency. But Ibn Taymiyya encouraged that the representatives' decision not be imposed on the public. Once their choice has been made, it should be offered to the public for ratification. In fact, he took pains to reject the supremacy of an elite core in Islam. Ultimate power over choice of leadership rests with the public. Only when they have approved the choice does the binding occur. Just as with any contract, neither side should be under compulsion.[38] It must be a matter of free choice on both sides and result from the reasonable expectation of mutual benefit, i.e., both for the leader and those who are led. The imam has the right to expect obedience so long as he leads in accordance with Shari'a, and the subjects have the right to expect the peace and social order that will inevitably result from proper Islamic leadership. Again, the implication is clear: If one party to the contract fails to live up to the bargain, the contract is effectively nullified.

What Ibn Taymiyya has done here is articulate a basis of Islamic unity that is not dependent upon political unity. He has upheld the Islamic ideal of solidarity through submission to the will of God and the communal effort to establish a just social order, which removes the responsibility from the leadership alone and places it in the populace itself. In so doing he provides a framework for Islamic unity despite the politically fragmented reality. This revolutionary attempt to accommodate the seemingly ineluctable forces of political fragmentation differ significantly from the Holy Roman Empire's attempts to deal with similar forces some three hundred years later. As noted in Chapter One, the Augsburg formula—*cujus regio, ejus religio*—was to keep religious solidarity tied to political control: Whoever is in political control gets to determine the religious policy as well. Ibn Taymiyya, by contrast, placed religious unity above politics. Rather than sacrifice the ultimate ideal of spiritual unity, he justified the parcelling out of political control. And in the process, again far ahead of his European counterparts, he laid the foundations for geographically limited political sovereignty. Clearly, if political leadership is democratically legitimated, then its extent is limited to the domain of the populace in question.

Ibn Taymiyya's separation of religious from political unity is not the same as what the Western world now calls secularism. He still maintained that leadership should be Islamic. He simply accepted the reality of multiple political entities in the Islamic world. Islamic unity no longer depended upon political unity, nor was Islam as such—*submission* to the will of God—to be judged by the soul of the imam or caliph. Though the ruler should still ideally be a good Muslim, it was no longer essential that he be. In fact, even if he is not he must be obeyed, at least on the civil level, which is really the extent of his province. On the spiritual level, submission to the will of God is the responsibility of every individual. Unlike Saint Augustine in Christianity, Ibn Taymiyya did not simply separate the spiritual and political realms, placing morality solely in the former. He maintained the essentially Islamic notion that piety not only may but must be pursued in the here-and-now. But for Ibn Taymiyya neither unified nor pious leadership was ultimately responsible for achievement of Islamic social goals. Even the most pious leader would be powerless to achieve Islamic goals among a wayward population, and it was obvious to him that mere political unity had little to do with Islamic solidarity.[39]

Thus Ibn Taymiyya heralded a future of rising regionalism or proto-nationalism and Islamic attempts to accommodate it without sacrificing

Islam's universalism. That is why Ibn Taymiyya is called the source of Islamic reformism (see quote at beginning of this chapter). But that future would take a long time to come. Ibn Taymiyya's voice would be silenced. Although he achieved high position and widespread fame in his time, eventually the Islamic government tired of his attacks. As historian Marshall Hodgson says, Ibn Taymiyya "was too radical for the established authorities."[40] His criticism of what he considered lax religious practices, of the reliance on the form rather than the substance of religious unity, and of the other *'ulama'* for their compliance with official policy landed him in prison more than once. Still, Ibn Taymiyya carried significant influence as an important reformer. He achieved respect and high position in the religio-political milieu of the thirteenth-century Islamic world—a world well on its way toward fragmentation and sorely in need of reform. He attempted to focus on the weak spots in the system, like Luther, not in an attempt to destroy it but to return to its original vitality. Ibn Taymiyya recognized the politico-economic fragmentation of the empire, but it did not overly concern him. The basis of Islamic unity lay in adherence to Islamic law, not subservience to a single ruler. But like most significant reformers, Ibn Taymiyya posed a threat to the entrenched authorities and therefore suffered for his convictions. He was eventually denied the right to express his views on paper, even from his prison cell, and died a lonely death. The Islamic authorities ignored his warnings, and the Arab world fell prey to further foreign domination, this time by the Ottoman Turks.

CHAPTER THREE

The Ottoman Interlude

*T*here was a continual tension between the central
government and its agents: the tax-farmers had to be
given enough power to allow them to do their job but
not so much that they became strong enough to defy government
regulations, to increase the rate of taxation, and to hold back a
significant proportion of the rural surplus for their own use. This
tension could be contained when the central and provincial
governments were strong, but once they began to weaken this
rapidly had a cumulative effect. Tax-farmers would keep back more
and more of that they owed to the Treasury, using the money to
augment their own power. Meanwhile, the government, deprived of
the funds it needed to maintain its own forces, grew steadily
weaker.

—Roger Owen[1]

The Ottomans Assume the Caliphal Legacy

The rise of the Ottoman empire only postponed the ultimate fragmentation of the central Islamic lands. Like the 'Abbasids before them,
the Ottomans were never free of the decentralizing forces at work in
the empire, especially in the Arab regions.[2] The Ottomans began as
a border troop on the western reaches of the Seljuq state in Anatolia.
The Seljuqs had followed the Buyyid precedent of caliphal investiture
to their throne, thus securing Islamic legitimacy while retaining autonomy. But by the second half of the thirteenth century, the Seljuq
state, too, was floundering under pressure from the Mongols. The Seljuqs
had established a system of these border troops, which were generally

seminomadic Turkic tribes, who acted as both defense units and vanguards of expansion in the name of Islam. The tribes were loosely organized around leading generals, the strongest of whom were often able to act as brokers in power struggles among the Seljuqs.

The Ottomans rose to power in just this way. The power of the border tribes was such that it could best be exercised through expansion. That, after all, was one of their purposes. An ambitious leader of the western border troops had a ready means to enhance his position: conquest of Byzantine lands. By the turn of the fourteenth century, 'Osman (Turkish for 'Uthman, whence "Ottoman") had emerged as such a leader. By 1373 the Byzantine emperor was forced to accept the dominance of the Ottoman Murad I (r. 1362–1389) in the Balkans. Even Christian leaders began to seek Ottoman protection in their feudal disputes. The Ottomans also became the power to reckon with in Anatolia, which was still under Mongol control. They claimed Konya, the old Seljuq capital, as their own and proclaimed themelves the Seljuqs' heirs. Under Murad I's son Bayezid, known as "the Thunderbolt," the Ottomans soon subjugated the remaining border tribes in western Anatolia.

Bayezid also reformed Ottoman government from a tribal model to the centralized administration of the classic Islamic model. Agents in the provinces (*sanjaks*) became answerable to the sultan himself. This was not particularly significant for the peasants in the countryside; their allegiance was generally to whomever could provide security from the various raids that had become common as central 'Abbasid control dissipated. But it did increase the efficiency of the administration and militate against rebellion by provincial leaders. To be an enemy of the Ottoman leader was one thing; to declare oneself an enemy of the Islamic leader, on the other hand, was to invite jihad. Although they had not yet formally declared themselves caliphs, the Ottomans had clearly revived the identity of the state and Islam, Ibn Taymiyya's efforts to distinguish between the two notwithstanding. And on that basis, Bayezid continued to expand Ottoman control.

Successive Ottoman sultans consolidated control in the Balkans and in the formerly Mongol and Mamluk lands. In 1453, after a nearly two-month siege, Constantinople was taken. It became the Ottoman capital, Istanbul, and Mehmed II ("the Conqueror," r. 1451–1481) became the most prestigious ruler in the Muslim world. He publicly proclaimed his expansionist policies in religio-political terms: "The *ghaza* [raid on non-Muslim lands] is our basic duty, as it was in the case of our fathers. Constantinople, situated as it is in the middle of our dominions, protects the enemies of our state and incites them against us. The conquest of this city is, therefore, essential to the future and the safety of the Ottoman state."³

Ottoman scholar Halil Inalcik cites a contemporary description of Mehmed the Conqueror that sounds strangely like Pope Boniface VIII's *Unam Sanctam,* which was issued some 150 years earlier (see Chapter One): "In his view, there should be only one empire, only one faith and only one sovereign in the whole world. No place was more deserving than Istanbul for the creation of this unity in the world. The Conqueror believed that thanks to this city he could extend his rule over the whole Christian world."⁴ With that in mind, Mehmed II destroyed former Byzantine leaders in the region; fought any and all contenders to strengthen his control of the Balkans, including the Hungarians, the Venetians, and the crusaders; and continued his conquests in the Black Sea region, in southern Crimea, and in Italy.

In consciously modelling itself on the Islamic caliphates, the emerging Ottoman power was not simply reviving a cherished tradition. As had occurred in medieval Europe, it was working within the intellectual context of the age. Theoretical foundations for the separation of religious and political power may have been articulated by Ibn Taymiyya, but they had not been accepted. Though few citizens concerned themselves with more than the security any given leader could provide, an administrative infrastructure conforming with the highest standards of the caliphal—religio-political—leadership no doubt provided a powerful incentive for loyalty. The Ottomans therefore invariably claimed their conquests in formerly non-Muslim lands to be the will of God. When they pursued dominance in an already Muslim land, however, they encountered a slight obstacle. Islamic law was formulated in the context of a single, potentially universal, and religiously justified state. It therefore frowns on war among Muslims as a weakening of the social fabric. The Ottomans therefore, as far as possible, sought the submission of Muslim leaders by peaceful means: simple annexation in the face of threats and the grant of rich estates (*timars*) in the Balkans when added incentive was needed. When peaceful means were not effective and war was required to subdue a Muslim leader, the Ottomans elicited legal justifications (*fetva;* in Arabic, *fatwa*) from the religious scholars for their actions. The victims were declared "enemies of religion" for not joining forces with the only Muslims faithfully performing the duty of *jihad*—as the Ottomans liked to describe themselves. This was how the Ottomans justified their subjugation of Muslim lands in western Anatolia and Persia. To further mollify subjugated Muslims, Mehmed's son Bayezid II (r. 1481–1512) returned a good deal of confiscated land, assigned the revenues of several properties in Anatolia for the support of the shrines in Mecca and Medina, ostentatiously followed the Shari'a, and intensified the Sunni orientation of the Shari'a in the face of the rising power in Persia, the Saffavid Shah Isma'il. In fact, it was in order to distinguish between these two expansive powers' respective domains—the border having been established in an Ottoman victory in 1514—that Shah Isma'il declared Persia thenceforth officially Shi'i.

But the Ottomans still had to acknowledge the caliph, who was by then a virtual captive of the Mamluks in Egypt. The Mamluks, in turn, considered the Ottomans' Islamic claims a challenge: There could not be more than one ultimate and potentially universal Islamic empire. Just as the Saffavids had had to distinguish their Islam from Ottoman Islam, now the Mamluks and the Ottomans had to come to terms. One had to usurp the other, and it was the Ottomans who were successful. Damascus and Palestine fell to the Ottoman leader Selim in 1509; soon Cairo was added to the Ottoman regime and with it the remnants of Mamluk control. The caliph became a captive of the Ottoman court. The Ottoman sultan assumed the former Mamluk sultans' title, "Servant of the Two Holy Sanctuaries" (*khadim al-haramayn al-sharifayn*).

It was not until 1727 that the Ottoman sultans began to call themselves the caliphs, but the claim was made retroactively. They said that the last 'Abbasid caliph (al-Mutawakkil, the one who had been captured in the battle with the Mamluks) had officially made Selim and his heirs caliphs of all Islam in 1517. One way or another, the Ottomans considered themselves the successors of universal Islamic government, rejecting separation of religious and political authority. They claimed to be restoring the glory of the Prophet's empire and thus fulfilling the will of God. Non-Muslims who refused to submit to Ottoman leadership were infidels; Muslims who did so were heretics. The most scathing condemnation the Ottomans leveled at the Mamluks was that the latter had been incapable of protecting Islam's holy places. Whether the term *caliph* meant the only or simply the most important Muslim ruler by the time of Ottoman ascendancy is immaterial. Ottoman power, just as that of the Umayyads, the 'Abbasids, and the Mamluks had been, was justified on the basis of Islam. As a result, there was clearly no room to develop theories of political power legitimated by any other source, as Ibn Taymiyya had attempted to do. Suleyman the Magnificent (r. 1520–1566) proclaimed openly that he had been brought to the throne by God. Ottoman control was complete; its legitimacy was not open for discussion.

For that reason, the Ottoman period is notorious for having produced virtually no philosophers of distinction. The intellectual decline had begun toward the end of 'Abbasid times. As noted above, in an attempt to stifle criticism of the increasingly inept and obviously no longer Islamic government, the "door of *ijtihad*," or fresh Islamic thinking, had been closed. The last major attempt to revive *ijtihad* had died with Ibn Taymiyya.

Ottoman Success Is Fleeting

In the early centuries of Ottoman control there seemed to be no pressing need to question their authority, at least not on the popular level. The Ottomans created a strong and stable government in the place of an unstable balance of competitive claims, and overall the populace was better off under Ottoman control. The ultimate strength of the Ottoman empire, like that of any other, was its economy, and that was very strong, at first. The Ottomans had built tremendous wealth through a series of financial measures, including periodic currency devaluation, creation of state monopolies on certain essential goods, and confiscation of massive amounts of privately held land as well as of *waqf* (pl. *awqaf*)—land or institutions bequeathed to the Islamic state for pious purposes (schools, shrines, etc.).

Despite any discontent caused by Ottoman policies among the former landowners, the religious establishment, and the merchants, Ottoman control initially enhanced the overall welfare of the provinces. The provinces had been languishing. When the Ottomans took over Egypt and Syria, both appear to have been emerging from severe economic problems. The Black Plague no doubt seriously affected the area, just as it had in Europe.[5] Even before then, however, in the declining days of central authority, coordinated efforts to maintain irrigation systems and rural security had been abandoned. Many fields had fallen into disuse, and the yields from those still under cultivation were down. The economic integrity of the former 'Abbasid lands had degenerated into a precarious system of treaties and alliances among autonomous and semi-autonomous local powers, resulting in a complex pattern of tariffs and taxes prohibitive of commercial development. Peasants had fled, from disease or oppression or both. The Ottomans, in an effort to maximize their investments, concerned themselves directly with rural security. They repaired dilapidated irrigation systems, dug wells, and streamlined and regularized tax collection. They also sought to increase productivity by encouraging commerce. They built caravanserais and estabished garrisons along trade routes. Ottoman tax registers indicate that these measures benefitted the peasants and the pastoralists. Population, agricultural output, and, as a result, tax revenues all show marked increases during the sixteenth century in regions subject to Ottoman control.[6]

Although, as we will see, these positive indications masked severe problems brewing in the provinces, for the time being Ottoman power flourished. With Europe preoccupied in its tangle of religious warfare at the beginning of the sixteenth century, Mehmed the Conqueror's son Suleyman was in a perfect position to become "the Magnificent." He continued territorial expansion, capturing Belgrade in 1521. When the French king asked him for help against the Hapsburgs, he was happy to oblige. He invaded Hungary and made its king a vassal. In 1529, under similar circumstances, he attacked Vienna and, although he withdrew after a three-week siege, he had put the fear of God into Europe. In fact, the Ottoman sultanate reached its pinnacle at this stage, as Europe's power broker. Only the Ottomans were considered capable of preventing a reimposition of Holy Roman hegemony in Europe by the Hapsburgs. Suleyman also gained dominance in North Africa and, if only briefly, the Mediterranean.

Suleyman played his position in Europe for all it was worth. When France sought a formal alliance against the Hapsburgs, he granted it and was able to gain even more European territory as a result. But in the alliance (1535) Suleyman made a fateful move. In a series of agreements referred to as capitulations, he granted France a privileged position in trade within the Ottoman empire in an effort to further encourage commerce. This move called into question the sultan's devotion to Islamic law. The French were Christians, and the privilege of semi-autonomy enjoyed by the communities they established in Syria was easily misinterpreted as a concession to their religion rather than their nationality. Even more importantly, although no one could have predicted it at the time, these capitulations were the first step in what would result in European commercial—and ultimately political—domination of the Arab world. Capitulations were also granted to the British in 1580.

For a while Ottoman policy remained successful. The empire flourished as the Ottomans spread their hegemony to Baghdad, albeit tenuously, in 1538. However, the eclipse of Ottoman power was becoming inevitable. Although the Portuguese were finally driven from East Africa (1585), the Ottomans never fully recovered Indian Ocean trade. At the beginning of the seventeenth century, the Dutch and the English, with their new ships and weapons, assumed dominance on the seas. At the same time, the Duchy of Muscovy, formerly a weak buffer between Poland and the Mongols courted by Istanbul, was becoming Russia. Ivan IV ("the Terrible") had become czar in 1547 and begun to expand southward into Ottoman and former Mongol territories. But Suleyman's successors were prevented from checking Russian expansion by troubles with Persia and Europe and, especially, by internal problems.

For one thing, the rising peasant population, particularly in Anatolia, eventually outstripped the supply of available land. Tax registers show an increasing number of landless peasants by the turn of the seventeenth century. The peasants therefore became available for mercenary bands modelled on the old ghazi troops that were forming along the borders as well as for service in the formerly slave-dominated Ottoman military. This was convenient initially because Ottoman expansion required a ready supply of soldiers. But when territorial expansion ceased and troops were called home, the economy was unable to reabsorb them. As Ottoman scholar Halil Inalcik describes it:

> Thousands of . . . students (known as *sukhte*, "burnt up" . . .) periodically left their schools in Anatolia on alms-collecting expeditions in the surrounding villages. Some of these *sukhtes*, whose numbers increased considerably from the middle of the [sixteenth] century, formed groups which descended on villages like clouds of locusts. Some were indistinguishable from bandits. The disturbances they caused became a serious danger to the state, particularly after the reign of Selim II.[7]

The influx of American silver via European merchants, which began toward the end of the sixteenth century, did not help matters in the Ottoman empire. It led to an inflationary spiral of depreciated currency, rising prices, increased speculation, and higher interest rates. This also played havoc with the Ottoman military institution, both for the slaves, whose fixed stipend from the sultan was devalued, and for the cavalry, whose income from agricultural land grants was threatened. Military revolts resulted, and many cavalry simply refused service. Those who continued to serve were severely restricted by decreasing income from their properties. This situation in turn led to oppression of peasants, who were often subjected to inflated taxes. Non-Muslims' taxes were also increased, and ever new taxes were imposed on the general populace.

Other problems were caused by the diminishing cavalry forces. The government was faced with the expense of hiring more infantry and providing them with new equipment. As the cavalry diminished, these troops—the Janissaries—came to be relied upon for security in Anatolia and the provinces. As representatives of the sultan's government, they formed a privileged class in the towns. Members of this class were resented and became a focus of local discontent. Thus when landless peasants sought military employment, they tended toward the local governors' forces. Local governors' forces swelled and, armed with muskets, came to be the principal arm of the Ottoman military. However, when they were not on campaign, unlike the Janissaries, they did not get paid. As a result, they were prone to banditry and extortion and, particularly when they organized into roving bands known as *jelalis,* came to be feared throughout the countryside.

Attempts at reform within the complex Ottoman military system resulted in a series of rebellions among its various factions. Not until the reign of Murad IV (1631–1640) was any semblance of order restored to the Ottoman military forces, and even that was short-lived. A series of weak sultans allowed the resurgence of Janissary influence, which in turn led to revolts among the provincial governors' militias. When the powerful and capable Koprulu family took over the Ottoman government (as "grand vezirs," or prime ministers/chiefs-of-staff), the Janissaries were once more brought under control, provincial rebellions were put down, and reforms stressing Islamic law were implemented.

Ottoman scholars are very insistent on the distinctions between the European feudal system and the Ottoman timar system. Indeed, there are differences, but the significant similarity lies in the tenuous balance between central control and provincial power. In each case, the central government distributed income-producing land in return for loyalty, whether such loyalty came in service or tribute. And in each case, the incentive for such loyalty was the key issue. Once all available land had been granted, what could the central government offer to keep the vassal beholden? So long as there was an external threat requiring a unified defensive front, or the promise of further wealth from external campaigns, or even a powerful and effective private central army to exact loyalty when it flagged, the system could remain intact. But in lieu of any of these, vassals gradually lost incentive to support a central government that had nothing more to offer.

By the end of the sixteenth century, the Ottomans had been forced to modify their administration of the provinces in an effort to increase both revenue and control. They had originally retained many Mamluks in Egypt and the Fertile Crescent, for instance, as local governors. They also employed salaried officials (*emins*) to collect taxes. In Syria, where control was not as well entrenched as in Egypt and the bedouin never really accepted Ottoman control, cavalry were maintained to protect peasants and pilgrims. But as foreign wars and inflation increased revenue requirements, the system of tax-farms (*iltizams*)—wherein the state retained ownership of a given revenue-producing unit but awarded the right to collect taxes in that unit, generally to whomever promised to deliver the highest amount—became increasingly common. This system itself was unstable, in addition to being exploitative of the taxpayers, who were subjected to arbitrary levies and various methods of extraction, including coercion. Just as in feudal Europe, in the absence of a strong central government (i.e., with no way to force the return of *iltizams* to the government), great estates were readily appropriated as the bases of power of local families. Thus, as in Europe, the struggle to balance centripetal and centrifugal forces raged.

The seventeenth century was the watershed for the Ottomans. Their northeastern borders were being pressed by the growing Russian power. Istanbul itself was raided in 1625. The Ottomans lost supremacy in the Mediterranean to the Venetians. Even when they hired English and Dutch ships—in exchange for further concessions to English merchants in Ottoman lands—their fleet was no match for the Venetians. The Ottoman attempt to draw the line at Crete dragged on for more than twenty years, at staggering financial and human costs, and ended up only checking further Ottoman expansion in the area. Their wars in Europe with the Hapsburgs were no more successful. In 1665 Ottoman forces were finally defeated at Saint Gotthard. Some gains were realized in Transylvania and the Ukraine, but for Europe the Ottoman threat was a thing of the past. The 1683 Ottoman effort to take Vienna was rebuffed by a combined Austro-German-Polish army. The Holy League— formed by the pope the next year with Austria, Poland, Venice, and Russia—finally imposed Austrian Hapsburg dominance on the border of the Balkans, while Russia expanded into the Ukraine and the Black Sea. From the turn of the eighteenth century on, the Ottomans abandoned efforts against their acknowledged European superiors.

Conditions in the Arab Provinces

While the sultan was preoccupied with foreign adventures and problems in the central Ottoman domain, control in the provinces began to slip. The North African provinces of Algiers and Tunis had become virtually autonomous during the seventeenth century, as had the Iraqi province of Basra. And trouble was brewing for the sultan in Egypt and Syria. Yet the impact of provincial developments registered slowly in Istanbul, for the significant measure—total tax revenues (Egypt's alone accounted for at least half)—remained relatively constant throughout the seventeenth and eighteenth centuries.[8]

Not only did the plague ravage the Arab world in the seventeenth and eighteenth centuries,[9] but there were deeper, systemic problems undermining the sultan's centralized claims. Despite provincial tax indicators, conditions for the general populace were deteriorating rapidly. No one had predicted the effect high-quality, industrialized European products would have on the Arab economy or the concomitant reduced competitiveness of local products when the Europeans were invited in to trade. Nor did anyone foresee the pivotal role that European trade— made so advantageous by the sultan's granting Europeans favored status in the provinces through the capitulations—would play in the creation of indigenous elites in the Arab provinces. And certainly no one anticipated the political or economic effects of that pivotal role: local autonomy would come to depend on this source of wealth, and local elites would therefore find their allegiances closer to European traders than to the Ottoman sultan. Perhaps most far-reaching, no one seems to have recognized that in pursuing mercantile wealth local elites would neglect to develop an indigenous industry. The most valuable products the Arab provinces had to offer Europe were agricultural. Mercantile wealth therefore was invested in land, not workshops or factories as it had been in Europe. Industry was not fostered and cities did not develop. Thus, as local elites sought the wealth necessary to secure their autonomy from the Ottoman caliph, they maintained the Ottoman provinces' nonindustrialized condition, a condition that would eventually make them vulnerable to the industrialized powers of the West and usher them into third-world status.[10]

An added source of tension in the cities arose from the growing resentment of both foreign merchants and the local merchants' association with them. The traditional bond between craftspeople and merchants was strained by these conflicting loyalties, dissipating potential urban political strength. In the seventeenth and eighteenth centuries, regular outbursts in the cities revealed the complexity of the realignment of traditional urban groups and their rural counterparts.[11]

Ottoman Egypt

Egypt entered the sixteenth century with a series of military rebellions against the Ottoman governors, while leftover or reconstituted Mamluk families competed with the military and the Ottoman governors for local dominance.[12]

A Mamluk faction eventually emerged over its competitors and brought stability to Cairo, but only by consolidating its own power. 'Ali "Bey" (a linguistic corruption of the Turkish honorific title *beg*) neutralized his opponents by outright seizure of their lands. He then set about strengthening his military base, hiring mercenaries and providing both cavalry and navy with advanced training and equipment. This was all very expensive, of course, as were the luxury items for which the Mamluks had developed a taste, which were purchased mostly from the French. The needed funds were raised by assessing special taxes on villages and on urban groups; by creating and exploiting monopolies; and, later, by hoarding foodstuffs to force up prices. These measures not only caused economic strain on the general populace, but also continued to keep both rural and urban surpluses of goods and/or capital unproductive. What indigenous investments the Mamluks did make were in land rather than industry, so they could exploit the high price of grain on the increasingly industrialized world market.

Further diminishing the role of industry and increasing that of commerce, the Mamluks directly involved favored merchants in tax-farming, trading what was supposed to have been inalienable state property (*miri*) for more liquid assets. Even members of the *'ulama'* were involved in the Mamluk mercantile economy. Some were merchants themselves; others acquired tax farms, obviously in return for loyalty; and some—especially those in charge of *waqf* (land or institutions bequeathed to the Islamic state for pious purposes) and therefore also in control of liquid assets useful to government spending programs— became trusted officials in the government.

Of course, the peasants and urban lower classes suffered under erratic and uncontrolled taxation by beys seeking to support their own power structure and also suffered from the effects of monopolies and hoarding. Not surprisingly, there were frequent protests and, where there was leadership, revolts against the beys' extortionary practices. Revolts were evident particularly during the last decade of the eighteenth century.

However, two factors prevented effective efforts at change. The first was Napoleon's invasion of Egypt in 1798. France was already in a favorable trading position in Egypt. Thanks to the capitulations, French merchants only had to pay a fraction of the customs fees and taxes that Muslim merchants paid, and they passed that advantage on to Christians living in Egypt (including many Syrian Christians who had moved to Egypt seeking favored trade status). However, a series of domestic grain crises in the second half of the eighteenth century increased France's dependence on agricultural imports. France therefore wanted to supersede the fluctuations in supply caused by competition among the Egyptian merchant elite, as well as to secure markets for French industrial wares. Those motivations, combined with the desire to offset England's expanding influence in the East, were behind Napoleon's invasion of Alexandria.[13] Claiming to be delivering Egypt from the Mamluks and the Turks, who had ruined "this best of countries . . . with their greed," and to be restoring true Islam, Napoleon soon set about undermining Mamluk power.[14] While the Mamluks hid in upper Egypt, Napoleon expropriated their lands and redistributed them to those members of the merchant elite and *'ulama'* who would cooperate with him. He was unsuccessful overall in gaining control of trade and breaking Mamluk strength; a series of military defeats, a British blockade, and urban uprisings against new income taxes, combined with defeats in Europe, forced French withdrawal from Egypt. But the occupation did have the effect of redirecting the focus of discontent from the Mamluks to foreigners. Thus, when the Ottoman sultan appointed a new governor of Egypt in 1805, Muhammad (in Turkish, Mehmed) 'Ali, he received full cooperation from the Egyptians.

This reassertion of Ottoman control, albeit nominal, clearly indicated the lack of revolutionary leadership in the provinces—the second factor that stood in the way of effective change in Egypt. The local elites were not interested in overthrowing Ottoman control, notwithstanding 'Ali Bey's proclamation in 1769 to the contrary. Their wealth depended on their political legitimacy, and the only political legitimacy the Mamluks could muster—even as they manufactured genealogies and forged alliances with indigenous groups—was through the Ottoman government. They were able to provide for their troops only by enrolling them in the Ottoman forces; the destruction of those forces would have thrown their own houses into total disarray.[15]

'Ali Bey's successor, Abu al-Dhahab, sought to enhance his position by claiming, in addition to the title of *sheikh al-balad* ("leader of the country"), that of Ottoman pasha (the sultan's governor), again showing the utility of Ottoman legitimacy. Prior to that, the Mamluk policy of keeping the Ottoman governor acquiescent had been successful; after the mid-eighteenth century, none of the Ottoman representatives wielded much actual power. But the Mamluks were devoted to their own autonomy, not Egyptian independence. They did not want so much to evict the pasha as to *be* the pasha.

Yet despite Egyptian leaders' exploitation of Ottoman legitimacy, Ottoman control continued to slip away. In 1728 the Ottoman governor of Egypt acknowledged the failure of the *iltizam* system. Most of the income-producing properties were already firmly in the control of local powers, and it was was too late to replace them with Ottoman agents. The Mamluks continued to rule the country as if it were their own, and in 1841 the Ottomans finally made it official. They not only declared Muhammad 'Ali the pasha, but made the office hereditary.

Syria

Ottoman control in Syria was even less secure. Headquartered in Damascus, the region included Palestine (now Israel and the Occupied Territories) and what are now Lebanon, Jordan, and Syria. Ottoman control of the area had never been a simple matter. From the time Sultan Selim I wrested control from the Mamluks through the seventeenth century, Syria ran through a series of at least 133 pashas.

As in Egypt, there were significant communities of foreign merchants—French and English—operating under the advantageous conditions provided by the sultan's capitulations. Syria entered the eighteenth century suffering from the combined effects of tribal uprisings and the plague during the sixteenth and seventeenth centuries. Formerly productive agricultural areas had been abandoned. As industrialized Europe had assumed dominance in world commerce, Syrian merchants and artisans had receded into virtual oblivion. Nor could Syria offer agricultural products on the scale Egypt could. Yet European merchants were busy in the region. Aleppo, former terminus of the overland trade route from India and the home of a Venetian colony since Byzantine times, saw the development of an important French settlement. Begun with the first capitulations in 1535, the settlement gained importance in 1740 when Sultan Mahmud I put all Christian visitors to Ottoman lands under French administration. The French later built some textile factories. Again as in Egypt, however, their most important activity was commercial. Later capitulation treaties brought the English into Syria, as well. And both groups fortified their establishments with missionaries and teachers. French Catholics and English (and subsequently U.S.) Protestants established schools that would later play a very important role in the region.

Meanwhile, local leaders sought, often successfully, to maintain their own control. For instance, in the western portion of Syria, known as Lebanon, local Druze leader Fakhr al-Din al-Ma'ni had managed to maintain control of his Lebanese holdings from the very beginning. When the Ottomans were fighting with the Mamluks for control of Syria, Fakhr al-Din remained neutral; for him the dispute represented only a change of distant masters. Upon the Ottoman victory, therefore, he expressed such sincere devotion that the sultan allowed him to keep his position, exacting only a light tribute. Both Druze (a sect of Shi'i Islam) and Maronite (a Christian sect) chieftains generally were allowed special freedom in their traditional realms, acting as vassals responsible directly to the sultan. Their properties and positions were passed on within families, and both were subject to tribute only, rather than the kind of service required in the regular timar system of the Ottomans. Fakhr al-Din's grandson, Fakhr al-Din II (d. 1635), utilized the Ma'ni relations with the sultan, expanding his control to include Beirut, Sidon, Tripoli, Baalbek, and the Beqaa. As his grandfather's had been, Fakhr al-Din's concerns were not with Istanbul's power but his own. He was caught conspiring with the crusaders against the sultan and was exiled to Europe for five years. When he returned, however, having demonstrated to the sultan that he was the only one who could faithfully deliver Lebanese tribute, he was reinstated with even greater powers. In 1624 he was dubbed the leader of the Arabs from Aleppo to the borders of Egypt.

Fakhr al-Din expended all possible efforts to develop his domain. He hired European engineers, architects, and teachers and welcomed more missionaries into his cities and villages. His independent behavior finally got him beheaded by the sultan, and his fiefdom was scaled back to its original size. But another branch of his family—the Shihabis— picked up where he left off. Beginning in the second quarter of the eighteenth century, the 'Azm family played a similar role in Damascus, Hama, Sidon, and Tripoli. And as had been the case with other locals who became too powerful, in 1757 As'ad al-'Azm was considered such a threat that the sultan had him assassinated.

In Palestine, a former bedouin leader, Shaykh Zahir al-'Umar, assumed dominance in Safad and Tiberias in the early eighteenth century. By 1750 he expanded his control to 'Akka (Acre), developing its agricultural sector as well as the silk and cotton industries. In 1772, with the collusion of 'Ali Bey in Egypt, he occupied Sidon, at the frontier of Shihabi power. The Shihabis sought and received support from the Ottoman governor in Damascus and attacked Zahir. A member of the Syrian contingent, Ahmad al-Jazzar ("the butcher"), then took control of Zahir's lands. In 1780 he was made governor of Damascus (in addition to Zahir's former domains of 'Akka and Sidon) in reward for his service to the sultan. He built up such an effective military machine that, with the help of the English fleet, he was able to turn back Napoleon's invasion in 1799.

European Attempts to Keep the Ottoman World Weak

The tendency toward autonomy in the Arab provinces, although stifled, was never eliminated by the Ottomans. But overly independent provincial leaders were not the only trouble the Ottomans had in the eighteenth century. They were at a stalemate in Europe, Russia was looming large in the north, and the Arab provinces were virtually uncontrollable. As if that were not enough, the Europeans took a leaf from Ottoman history. Just as Suleyman the Magnificent had tried to keep the Holy Roman Empire from reasserting itself in Europe, Europe—newly reorganized and prosperous—worked to keep the Ottoman lands divided and therefore weak. But the European strategy was different. Suleyman had viewed the Hapsburg pretenders to the Holy Roman emperorship as the major threat; he thought they were the only ones who could reunite Europe and make it a power rivalling his own. In contrast, the nineteenth-century European states saw the Ottoman emperor as the *weak* link. They were willing to support his governors to the extent that it improved their trading positions, but they had no intention of seeing the weak sultan replaced by a strong regional leader capable of reunifying the Ottoman empire or even a significant portion thereof. Such a leader was Muhammad 'Ali (r. 1805–1848) of Egypt.

As noted above, this Albanian-born officer in the Ottoman army had been made the Egyptian pasha in 1805, charged with the task of restoring order in Cairo after the French occupation. He quickly set about consolidating his power within the Mamluk system. He confiscated private property and placed *iltizams* (tax-farms) under his direct control. He then abolished the positions of the *multazims* (tax farmers) and replaced them with state agents. He centralized control of all *waqf* properties, including the institutions that depended on them, such as the center of Islamic learning, al-Azhar. He monopolized Egypt's major products, agricultural and industrial. He restored Egypt's irrigation systems and promoted modern agriculture under the direction of European experts. He introduced the cultivation of long-staple cotton, which had a ready market in British textile mills, and was ready to fill in the gap when the U.S. civil war caused a world cotton shortage. He took as much control as he could of foreign trade, undercutting the favored French position by selling huge quantities of wheat to the English when their Russian wheat supply was cut off in the early nineteenth century. He created a ministry of education to begin the long task of reforming Egyptian education, which, like that in the rest of the Islamic world, had gone stagnant with decline of the 'Abbasids. He founded the first schools of engineering and medicine in Egypt with instructors from Europe. He hired military advisers from Europe to reorganize and modernize the Egyptian army and navy and sent Egyptian students to do their advanced studies in Europe. Then, in 1811, once he had risen to the pinnacle of the Mamluk system, he abolished it by inviting the remaining Mamluk dignitaries to a party at which they were assassinated.[16]

But like 'Ali Bey before him, Muhammad 'Ali was no revolutionary. He did not change the Mamluk political structure; he just took control of it. Although he is known as the founder of modern Egypt, he was not an Egyptian nor even an Arab nationalist. He was a faithful servant of the sultan so long as it suited his own power structure. For instance, among his first imperial assignments was to stop the growing power of the Wahhabis in Arabia, the first real reformers of modern Islamic history.

The Wahhabi Affair

Muhammad ibn 'Abd al-Wahhab (d. 1792) had travelled out of his native Arab heartland in the Nejd (in the Arabian peninsula) to the Islamic centers of Iraq and Syria in search of religious education. In

Baghdad and Damascus he was inspired by the remnants of Ibn Taymiyya's Hanbali teaching, all but overcome at the time—in the vacuum of religious learning that characterized the Sunni Islamic world—by Shi'i dominance in Aleppo and Basra and by popular Sufi practices that had taken root throughout the Islamic world. 'Abd al-Wahhab was horrified by the laxity he saw around him, particularly the elevation of human beings to positions competitive with the divine. This was how he saw Shi'i devotion to 'Ali and his family and to the imam, believed by the Shi'is to be the mouthpiece of divine leadership. It was also how he saw Sufi devotion to saints and spiritual guides, which had permeated not only Shi'i but Sunni Islam as well. In both cases he felt social responsibility had been relegated to the supernatural realm, which he considered antithetical to Islam. Belief in the one God and submission to God's revealed command to create a just society—prescribing good and proscribing evil—were being compromised by saint worship and cultic practices, he concluded. He believed that was why the sultan was able to impose his barely Islamic regime on a sheeplike populace.

'Abd al-Wahhab forged a relationship with a central Arabian tribal leader, Muhammad ibn Sa'ud (d. 1765), and together they set about creating the type of political order they believed God had mandated. But unlike Ibn Taymiyya, they were not susceptible to caliphal censure: Arabia had never been fully under Ottoman control. Soon the Wahhabi system of strict adherence to Islamic law and utter devotion to God was dominant throughout central Arabia. Aspiring to emulate the Prophet's example, they tried to replace tribal solidarity with religious solidarity and eliminate devotion to saints, whether Sufi or Shi'i. Upon the deaths of 'Abd al-Wahhab and Ibn Sa'ud, the movement gained strength under the latter's grandson, Sa'ud ibn 'Abd al-'Aziz. He spread Wahhabi-Sa'udi influence to Shi'i Karbala' (1801), Mecca (1803), and Medina (1804), destroying saints' tombs wherever he went, forbidding any pilgrimage except the annual Hajj sanctioned by the Prophet, and issuing the death penalty to any who refused to submit to the new order. When they invaded Syria and Iraq in 1805, thus spreading the Wahhabi regime from 'Oman to Palmyra, Sultan Selim III (r. 1789–1807) decided it was time to act. Not only was this the most formidable Arabian power since the time of the Prophet, but in challenging the accepted religious order the Wahhabis were challenging the very basis of the Ottoman claim to political legitimacy. The threat posed by the Wahhabis was not simply a matter of an overly ambitious vassal who could be pacified with a greater share of power. An attack on prevailing religious practice was an attack on Ottoman power overall. That was why the sultan ordered Muhammad 'Ali to stop the Wahhabi threat, and Muhammad 'Ali eagerly grasped this opportunity to enhance his own power. By 1818 the Wahhabi threat was effectively contained and the Ottoman status quo restored.

Thus the Ottomans were granted a brief reprieve. 'Abd al-Wahhab did not challenge the theory of unified religio-political power. An activist rather than an intellectual, he did not question the theoretical structure of the caliphate. He only questioned the Ottomans' qualifications for the title. Like Luther, he believed in a political order established by a pious leader; he just rejected the claims to piety of the current leader. Unlike Luther, however, he went so far as to wage an armed struggle to establish an order based on his interpretation of orthodoxy. Before his movement could effectively threaten the sultan's position, it was checked by a faithful servant of the system. Muhammad 'Ali, however, cherished greater ambitions than his predecessors had. 'Ali Bey had only wanted to take over the Egyptian pasha's domain; Muhammad 'Ali—flushed with the success of his Arabian campaigns—soon felt capable of taking over the sultan's domain, or at least the greater portion of it. Soon after defeating the Wahhabis and gaining dominance over western Arabia, Egyptian troops marched into eastern Sudan and established Egyptian control (which was later bequeathed to the British). The sultan next asked his pasha to help put down rebellions in Crete.

By this time Europe was beginning to worry about the prospect of a reconstituted Ottoman empire. Sultan Mahmud II (r. 1808–1839) seemed to be staging an Ottoman comeback. At the time that he ascended the throne, there were mutinies, rebellions in virtually all the provinces, and the Ottoman treasury was depleted. Mahmud II overcame most of the provincial rebellions, abolished the Janissaries and created an entirely new army to be instructed only by Muslims (rather than by the European Christians who had been brought in to modernize the system), and forged an alliance with his clever lieutenant in Egypt, Muhammad 'Ali. When these two extremely competent Ottoman leaders joined their navies to put down the rebellion in Crete, therefore, England, France, and Russia sent a combined fleet to make sure the Ottomans were defeated (Navarino, 1827).

But the sultan had promised Muhammad 'Ali control of Syria in return for his efforts. And despite the defeat, Muhammad 'Ali meant to get paid. In 1831, therefore, he sent his son, Ibrahim, to Syria to establish hegemony. Bashir II Shihab (d. 1840) was in charge in the Lebanon, and no love was lost between Bashir and the sultan's man in Damascus, Ahmad "the Butcher." So when Ibrahim arrived and quickly occupied Jaffa and Jerusalem, Bashir and his army helped Ibrahim take over 'Akka and Damascus. Soon the Egyptian forces had defeated Ottoman troops and advanced all the way up to Konya, halfway across Anatolia toward Istanbul. Again Europe took action to maintain the status quo. Russia, England, and France joined together and forced Ibrahim to withdraw from Anatolia.

At first the European powers allowed Muhammad 'Ali to retain Syria, which he ruled through Ibrahim. But following a brief honeymoon during which social reforms were introduced and Shihabi Lebanon was accorded special privileges, Ibrahim began to treat Syria as an Egyptian colony.[17] Taxes were tripled, monopolies were created on local produce and industry, and forests and coal mines were exploited to rebuild the Egyptian navy. Local rebellions against Egyptian rule began as early as 1834. To maintain stability, Sultan Mahmud II tried to send Ibrahim home in 1839, but Ibrahim's forces crushed the sultan's army in northern Syria.

For a third time the European powers intervened. France considered Muhammad 'Ali's strong control conducive to its own interests. Egypt's economy had been transformed from a primarily subsistence-level agrarian system to a net exporter of grains. It had become integrated into world trade and was therefore dependent upon fluctuations in the world market. France was aware that, as the major market for Egyptian grain, it was in the dominant position. So the Egyptian government did not appear as a threat to the French. But England and Russia felt far more comfortable with the "sick man of Europe," as Czar Nicholas would call the sultan.[18] They therefore wanted to intervene to limit Muhammad 'Ali's power. Lest either England or Russia get the jump on them, the French went along with the plan to limit Egyptian/Ottoman power. British agents were allegedly sent into Syria to contact opponents of the regime and foment insurrection. Proclamations were issued demanding freedom from Egyptian control. Thus, though the impulse toward Syrian independence was strong, multiple layers of foreign intervention kept the movement from being strictly nationalist. The immediate goal was to get rid of Egyptian control. To that end, the protesters proclaimed their obedience to the sultan, and the French ambassador was openly courted to help force Ibrahim out in an attempt to restore the status quo. Finally, in 1840 Britain sent a fleet to convince Ibrahim he had best go back to Egypt, and the European goal was achieved.

The First Stirring of Arab Nationalism

If Muhammad 'Ali, despite his progressive strategic measures, was a political conservative, two of his reforms would nevertheless initiate irrevocable changes in his Egyptian and Syrian domains. First, he introduced conscription. The original rationale was simple. The sources of mamluk or slave soldiers had dried up. Russia had conquered the trans-Caucasus and Catherine the Great had closed the borders to mamluk trade. African slaves had been tried, but their high mortality rate made them unsuitable for the military. So Muhammad 'Ali tried the French model and began conscripting soldiers. In both Egypt and Syria the measure was despised; as historian Philip Hitti points out, from 1840 on, conscription was listed (along with disarmament) among the major grievances in Syrian uprisings against Ibrahim's rule.[19] But local conscription had the unprecedented effect of creating a basis of local solidarity within the provinces. Egyptian order had been maintained by foreign soldiers since the fall of the 'Abbasids in 1250. And Syria had seen a succession of foreign overlords, followed by the localized rule of feudal and semi-feudal warlords. Even in the latter case, the Ottoman millet system (wherein everyone was subject to Ottoman civil law, but family law was left to religious courts: Rabbinic/Jewish, canonic/ Christian, or Shari'a/Muslim) had assured that the population would be divided into religious communities. Now, for the first time, Egyptian and Syrian peasants were being made into regional corps on the basis of nothing other than a shared homeland. The soil was finally prepared for national solidarity to grow.

The second measure taken by Muhammad 'Ali that would yield revolutionary results was his educational missions. As mentioned above, in his desire to update the curriculum of his charges, he imported European (mostly French) instructors and sent hundreds of advanced students to study in Europe. He even maintained a house in Paris for these students at state expense. Europe at this time—the first half of the nineteenth century—was just assimilating the effects of the French Revolution. Having spent some three hundred years trying to figure out a basis of political order after the demise of centrally organized and religiously legitimated government, Europe had become an association of economically independent, politically autonomous, geographically limited states. A new name would be devised for this phenomenon: nationalism. At first a pejorative term, nationalism was used to describe the Calvinists and—interestingly enough—the "Mohammedans" in their insistence on independence; but in the mid-nineteenth century, nationalism quickly became normative. And visiting Arab students eagerly learned its lessons.

There are so many aspects of nationalism that, as the saying goes, one attempts to clarify them at one's own risk. But its essential feature in this context is that it provided a new sense of social or cultural identity congruent with the new, limited geopolitical formations. In the Holy Roman Empire, the ultimate basis of social organization had been the church. Catholicism was the official religion of the realm;

anyone who was not Catholic was not a full citizen. The pope was in charge of legitimating the emperor; bishops and priests taught obedience based on religious orthodoxy. Since the time of Saint Augustine the political formation had been nowhere near so important as the religious. The official language of the realm was Latin; vernacular literature did not begin to appear until the late thirteenth century. One was not so much French or German or Italian as one was, first and foremost, Christian. As regions had begun to pull away from the empire, their primary concerns had been economic, military, and political. They had to defeat the emperor's forces and get him to recognize their independence somehow. Only when that was done did they set about reidentifying themselves, creating new criteria of citizenship, and dealing with the consequences of the redefinition. This was when nationalism became acceptable. Citizenship could no longer be primarily a function of religious affiliation; religious affiliation now transcended the new, limited state boundaries, because it could not be geographically bounded. As we saw in Chapter One, the Hapsburgs' claim to the Holy Roman imperial title kept them pressing political claims far beyond their Spanish and Austrian borders. Nor could a stable political entity be created within a given geographic unit if full citizenship rights were limited to one or two religious factions. As the Age of Religious Warfare had demonstrated, a new definition of citizenship was required—one that reflected a social formation cohering on something analogous to shared birth, but within a geographically limited state. A new cultural identity had to be devised to answer the question, "What is it to be French, or German, or Spanish?"

This was among the major issues occupying intellectual center stage in the Europe to which Muhammad 'Ali sent his best and brightest students. They found European scholars discussing the origin and nature of civilization and arguing about which nation-state best exemplified "true" civilization. Others debated whose language was most pure or whose literature was most edifying.[20] These questions were all directly related to the new bases of political legitimacy articulated by the Enlightenment thinkers (see Chapter One). Europeans were revelling in their newly defined values. Locke, for instance, had said that the only reason a ruler is invested with authority is "for the good, preservation and peace . . . in that society over which he is set." Accordingly, that is the only measure by which a ruler's legitimacy may be judged.[21]

And Rousseau had said that government is only legitimate when people freely choose it. But that entailed social responsibility, each individual having to make an informed choice. The best means to elicit that sort of devotion, he felt, was love of country, or *l'amour de la patrie*, the greatest virtue. When human beings are working together for the common good, they cannot help but make virtuous choices. Thus, people must be educated in virtue, trained in the joys of patriotism. But that *patrie* was now limited. And it was very important to the Europeans to identify each unit distinctly from the others.

This was the culmination of the development of nationalism in Europe. It was the final step in the process of transferring ultimate loyalty from the church, as an institution separate from the people, to the people as guardians and executors of the values the church taught. It was by no means a mitigation of religious values. It was rather the assumption of the guardianship of those values by a populace who believed their leaders had failed in that task; in light of that, the populace was defining itself anew. But in Europe the articulation was taking place *after* the fact: the geopolitically limited states were already free and independent. In the Arab world, the ideas were being discussed at the same time independence was being sought.

The European discussions therefore struck an extremely resonant chord with the young Ottoman visitors. They clamored for European learning. As early as 1816, the works of Voltaire, Rousseau, and Montesquieu could be found in Arab libraries.[22] The Arabs recognized that they, too, were experiencing the decline of an old order. Their discontent was expressed in the rebellions and uprisings that had become common during the second half of the nineteenth century. They had lived with oppressive taxation from a distant master for years. But the French and British occupations, as well as Europe's repeated interventions, finally made it clear that something had to change. The rising popularity of Sufi orders represented one avenue of approach to the crisis. But there were others. Associated with the Sufi orders in Egypt, for instance, were literary salons that fostered a growing interest in Arabic language and cultural heritage—literary and historical as well as religious. This phenomenon can no doubt be interpreted as a natural correlative to renewed interest in religious literature. It has also been viewed as indicative of social transformation, particularly relative to a growing middle class.[23] And it is no doubt related to the introduction of printing presses into the Ottoman world, which occurred when Napoleon brought the first Arabic press into Egypt.[24] When printing in Arabic was finally made legal in 1727, there was a tremendous upsurge of interest in Arabic learning.

But in the present context, just as in Europe of the same time, revived interest in the language and classical heritage of the society clearly reflects a growing self-awareness, a rejection of the Arabs' administratively defined identity as Ottoman subjects, and a search for a chosen self-identity. In Europe the search for cultural identity often centered on language. Vernacular languages were a relatively late development in Europe (see Chapter One), having arisen from the various peasant populations to eventually replace Latin as the official language in each realm. Therefore, "official" forms had to be established. The French and the Germans loved to trade barbs over whose language was "purer." The Arabs did not have that problem, of course. "Pure" Arabic was and remains Qur'anic Arabic. However, in the years of intellectual stagnation, the language's classical forms had all but fallen into disuse, replaced by Turkish in the royal court and by colloquial dialects in the home and marketplace. Classical forms needed to be revived and studied anew. In the eighteenth-century Arabic literary circles, modern usage became apparent as well. The significance of using colloquial Egyptian to achieve broader understanding of religious teachings was even discussed. This activity, combined with the scrutiny of local dialects and usage, no doubt reflects a trend toward self-identity characteristic of emerging nationalism.

The revival of classics of Arabic literature was particularly evident in historical studies. Several scholars have discussed, for instance, the renewed interest in the writings of Ibn Khaldun.[25] Ibn Khaldun (d. 1406) was born at the height of the Spanish Islamic caliphate and witnessed the decadence of the eastern caliphate during the time of the early Mamluks and the Mongols. He is best known for his history of the Muslim world, wherein he articulates for the first time in history a theory of the development and decline of nations.[26] Here was a theoretician of national progress and decline who might shed some light on the current predicament in which the Arabs found themselves. This critical self-awareness is also discernible in the history written at the time, such as that of 'Abd al-Rahman ibn Hasan al-Jabarti (1756–1825).[27] A religious scholar at the center of Islamic learning, al-Azhar University in Cairo, when Napoleon landed, his work is full of references to Egyptian suffering and examinations of past tribulations suffered by the Islamic world, in order to understand the contemporary predicament.

Thus there was a growing awareness in Egypt that something was amiss. There was palpable discontent with Ottoman rule and a concomitant scrutiny of Egyptian identity, in an effort to understand not only how they got into the situation but what kinds of resources they could muster to get out of it. This was the intellectual milieu that made Egyptian students so open to the examinations of national identity and democratic rule that they discovered in Europe. In Syria the situation was very similar.[28] Syria and Egypt, the traditional centers of Arab culture, have a long history of close association, of course. Periodically, pharaonic Egypt ruled Syria; each was under Greek and then Roman rule for a time; the Islamic caliphates ruled the two areas jointly except during the Egyptian Fatimid caliphate; and the Mamluks ruled both

Egypt and Syria. But each nonetheless has a unique identity, which became even more pronounced during the decline of the Ottoman empire. Syria, the birthplace of Christianity, traditionally had a far larger Christian minority than did Egypt. In eighteenth-century Syria, the various Christian sects made up nearly one-third of the population, whereas Egypt's Copts numbered less than 10 percent of the total. The effects of the Ottoman millet system of administration, combined with the capitulations made by the sultan to European powers since the sixteenth century, resulted in a unique and highly visible position for Christians in modern Syria. In fact, it was through the various Christian communities that European learning first took root in Syria, a fact that heightened the distinctions between Egypt and Syria in the modern age.

As early as the sixteenth century, Rome sent emissaries to Syria in an effort to unify its Christian communities. Jesuits were sent, for instance, to conform the teaching of the Maronites, that group living in the Lebanon who alone among Christian sects accepted the so-called monothelite heresy—an attempt to explain the belief that Jesus was both God and man that suggested that Jesus had two natures but only one will, which was divine. Almost immediately the effects of European association began to be felt in Christian Syria. The Vatican had established a special college in Rome in 1584 to train Maronite clergy. In the seventeenth century, the Vatican turned its efforts to studying Eastern Christianity as well, in the process greatly increasing Syria's self-knowledge. One of its earliest prodigies was Istifanus al-Duwayhi (d. 1704?), who produced a history of the Maronites that is now claimed by Lebanese nationalists as the first identification of Lebanon as a distinct territorial unit. The next generation produced Yusuf Sim'an al-Sim'ani ("Assemani," d. 1768), whose four-volume compilation of Christian documents remains a major source of Syrian history.[29]

Under the protection of France, Catholic schools and monasteries were established throughout Syria, particularly in the Lebanon and at Aleppo. The overall effect of these measures was to elevate the standard of education in Syria, first among Christians but quickly transcending religious distinctions. Early in the eighteenth century, for instance, although the new Christian education was generally carried on in Italian or French, Christian learning in Aleppo generated intense interest in the Arabic language. Educated Christians began to study with the acknowledged masters, the Muslim *'ulama'*, and revived the love of Arabic literature in Syria. They set an example that would be emulated in the next generation, just as the histories of Syria would be, laying the groundwork for a rise in national consciousness in Syria paralleling that in Egypt.

CHAPTER FOUR

The Emergence of National Self-Awareness in Syria and Egypt

he intellectual and social life of the East is today undergoing a process of transformation at the close of an historical epoch in which religion and a religious moral code dominated the whole inner life, and at the beginning of a new epoch in which, upon the European model, nationalism is destined to succeed to the role of religion. In Europe the Thirty Years' War heralded the passage from the religious to the nationalist principle. Here we are confronted with the remarkable spectacle of an epoch ending, not with the fading away of its distinguishing characteristics, but with their final extreme intensification.

—Hans Kohn[1]

Education as Catalyst

With Ottoman power clearly on the wane, the Arab provinces quickened their efforts to determine and defend their self-identity, at the same time developing political forms to preserve that self-identity. In the nineteenth century several developments led to a tremendous explosion of modern education in the region, reaching far beyond the Christian communities of Beirut and Aleppo. For one thing, other religious groups

Parts of this chapter were published under the title "Secularism and National Stability in Islam" in *Arab Studies Quarterly* Vol. 9, no. 3 (Summer 1987):284–305.

began to enter the region to compete with the Catholics for converts—U.S. Presbyterians, for instance. But even more important were the reforms introduced by Ibrahim in Syria (see Chapter Three). Most significantly, he reformed the legal system to give members of all religious denominations equality before the law. This vastly expanded the scope of activity available to the Christian missionaries. Furthermore, following his father's example in Egypt, Ibrahim initiated a policy of educating all boys in the realm. These two reforms had a ripple effect in the Muslim community. The Christian community was already receiving special privileges due to the capitulations. With their new legal equality they posed a palpable threat to the entrenched Muslim establishment, which was then motivated to revive its own schools in order to keep up. The fact that Ibrahim's schools were actually designed to produce competent recruits for the hated conscription policy provided further incentive for the Muslims to open their own schools. If there was going to be a standing army, its members could at least be imbued with Islamic rather than Christian loyalties.

The cumulative effect of Christian missionary activity and Ibrahim's reform policies was unprecedented educational activity in Syria, which would benefit Syria as a whole. Before the Egyptians were forced to evacuate in 1840, their agents had seen to the establishment of primary schools throughout Syria, as well as of colleges in Damascus, Aleppo, and Antioch. Despite the collapse of Ibrahim's system, many of the schools survived, under new administration. And the U.S. missionary schools introduced schools for girls, as well as schools for training teachers among the native population. Perhaps most significant, the U.S. missionary schools created Arabic textbooks to foster teaching, not in Turkish or in European languages, but in Arabic.

Syrian Arab Nationalism

It was through these combined influences that learning in general and Arabic learning in particular regained their former position of dominance in Syria. After the centuries of stagnation under 'Abbasid and Ottoman anti-intellectualism, erudition began to recover its respect and educated people again became leaders in society. With the respect for learning came pride in the national heritage; indeed, the history of this new generation of prominent Syrian intellectuals would turn out to be the history of the emergence of a new kind of national consciousness in Syria. It is full of the names of legendary leaders of Arab or Syrian nationalism, such as Butrus al-Bustani (d. 1883). Al-Bustani was from a Maronite family who studied and then taught at Christian colleges in Syria, and he became the most famous Arabist in the region. A linguistic prodigy (he was also proficient in Hebrew, Aramaic, Syriac, Greek, Latin, French, Italian, and English), al-Bustani translated the Bible into Arabic; created the first modern Arabic dictionary (*Muhit al-Muhit*, literally "circumference of the ocean," a title whose grandiosity itself reveals the regard in which knowledge was held); began an Arabic encyclopedia; founded a literary society to encourage the study of Arabic; created a weekly newspaper and a biweekly literary and political supplement; and, most importantly, founded Syria's first school open to students of all faiths, called *Al-Madrasa al-Wataniya*, the National School.

The National School symbolizes the unique thrust of al-Bustani's work. In a region whose administration was based on separating religious communities from one another and whose recent commercial trends (thanks to the capitulations) tended to pit those communities against one another—in a cultural milieu wherein one's primary identity was still religious—al-Bustani opened a school for all Syrians regardless of religious affiliation. The motto of his biweekly, *al-Jinan*, was *"hubb al-watan min al-iman"*: "Love of homeland [or patriotism] is an article of faith." *Hubb al-watan*, a direct translation of Montesquieu's *l'amour de la patrie*, became the overriding theme in all al-Bustani's work. He by no means denigrated religious affiliation or denied differences among the various confessions; he simply added national awareness to religious awareness.

Al-Bustani's articulation of this principle was particularly significant in the Syrian context. In Syria the national identity could not simply be a matter of limiting religiously legitimated government to a specified social or geographic unit, as it had been in Christian Europe. Unlike Christianity, Islam accepted its religious minorities—Christianity and Judaism—as legitimate. Their communities were as Syrian as the many Islamic communities were and could not legitimately be relegated to inferior positions. Syria needed to supersede religious identity—to focus on those things the three groups had in common rather than those that separated them. Religious identity itself had to be augmented by national identity, al-Bustani held.

Furthermore, al-Bustani was convinced that national consciousness could be achieved through learning. He was completely animated by pride in Arab cultural heritage. His extensive education had familiarized him with the advances made by European society, but he believed Arab culture was superior. He said the Arabs had created the highest culture the world had known, but then had lapsed into lethargy and allowed Europe to take the lead; now they had to regain their cultural superiority. This was not an unusual sentiment, under the circumstances. As noted in Chapter Three, when the various European national identities were emerging as distinct from one another, each had spokesmen articulating the things that made it superior to the others.[2] But in Syria, the belief in national superiority had an added importance: It was the only thing that could provide the incentive to overcome religious differences. People would retain primary religious identity so long as it was comfortable. A new or expanded identity would only be accepted if it was made attractive enough. Pride in shared cultural heritage was all Arabism had to offer. And as in the case of renewed interest in the Arabic language, regaining cultural pride was not a matter of creating something anew. Instead, it was reviving what had already been achieved. Al-Bustani motivated his audiences to reclaim the cultural leadership that had been theirs to begin with, to regain dominance in the fields of science and learning. He did not advocate wholesale adoption of European culture—far from it. He was thoroughly critical of certain aspects of European civilization, particularly with regard to sexual mores. But he did want his compatriots to assimilate the scientific advances made by the Europeans. He wanted them to share the intensity of his pride in "Arab blood" and thus be able to overcome their differences.

Indeed, al-Bustani believed that religious fanaticism and its attendant spirit of revenge were destroying Syria.[3] He was convinced of the ultimate unity of all religions. It was not that their differences were unimportant. He himself had considered the differences important enough to convert from Maronite Christianity to Presbyterianism. It was simply that all people were created by the same God, that God had created all people equal—a doctrine none of the religious communities involved could dispute—and that this equality before God must be reflected in society. Al-Bustani was not a religious reformer, as had been the critical leaders during Europe's turbulent breakdown of religiously legitimated imperial structure. Instead, change was being advocated among Arabs as such, not as members of any religious group. Al-Bustani wanted to see the new attitudes of pride and equality—both founded in Arabism—reflected in the Syrian government. He wanted laws guaranteeing justice based on the equality of all, and he wanted that equality emphasized by a state system of education in Arabic. To guarantee that no religious group would be able to control another, he wanted religious matters treated separately from civil matters.[4]

These reforms sound far more revolutionary in today's Arab world, where religious reaction has set in, than they did in nineteenth-century Syria. Ibrahim had just legislated equality among religions, and although it was opposed by many—especially those for whom it meant greater competition for already scarce resources—it was accepted by many more as actually reflecting both Islamic and Christian beliefs. There is no denying that in Islamic regimes non-Muslims had frequently been treated as inferiors. But there had always been reformers who rejected such prejudicial treatment as alien to true Islam.[5] In fact, those caliphs considered most pious often gained that reputation for their fair treatment of non-Muslims. And certain ages of Islamic history—most notably, that of Islamic Spain—are known for the high places achieved by Jews and Christians.

Furthermore, although al-Bustani's call for legal separation between religious and civil jurisdictions amounts to a call for secularism, two things must be borne in mind. First, Ottoman administration at the time was theoretically based on a distinction between religious and civil matters. Each millet was in charge of its own people religiously, but all were subject to Ottoman civil authority. Second, there was no common conception of secularism at the time to which al-Bustani's descriptions would conform. As noted in Chapter One, the term *secularism* itself did not exist yet. The European precedent of separating religious from political sovereignty had been set "not to diminish the role of religion, but to establish it more firmly at its proper level";[6] from the perspective of nineteenth-century subjects of the Ottoman caliph, this seemed a successful plan—particularly in view of the sectarian conflicts that were overtaking Syria at the time.

Sectarian Rivalry Invites European Intervention

Discontent in Syria had been building since the capitulations and the reforms of Ibrahim. The privileged position of the Christians associated with foreign influence and outright intervention pitted the Ottoman millets against one another. The discontent was heightened by Ibrahim's insistence on modern education—which also appeared to be foreign— and mandatory conscription. The expulsion of Ibrahim alleviated the pressure, but it did not cure the causes, for underlying the tension was the old feudal socioeconomic system whose increasing obsolescence was only highlighted by the Christians' successful mercantile activity. In particular, the Maronite and Druze (a sect of Shi'i Muslims) fiefdoms on Mount Lebanon were feeling the pressure. Competition between the two feudal powers eventually established a rather uneasy pattern of Maronite control in the northern region and Druze control of southern Mount Lebanon. Their differences were briefly buried in 1858, when the Maronite peasants rebelled against their feudal chieftains and the Druze chieftains came to the aid of their social peers. However, when the peasants—some of whom were Christian—subsequently rebelled against the Druze lords as well, the Druze had to defend their own interests. The conflict soon took on the form of a religious clash, with

Druze fighting a battle to the death against the Maronites.[7] The other religious communities—Sunni, Shi'i, Catholic, and Orthodox Christian—also became involved, although not in consistent patterns. The disturbances reached appalling proportions. Syrian historian Philip Hitti refers to the "massacre of 1860, a year which will remain infamous for all time in the annals of the land," claiming eleven thousand Christians, mostly Maronite, were killed.[8]

The chaos resulting from sectarian rivalry gave the Europeans the opportunity to again intervene in Syrian events. French troops briefly occupied the Lebanon and imposed a settlement whereby the region was declared an autonomous administrative unit, Jabal Lubnan (Mount Lebanon). It was to be ruled by a Christian, who would be appointed by the sultan but had to be approved by the European powers (France, England, and Russia). The Christian ruler also was to be advised by a governing council that included Maronite, Greek Orthodox, Greek Catholic, Druze, Sunni, and Shi'i members. Mount Lebanon would pay no Ottoman taxes, have no Ottoman troops, and render no military service to the sultan. Although relative stability was maintained on this basis in the region until World War I, as had happened in Egypt, the sultan had effectively lost control of the area. Resentment of Christian dominance and the Ottomans who imposed it continued to mount. Many Druze simply left, entering the Druze community in Huran to the east of the Lebanon, which allowed expansion of Christian claims into former Druze lands. Significantly, in lieu of what were considered equitable political forms, secret societies began to form. These secret societies promulgated the ideas exemplified in al-Bustani's work and laid the groundwork for later developments.

Egyptian Nationalism

Meanwhile, in Egypt events were taking a different course. The Egyptian ruler Muhammad 'Ali remained in full power until shortly before his death in 1848. He continued his modernization programs and openness to European learning. During this period Egypt produced its own intellectual father, Rifa'a Badawi Rafi' al-Tahtawi (d. 1873). Al-Tahtawi spent five years in Paris as spiritual leader of one of Muhammmad 'Ali's educational missions, studying and translating into Arabic everything he could get his hands on: philosophy, history, geography, literature, and mathematics. When he returned to Egypt he wrote a diary of his observations on French life, which became required reading for Egyptian civil servants.[9] In the diary he describes the French political process simply and approvingly, laying special stress on its insistence on justice and equality. The French, he says, believe that "justice and equity are the cornerstone of civilizaton and of the well-being of the inhabitants." Both rulers and ruled accept this, he reports, "with the result that their country developed, their learning increased, their prosperity multiplied and their hearts dwelt at peace. For you hardly ever hear anyone complaining of injustice; justice is indeed the foundation of civilization."[10] Al-Tahtawi believed the Egyptians could follow the same course and, for that reason, insisted on the importance of acquiring modern knowledge. And like al-Bustani, he claimed European knowledge was all derived from the Arabs anyway. The Europeans "even admit to us that we have been their teachers in many branches of knowledge, and they acknowledge that we came before them. And it is obvious that the one who is the first to achieve deserves the merit."[11]

Just as al-Bustani had done with the Syrians (and as others would do in the future), al-Tahtawi appealed to Egyptian pride in order to reawaken it. In Europe, the compulsion to self-identity resulted from the recognition of an "other." Europeans were all Christians, but the French were somewhat different from both the Germans and the Spaniards, who were also different from one another. The challenge was to articulate the basis of their differences, to give voice to a unique national consciousness. The "others" facing the Egyptians at this stage were the Europeans. The Egyptians, like the Syrians, knew immediately they were not Europeans, but that brought them to question what they really were. When the technically accurate answer—Ottoman subjects—was articulated, it was somewhat less than satisfying, to Muslims and Christians alike. That was what set into motion the search for a national identity based on something other than religious affiliation, and cultural uniqueness became the subject of the day. Although al-Tahtawi dedicated his diary to all Muslims, it soon became very apparent that his concern was with Egypt.

Al-Tahtawi's official position in Egypt when he returned from Paris was as translator of educational materials. Although military works were the main emphasis, philosophical and literary works were among the more than two thousand books translated by al-Tahtawi and his staff.[12] Al-Tahtawi personally translated Voltaire, Fenelon, and Montesquieu. And, like al-Bustani, he translated *l'amour de la patrie* as *hubb al-watan*, love of homeland. The term *watan* in this context is of utmost importance, because it refers to a geographic area rather than a religious community. Up until this point, the community with which Muslims primarily identified was the *umma*, the community of believers. Clearly, such a designation transcends geographic borders. Al-Tahtawi used the geographic term instead and went on to specify:

For there is a national brotherhood among [members of the same *watan*] over and above the brotherhood in religion. There is a moral obligation on those who share the same *watan* to work together to improve it and perfect its organization in all that concerns its honor and greatness and wealth.[13]

Al-Tahtawi certainly did not abandon Islamic identity. In fact, his writings are traditionally Islamic in form. The purpose of society, he says, is to do God's will by striving to establish *maslaha* (social well-being) in this world, which will assure happiness in the next world. Yet al-Tahtawi describes *maslaha* as a just and *progressive* society founded not only on religious training, but also on "the economic activities which lead to wealth and the improvement of conditions and contentment among the people as a whole."[14] In addition, he says, Islamic law varies little from the natural law on which European civilization is based, so Islamic law could also produce a society capable of modern advancements.

The source of *hubb al-watan,* al-Tahtawi says, is freedom, and its locus, Egypt. It is not the Islamic *umma* or even the Ottoman caliphate; the sense of community cannot be limited only to Muslims, because although Egypt is Muslim, it is not exclusively so, al-Tahtawi says. Not only is its pre-Islamic past distinctly relevant to Egypt's modern character and ultimately worthy of study in its own right, but Islamic Egypt itself includes Jews and Christians as well as Muslims. Therefore, religious differences must be transcended for the good of the country. In fact, the nation must be redefined. It is no longer the worldwide Muslim community alone. It is Egypt. Again, this is not to denigrate the importance of the Islamic *umma;* it is simply a conviction that the most expedient way to ensure worldwide *maslaha* is region by region. Religious differences weaken the country and therefore can only be detrimental to all involved.

Since a society is only as strong as its weakest link, the welfare of the Muslims in Egypt depends on the welfare of all of Egypt. This brings al-Tahtawi to the second implication of Egyptian *maslaha.* Just as al-Bustani had concluded regarding Syria, al-Tahtawi says all members of the Egyptian nation must be guaranteed welfare through legal equality. The *ahl al-dhimma* (protected peoples, i.e., non-Muslims) are every bit as important in the *watan* as the Muslims. They must also contribute to *maslaha* and so should have complete freedom and equality with Muslims.[15]

Europe as Catalyst to Emerging Nationalism

It is therefore with the likes of al-Bustani in Syria and al-Tahtawi in Egypt that nationalism in the Arab world can be said to have started. Despite an undeniable sense of regional identity, both areas had been under some form of Islamic government for twelve hundred years, and that transnational identity was foremost. In the late nineteenth century, both regions still had much in common. Most peasants still lived under feudal or semi-feudal conditions. Some form of tribute was paid to a distant Muslim ruler, but communications were primitive and if the caliph had walked down a village street in either area, he would have been identifiable only if his courtiers accompanied him. Family and tribal kinship systems were the operative social order on the local level. But it was a time of transition. Mercantile activity, particularly under French influence, had produced changes in the social order. In Egypt, as discussed in Chapter Three, such transformations were discernible on the popular level in subtle shifts in religious orders; on the government level, in changing alignments of wealth and power. Overall, these shifts produced a government with a level of cohesion and power unprecedented in the modern period: that of Muhammad 'Ali. In Syria, however, the changes were far more chaotic. The heterogenous religious make-up combined with the plethora of competitive foreign missions resulted in a severely fragmented society. As each region sought independence from the increasingly Turkish (as opposed to Ottoman) government, it focused on the key ingredients of nationalism. Intellectuals in both Syria and Egypt recognized the importance of transcending the strictly religious sociopolitical identity that gave the Ottomans legitimacy and realized this implied legal equality of all—regardless of religion—within a given region. The differences between the two emerged, however, when thinkers and activists from each region set out to elaborate a new identity, i.e., to answer the question "What is an Egyptian?" or "What is a Syrian?"

That was exactly the question asked by Butrus al-Bustani's son, Selim (d. 1884). In an article entitled *"Man Nahnu?"* ("Who Are We?") he said, "Instead of constantly bragging about ourselves and our great past, let us try to find out something about our [present] condition."[16] He was referring to the kinds of claims made by his father: that everything worthwhile that had ever been done was done by Arabs first.

But there was an added element of self-defense involved in the Arab assertions. European self-aggrandizement had not abated with the settling of national borders. It survived through the so-called Age of

Discovery, when European nations established their respective empires around the world; it became, in fact, their rationale for exploiting other peoples' natural resources. Whether it was the British "white man's burden" or the French *mission civilizatrice* ("civilizing mission"), the justification for imperialism turned on the simple matter of cultural superiority based on religious superiority. It was for the natives' own good, the Europeans claimed, that they came in and taught European languages, for then the natives could be taught "civilized" religion and culture. Europeans considered the indigenous religions either non-existent, "pagan," or inferior and believed these religions explained why the societies were so primitive. If the natives had been Christian, the Europeans thought, surely God would have rewarded them with technology and wealth. The next task was teaching the natives that technology and wealth were ultimate values; it was unthinkable to the European mind that failure to value those things was a reflection of anything but utter ignorance. European thinkers such as Max Weber and Ernest Renan were well known for their denunciations of Middle Eastern culture as backward and antithetical to the development of human potential. It was in response to these accusations that many orations on the glories of Islamic or Arab culture were pronounced. The Arabs—with their love of eloquence and long tradition of hyperbole in extolling tribal virtues—therefore readily mixed self-defense with a genuine search for self-identity.[17]

Al-Afghani

Perhaps the most vociferous defender of Islam against Christian aspersions was Jamal al-Din al-Afghani (d. 1897). He is quoted as having described the English as people of "little intelligence but great perseverance; . . . greedy, avaricious, stubborn, patient, and supercilious."[18] Among the things al-Afghani wrote was *al-Radd 'ala al-Dhahriyyin* (*The Refutation of the Materialists*), in which he attempts a point-by-point response to Renan in defense of Islam.[19] Later political reactions against Western imperialism would have a very different tone from this type of religious defense. At this point it was simply part of the twofold process of self-defense and self-identity. Like others at the time, al-Afghani's primary concern was creating a strong and stable society in the Islamic world of his birth. Since religion was the defining characteristic of that society, the reformers naturally sought to buttress it. Religion was considered the source of strength needed to cast off imperialism. Al-Afghani addressed himself specifically to India and Egypt, both of which were under British occupation. Concern over the need to buttress religion so that its strength would be sufficient to cast off imperial control forms the unifying element of his thoughts.

Al-Afghani is quoted as saying the goal of Islamic reform was to "end political disunity by reconstituting religious unity."[20] He is also said to have claimed, "Muslims form one nation because they belong to one faith."[21] However, in his *Refutation of the Materialists* he speaks of the kind of society that "higher" religions—not just Islam—can produce. Any religion, he says, that provides a standard of religious law by which the people can judge the virtue of the ruler can produce a just society.[22] He claims that Islam is "the strongest bond" of social solidarity. *Al-'Urwa al-Wuthqa* (*The Strongest Bond*) was the name of the periodical he and his disciple, Muhammad 'Abduh, produced while in exile in Paris.[23] But al-Afghani did not mean that Islam is the only bond or even the best bond. It is only the source of the strongest social bond for Muslims. Actually, he said, language is the essential element of communal stability: Without it no group can forge solidarity and with it a group can maintain solidarity even through religious changes.[24] In fact, as al-Afghani concludes in *Refutation of the Materialists,* it is language that ultimately defines and distinguishes among nations.

Accordingly, although al-Afghani is often called the "father of pan-Islamism," he did not call for a united Islamic nation from China and the Philippines to Morocco. The revived Islamic sentiment he advocated would produce one spiritual community, but on the political level he limited his call to Arab unity. Yet even that was not his ultimate aim. Al-Afghani frequently called for elected assemblies. He thought obedience was owed to just leaders, but more important was the nature of the leadership. It would be the task of the elected assemblies to monitor the ruler's dispensation of justice. What was more, their approval of the leader would establish his legitimacy so strongly that a nation of sufficient strength to repel foreign incursions would result. And the elected assembly would have the responsibility to remove the leader if his actions were not in the best interests of the Islamic community.[25] The significance of this proposal—just as it had been in the development of democracy in Europe—is that it effectively limits the leader's legitimacy to the extent of his popular support. The principles by which the leader's actions are judged—the principles of "higher" religions, including Islam—remain universal, but his sovereignty does not. Instead, that sovereignty is limited to the geographic area inhabited by those who legitimate the leader. And within that geographic area, social strength through unity is the ultimate principle.

Al-Afghani claimed both India and Egypt were susceptible to occupation by the English precisely because of their lack of unity, which was caused by religious factionalism. Therefore, like al-Bustani and al-Tahtawi, he condemned religious factionalism as the basis of weakness in the Islamic world. His main concern was transcending the differences between Sunni and Shi'i Muslims. But the principle of subordinating religious differences to national unity is the crucial point. As Arabic intellectual historian Albert Hourani points out, al-Afghani even praised the Germans for having overcome their religious factionalism.[26] His concern for unity in the Islamic world moved him to place that unity above even sectarian differences. Speaking of Egypt and India, he said there should be "good relations and harmony in what pertains to national interests among you and your companions and neighbors who adhere to diverse religions."[27]

Therefore, though al-Afghani called for unity among Muslims, his goal was not Islamic political unity as such; even though he said linguistic affinity is the most natural social bond, he did not call for a single Arab state. His goal was social solidarity sufficient to repel tyranny and imperialism whatever their sources: "[T]hrough their unity [the believers can] create a dam to protect them from all the floods streaming towards them! But I do not mean to insist that all Muslims should have a single ruler, since this would probably be difficult to achieve."[28] The social strength he sought was founded on virtue, but the source of virtue was not limited to Islam, to religion in general, or even to Arabism. He said that even a society based only on human reason could be virtuous. It is easier to establish a stable society based on the gift of revelation, he said, but it can also be achieved through "thought and study."[29] After all, he claimed, "Neither the individual nor the nation . . . nor scientific knowledge has any value except in its use."[30] In other words, there is no ultimate value in any given social or political form; its only value derives from its ability to achieve stability. Arabs, Muslims—all victims of tyranny and imperialism—had to revive and cultivate social solidarity wherever it was available. Al-Afghani, in offering a variety of suggestions, represented a colonized peoples' search for a new identity, one that could strengthen them sufficiently to throw off the old identity.

Al-Afghani's Legacy: 'Abduh

Al-Afghani's disciple and collaborator, Muhammad 'Abduh (d. 1905), was a far more specific in his concern. Again, the themes so prevalent in attempts to distinguish limited national entities from regimes claiming universal jurisdiction are apparent in his work. Like Rousseau in France and al-Bustani in Syria, 'Abduh said laws must suit the society they are to govern.[31] The purpose of his argument was to discourage the popular trend of importing European laws for application in Islamic lands. But the salient point in this context is that it is not the non-Islamic nature of such laws that makes them inappropriate. 'Abduh believed it was a simple fact of sociology that made application of foreign laws unfeasible. Effective laws must emerge from the cultural milieu of those they are to govern. In particular, Muhammad 'Ali and his successors came under attack for revising Egyptian law in accordance with European law. 'Abduh's argument could apply to any society, of course, but his real concern was Egypt. And unlike his predecessors, he felt no need to try to make his suggestions generally applicable.

In criticizing Muhammad 'Ali's reforms, however, 'Abduh did not mean to imply that Egypt was not in need of legal reform. On the contrary, he began his autobiography by stating that "to liberate thought from the shackles of *taqlid* [indiscriminate imitation of precedent]" was the first task he set for himself.[32] In his *Risalat al-Tawhid* (*Epistle on [Divine] Unicity*) he attacked "the Turks" for inculcating the ethic of *taqlid*.[33] In referring to the Ottomans as Turks, rather than as caliphs or sultans, 'Abduh was deliberately ignoring the basis of their claim to political legitimacy outside Anatolia. He saw Turks and Egyptians as two distinct national groups and, in fact, wrote "Every Egyptian . . . hates the Turks and detests their infamous memory."[34] He went on to identify the rights of a governed people. The Turks, he said, advocated blind imitation of precedent not simply because of their defective understanding of Islam, although that was a factor. Even more reprehensible, he said, they did it to keep their subjects under control.

The implication here is significant. Keeping people in ignorance is not only unjust, 'Abduh thought. If people's rights to acquire and act upon knowledge were restored, the Turks' political control would be threatened. Therefore, 'Abduh obviously felt a well-informed populace should exercise some control over leadership. In fact, he stated this belief explicitly in his autobiography: "There is still another matter of which I have been an advocate. . . . This is the distinction between the obedience which the people owe the government, and the just dealing which the government owes its people. I was one of those who called the Egyptian nation to know their rights vis-à-vis their ruler."[35] Although 'Abduh stated in several places that the establishment of such a government would come only gradually to Egypt after careful training of the citizenry and *'ulama'*, there is no doubt here a nascent theory of democratic legitimation of government. As al-Afghani had done, 'Abduh implied that if the leader was not working in the best interests of *maslaha,* then it was the duty of the community to replace that leader.[36]

Once more, the exercise of this power by the nation requires its unity, 'Abduh thought. Al-Afghani had said that the strongest bond lay in Islam, although language was the ultimate determining factor of nationality. 'Abduh said the strongest type of unity was geographic. Those who live in the same place and share the same national sentiment form the basic social unit.[37] But in order for geographic unity to be effective, all members of the nation had to be equal. Therefore, there should be no distinction between the civil rights and duties of Muslims and non-Muslims.[38]

To reiterate, 'Abduh, like the other reformers of his day in both Syria and Egypt, claimed that a given populace should judge the legitimacy of its political leadership and thus established bases for the effective limitation of political legitimacy to a given national entity. And these reformers did so—just as the Europeans had when they were struggling to free themselves from the Holy Roman Empire—by separating the universal claims of religious sovereignty from the limited sphere of political legitimacy. Because the basis of universalism in political claims was religious, the universality of religious claims had to be removed from politics. However, this did not mean removing religious principles from society. It was taken for granted that the standards by which leadership was to be judged were the province of religious teaching. The reformers were not separating religious values from political values; they were separating religious sovereignty from political sovereignty. Religious claims were no longer the source of political legitimacy; the people were. Therefore, a government could only extend over the geographic area inhabited by the consenting populace. Furthermore, this new system of legitimacy took political protest out of the category of religious heresy. If approval by the populace was the source of political legitimacy, popular disapproval was justification for changing the government. In other words, replacing religious legitimacy with popular legitimacy—which could only be done by separating religious authority from political authority—provided geographic limits to sovereignty congruent with the boundaries of a self-defined peoples' nation and provided a means for orderly change of government.

But there is still another element discernible in the work of 'Abduh. With him, the demand for national self-identity had gone beyond the comparisons with the newly discovered, "modern" European civilization and the defense against European criticisms that characterized the thought of his predecessors. Arab efforts at self-identity were growing more specific. As part of the process of replacing the withering Islamic political order, the Arabs distinguished themselves from Turks and, at least theoretically, from other Arabs as well. 'Abduh had a keen interest in Ibn Khaldun's writings on the nature of Islamic society and the rise and decline of political forms in general. He also read and taught François Pierre Guillaume Guizot's *Histoire de la civilisation en Europe* (Paris, 1838), which claims that human society governs the world and, therefore, that the condition of the world depends on the condition of society. The condition of society depends on the its individual members forming an effective unit by accepting a set of rational and moral principles. 'Abduh applied these concepts to Egyptian society. It was fragmented and culturally schizophrenic, he said, because it had lost its commitment to true Islamic values. True Islam is true civilization, as he put it, setting up as an example the community established by the Prophet and his companions (the Age of the Salaf [pious ancestors]). To return to that standard of a vigorous and strong society, Islam needed to renew itself, to learn what was valuable from Europe and apply it in accordance with Islamic principles. In all this the language is Islamic and therefore universal. But 'Abduh's specific application was always to Egypt in particular. The other Ottoman subjects could do the same for themselves, but he was working on Egypt.

Europe Exploits Waning Ottoman Power in Egypt

Of course, al-Afghani and 'Abduh had good reason to worry about Islamic society. The demise of Ottoman rule was becoming increasingly obvious and the need for reform more crucial. Despite the reforms initiated by Muhammad 'Ali, reactionary tendencies had set in with his grandson, 'Abbas (r. 1848–1854), and the latter's successor, Sa'id (r. 1854–1863). They abolished foreign schools and sent the foreign advisers home. Then Isma'il (r. 1863–1879) renewed interest in development and invited in U.S. advisers. He started the first schools for girls in Egypt, opened a national library that still exists, and initiated development plans of unprecedented ambition. His most spectacular project was the Suez Canal. Linking the Mediterranean and Red seas, it eliminated the need for Europeans to travel around Africa to get to the Orient. It was opened with great fanfare in 1869; Giacomo Puccini even composed a new opera—*Aida*—to celebrate the event. Isma'il thus gave new life to the Egyptian economy. Unfortunately, however, in the process he made Egypt all the more valuable to Britain and France. Not only was Egypt now *literally* the gateway to the "jewel in the [British imperial] crown," India, but Isma'il had heavily mortgaged Egypt to finance the project. The hundred-mile canal was financed mainly through the public sale of shares in France. Isma'il sold the roughly one-seventh interest he had retained to Britain in 1875. His alleged claim that Egypt was part of Europe, then, and not the Orient, became true. His extravagance utterly bankrupted Egypt. So despite the sultan's granting him the title *khedive*—virtually autonomous ruler—he became in fact a pawn of joint British-French administration. Indeed, they deposed him in 1879 and put in his place a ruler of their own choosing, Tawfiq (r. 1879–1892).

These were the circumstances under which al-Afghani and 'Abduh worked. Their insistence on the need for change in Egypt was shared by virtually all segments of society. In 1882 the combined grievances of the Egyptian military and the peasants burst forth in an uprising named for its leader, Ahmad 'Urabi. The British ended the insurrection by bombing Alexandria; they and the French then took full control of the country. Egypt remained nominally under the control of the Turkish sultan during the reigns of Tawfiq and his successor, 'Abbas Hilmi II (r. 1892–1914), but the British Lord Cromer was the unquestioned autocrat in charge. 'Abduh's criticism of the government got him jailed on more than one occasion; both al-Afghani and 'Abduh were exiled for their alleged support of the 'Urabi movement. Al-Afghani ended his days in forced retirement in Istanbul. 'Abduh was allowed back into Egypt in 1888 and spent the rest of his life quietly working to reform Egyptian education.

Renewed Ottoman Pressure Boosts Syrian Nationalism

Meanwhile, Syria was continuing its struggle to break with the empire and identify itself as a unique sociopolitical entity. But the sectarian disputes of 1860 had resulted in intensified—and unwelcome—attention from the Ottoman capital. As a result, most reform activity had to take place underground, in the form of secret societies. Actually, these societies grew out of the work of the educational reformers discussed above. As early as 1847, al-Bustani and his principal collaborator in the revival of Arabic studies, Nasif al-Yaziji, established the Society of Arts and Sciences (*Jam'iyyat al-Adab wa'l-'Ulum*), with a membership that included mainly Christian Syrians, as well as some Americans and Europeans. Then the Jesuits set up the Oriental Society in 1850 with an exclusively Christian membership. The goals of both societies were to encourage modern education and revive the Arab heritage in Syria.

Although these two societies had limited membership, they set an example that was soon emulated by the population at large. In 1857 the Syrian Scientific Society (*al-Jam'iyyat al-'Ilmiyyat al-Surya*) was established for Syrian intellectuals of all religions. Unlike its predecessors, the Syrian Scientific Society survived the massacres of 1860. It was granted official recognition by the Ottoman regime in 1868 and, bound together by its members' pride in their Arab heritage and concern for Syria in particular, it continued to attract members from across the religious spectrum. However, it was in the society's secret meetings that its most significant work was done. It was there, as Syrian historian George Antonius recounts, that Ibrahim al-Yaziji promulgated his ode to Syrian unity and independence, which would be passed by word of mouth throughout Syria: "With its utterance the movement for political emancipation sang its first song."[39]

As discussed above, the incidents of 1860 resulted in European intervention and the imposition of a new administrative order, called the *Reglement Organique* of 1864. Syria was divided into three administrative districts: Damascus, Homs, and the Lebanon. The governor of each was responsible directly to the sultan; in the Lebanon, the governor was to be Christian and the entire province was granted special privileges. One immediate effect of this series of events was to awaken any who yet remained oblivious to the fact that Syria's factional infighting had made it incapable of self-defense against foreign intervention. This awareness was further heightened during the administration of Sultan 'Abd al-Hamid II (r. 1876–1908).

'Abd al-Hamid II assumed control of the Ottoman empire in the wake of two incompetent predecessors and determined to reinstate central control over the provinces. Besides turmoil in Egypt and Syria (as well as in the Balkans), he was faced with an empty treasury, mounting European intervention, and a group of well-placed Turks calling for constitutional reform. The wily sultan decided to mollify everyone concerned by ostentatiously granting a constitutional government in 1876. Then, with somewhat less public scrutiny, he exiled the leader of the constitutional movement and, when Russia declared war in 1877, suspended the constitution. The results of the war were not favorable for the sultan; in the Treaty of Berlin (1878) he lost considerable control over his Balkan provinces. This, combined with the loss of Algeria and Tunisia to France (1830 and 1881, respectively) and Egypt to England, resulted in desperate attempts to increase control of the Arab provinces.

The first thing 'Abd al-Hamid II did was try to tighten control over Syria by further dividing it into districts governed by his special agents. In 1887 he ordered the threefold division increased to a fivefold division: Aleppo, Beirut, Eastern Syria, the Lebanon (south of Beirut), and Jerusalem. He followed the same strategy in Iraq, which had previously been virtually autonomous. It was divided into three administrative units: Mosul, Baghdad, and Basra. The sultan even tried to reimpose control in Arabia, but that was impossible: The shariff of Mecca was the only respected leader in the two holy cities of Mecca and Medina;

the Wahhabi Sa'ud family and its competitors, the Rashidis, were in control inland; and Britain and France had control over the southern coast.

Simultaneously, 'Abd al-Hamid II began a campaign of religious activity—founding colleges, supporting *madrasas* (Islamic schools), publishing journals—to strengthen his claim to the caliphate. By the time he became sultan, however, the position of religious leadership that had always been the basis of the Ottoman claim had fallen into disrepute. Previous sultans had flagrantly violated Islamic law in public and private life. 'Abd al-Hamid therefore wanted to undermine the basis of religiously inspired criticism growing in the Arab provinces. He was keenly aware that there was a very thin line between accusations of impious leadership and political revolt leading to independence movements. 'Abd al-Hamid therefore tried to demonstrate to the Arabs his devotion to Islam by beautifying their mosques and opening a railroad from Istanbul to Mecca. The Hijaz Railway was heralded as a great boon to pilgrims making their pious trips to Islam's capital. More important to the sultan, it provided an overland route for his troops to Arabia, should the need arise. He also began giving Arabs high positions in his court. If they did not accept, he forced them to reside in Istanbul. Such was the case of Shariff Hussein of Mecca and his three sons, who would later play crucial roles in the Arab uprising. They lived under the sultan's watchful eye from 1893 until 1908.

Syrian and Egyptian Nationalism Progress

The sultan's suspicions of Arab disloyalty were not unfounded. By 1880 anonymous placards were appearing on the streets of Beirut, Tripoli, Sidon, and Damascus, calling on the Arabs to overthrow their Turkish masters and create an independent Syria. 'Abd al-Hamid II's increased vigilance—he is said to have sent in spies posing as Muslim teachers to report on antigovernment activity—and censorship only amplified Syrian disaffection. By the 1890s the situation had produced another Syrian nationalist activist, 'Abd al-Rahman al-Kawakibi (d. 1903).

Al-Kawakibi was jailed in Syria for his outspoken criticism of the government; upon his release in 1898 he moved to Cairo. There he joined Muhammad 'Abduh's circle and anonymously published scathing attacks on Ottoman tyranny and pretensions to piety. But he was far more specific in his condemnations of the government than 'Abduh could afford to be. He expressed appreciation of the Egyptian regime (which, under British control, was giving him asylum from 'Abd al-Hamid's police) and utterly condemned the Turks' oppression in Syria. The Turks were incapable of carrying out the duties of the caliphate, he said, and had only been able to exercise their power so long because of the Arabs' ignorance. The Arabs therefore had to throw off the shackles of blind imitation (*taqlid*) and exercise their ingenuity (*ijtihad*) in establishing true Islamic rule anew. That meant, for al-Kawakibi, taking the caliphate back into Arab control.

Because of his emphasis on Islam, al-Kawakibi is often regarded as a religious revivalist. Others consider him a nationalist because he distinguished the Arab community from the Islamic *umma*.[40] But, in fact, it is anachronistic to try to characterize him as either a revivalist or a nationalist, strictly speaking. Because of the nature of Ottoman rule, attacking it involved what are now considered both religious and political issues. In al-Kawakibi's context, the two were one. As a devout Muslim, he could hardly be expected to call for the abolition of the caliphate, any more than Christian reformers would have called for the abolition of the papacy. Instead, it was simply a matter of orienting the caliphate properly toward moral issues. Al-Kawakibi said the caliph should be elected every three years, his power should be strictly limited, he should have no military force, and he should not interfere in the affairs of autonomous nations. What was more, al-Kawakibi said, there should be equality among all citizens of the "autonomous nations"—whatever those nations were—regardless of religion, for the sake of national solidarity.[41]

There were other Muslim leaders at the time who concentrated more on religious matters of a sort not considered threatening to the government. But their work differed from that of the likes of al-Kawakibi and 'Abduh more in sophistication than in motivation. It was all part of the growing effort to break the Ottoman hold on their religio-political reins and come up with something to replace it.

Another thinker who took for his starting point the horrors of tyranny—like al-Kawakibi, using it as a blanket condemnation of both indigenous and foreign control of Egypt—was Qasim Amin (d. 1908). Amin is perhaps best known as a proponent of women's liberation. True civilization would only be reached, he taught, when women were given their full rights.[42] The Muslim community has yet to fulfill its Qur'anically mandated command to implement a system of government based on *shura* (leaders' consultation with the people), which Amin considered a clear-cut principle of democracy.[43] Nor did Amin share 'Abduh's conviction that Islamic civilization, conforming to all the highest principles of freedom and democracy, was the highest or "true" civilization. For Amin there was no such thing. He concluded logically from 'Abduh's contention that laws must emerge from the society to which they apply that different societies require different laws. The Qur'an itself states that it was God's plan that people be separated into different nations (35:24; 13:7; 2:213; 11:118; 10:19). That was why each group was sent its own prophets. Instead of emphasizing the need to return to a glorious standard of Islamic life, Amin emphasized the need to establish Islamic principles in the modern context.

Amin's work was the culmination of the early reform movement in Egypt. Even in this brief survey, it is apparent that a reorientation toward Islam's role in politics was under way. Islam was an integral part of the culture, but it was no longer the sole identifying characteristic. Egyptian identity and independence were beginning to take center stage. This did not mean diminishing the role of Islam in the country. Islam remained the source of social strength and the language of the development of that strength. But Egyptian independence required something more than the religion it shared with so many others, including its oppressors. Egypt was breaking away from the rest of the Islamic caliphate and, by the time of Amin, no longer even felt the need to justify that break. Instead, there was a growing tendency toward strategic concerns. The sultanate that used to be justified by Islam had been rejected; it had been redefined as tyranny. Now all that remained was to actually eliminate the vestiges of the caliphate and replace it with Egyptian government. This was very practical work that required the type of organized effort evident in the next step in Egypt's development—the establishment of political parties.

Egyptian Political Organization

The first actual political party in Egypt was formed around remnants of Ahmad 'Urabi's group in the 1870s: the National Party (al-Hizb al-Watani). By that time the term *watan* had obviously been accepted as referring to Egypt both as an integral whole and as the central concern of Egyptians, rather than to the entire Islamic *umma*. In fact, *al-Watan* was the name of an Egyptian newspaper founded in 1877. This use of *watan* was the subject of a book written in 1881.[44] And "*Watan*" was the name of one of the first plays ever written in Arabic.[45]

The followers of 'Abduh also came to be known as a *hizb*, the Hizb al-Imam (the Imam's Party). Among them was a major figure in Egyptian history, Ahmad Lutfi al-Sayyid (d. 1963), who helped found another party, the Hizb al-Ummah or People's Party, and really articulated the transition between Islamic universalism and Egyptian nationalism. In his work it is evident that Islam is no longer the immediate constituent of Egyptian identity. Just as the French and Spanish, for example, remained Catholics, so Egyptians did not cease to be primarily Muslim, but Islam was not the defining factor (in the literal sense of the term: determining the boundaries) of their identity. This specific Egyptian concern does not make Lutfi al-Sayyid categorically different from his intellectual ancestors, al-Afghani and 'Abduh, as many scholars have claimed. He simply represents a further development of their thought. Al-Afghani and 'Abduh were pioneers in reshaping Egyptian consciousness. Their starting point was a twelve-century heritage of expansive Islamic consciousness. Naturally, Islam played a major part in their works. In addition, they were religious scholars, whereas Lutfi al-Sayyid had gone to one of Muhammad 'Ali's modern high schools (after Qur'an school) and then to law school. But this is not the reason Islam plays a secondary role in his works. The fact that a layman became a political leader in Egypt in the first place is the significant issue here. Lutfi al-Sayyid did not dictate beliefs to the Egyptian people; his popularity reflected their beliefs. As Albert Hourani put it, "By [Lutfi al-Sayyid's] time the idea of an Egyptian nation was a commonplace universally accepted."[46]

Indeed, the importance of religion is evident throughout Lutfi al-Sayyid's work, but not sectarian religion as such. As he put it, "Since for us Egyptians the principle of good and evil is grounded in belief in the essence of religion, it follows that religion, seen from this ethical point of view, must be the basis of general education."[47] Still, there is a distinctly Islamic content to Lutfi al-Sayyid's writings. He said that government is binding only when it is in accordance with the people's sense of justice. This reflects essentially the two basic principles of Islamic political thought: *shura* and *bai'a*. As noted above, *shura* is government in consultation with the people, which was imposed by the Qur'an even on the Prophet Muhammad; *bai'a* is the principle of binding agreement by which the populace pledges to abide by duly chosen leadership. But Lutfi al-Sayyid did not feel compelled, as the earlier thinkers had, to stress the conformity of his ideas with Islam or the Islamic legitimacy of nationalism. In fact, he was quite conscious of the incongruity of a universal political claim based on Islam. "The idea that the land of Islam is the home-country of every Muslim," he said, "is an imperialist principle, the adoption of which could be useful to any imperialist nation eager to enlarge its territory and extend its influence."[48] Instead, Lutfi al-Sayyid took the legitimacy of Egypt for granted without having to justify it religiously. He said that Europe's recognition of Muhammad 'Ali's hereditary rule of Egypt was in effect a recognition of Egypt's right to sovereignty.[49]

For the next generation of political activists, theoretical justification of nationalism was no longer even an issue. As we will see in Chapter Seven, there were those who continued to insist on Islamic unity—"pan-Islamism"—but at this stage they had not developed political programs or taken any practical steps toward realizing their goals.

Those who were active concentrated almost entirely on the next logical step in the quest for Egyptian independence—ridding the country of foreigners. It was not that they considered the question of Islamic unity vis-à-vis national unity unimportant; it was simply that this question had already been answered in 'Abduh's "brotherhood over and above religious unity." That was what allowed the new young leaders with their modern educations to form new organizations to achieve their goals, organizations no longer based on religious affiliations alone, but also on national commitment. Such was the party established by Mustafa Kamil (d. 1908), which took the name Hizb al-Watani (the National Party). Like their predecessors, the group that had formed around Ahmad 'Urabi, this was a group of single-minded activists with a strategic goal. For them, Egyptian independence under whatever justification was the most important issue.

This was demonstrated in their first public act. The language of Arab unity had been very important in breaking the bond with the Turkish sultan. But when Arab unity conflicted with Egyptian independence, that unity took second place. That was why Kamil's group attacked the newspaper *al-Muqattam*. The paper was run by Lebanese Christians opposed to 'Abd al-Hamid's Syrian policies, but, in gratitude for their safe asylum in Egypt, they were generally supportive of British rule there. Many Egyptian activists, on the other hand, saw British rule as the primary obstacle to independence. They would cooperate with the French and/or even the Ottoman sultan if it would help achieve their goal. At that time the Egyptian *khedive* was 'Abbas Hilmi II, who himself resented having to take orders from Lord Cromer. He and Mustafa Kamil therefore became co-conspirators with the French against British rule.

But this was only a transitional stage in Egypt's political maturation. By the first decade of the twentieth century the cumulative effects of modern education combined with continued foreign rule began to appear in a greater self-reliance on the part of Egyptian nationalists. Two events were decisive in accelerating development of Egyptian political consciousness. First was the promulgation of the *Entente Cordiale* (1904), in which Britain and France acknowledged each other's spheres of influence in Egypt and Morocco, respectively. Despite benefits brought to Arab lands by the Europeans and any strategic advantage French and British competition might have had for Arab nationalists, the *Entente Cordiale* severely discredited both France and England in the Middle East. It became clear even to many who had labored under the myth of European magnanimity that England and France meant to take control of their lands and had no intention of helping either colony achieve independence.

Second, in 1908 Lord Cromer retired as British governor of Egypt and was succeeded by the more moderate Sir Eldon Gorst. Because Gorst's style was far less autocratic than that of his predecessor, the reigning 'Abbas Hilmi II gained greater leeway from the British and, as a result, lost his need for Mustafa Kamil and his supporters. But Kamil's National Party had no intention of fading into oblivion, especially in light of the events in Dinshawai in 1906. Dinshawai was a village in the Nile delta where a British pigeon-shooting excursion led to a fight between the villagers and the British. One of the British officers died during the fray; when he was found, his cohorts beat a peasant to death. They then set up a special court that condemned several villagers to public flogging and others to public hanging. As so often happens, this blatant cruelty finally galvanized the sentiments that had been developing among the Egyptian populace for generations. It was then that political parties became the accepted avenue of public protest. Lutfi al-Sayyid's People's Party became official, and supporters of the *khedive* started their own party (the Constitutional Reform Party). But most productive was Mustafa Kamil's National Party.

Mustafa Kamil was not anti-European. He quoted approvingly Isma'il's assertion that Egypt is part of Europe. He believed European civilization held many things of value for the rest of the world and that it would be self-destructive to ignore these opportunities. Most important, Europe could teach Egypt the secret of its strength—*wataniyya,* patriotism or nationalism: "Everything that exists in those regions, by way of justice, order, freedom and independence, great prosperity and great possessions, is undoubtedly the product of this noble feeling which spurs the members of the nation in their entirety to strive for a common purpose and a single goal."[49] What was more, Egyptian patriotism was essentially Islamic, he said; Islamic principles, if correctly understood, actually require *wataniyya,* "patriotism and justice, activity and union, equality and tolerance."[50] Religion and national life were two spheres, not separate so much as they were concentric. The core is true religion, but true religion is far greater in extent than nationalism. If Egyptians simply concentrated on their own religious heritage they would be able to assimilate all that is valuable in scientific and intellectual discovery and thereby strengthen their own country. Of course, the immediate goal of *wataniyya* was ridding Egypt of foreign intervention. Included in the category of foreigners were Arabs who had been taking advantage of Egyptian trade since the capitulations and those who were taking advantage of British occupation—in particular, Syrians. But the British were no doubt his main target. The main plank of the National Party's platform was immediate and unconditional evacuation of Egypt by Britain.

These two considerations—the importance of independence from Britain and the centrality of Islamic heritage—shaped the National Party's policy of supporting the *khedive*. The way Mustafa Kamil saw it, Egypt's independence depended on the sultan's independence. If the *khedive* was weakened by opposition in Egypt, Ottoman strength in general would be diminished. That was how the sultan had been forced to let Britain take over Egypt in the first place. But Egyptian nationalism was so far developed at the time that Kamil encountered severe criticism for this policy. He had to defend himself against accusations that he was trying to save Egypt for Turkey. He called those who held this opinion slanderers. The idea was so ridiculous, he said, that it was "an insult to civilization and civilized men, and an indictment that the Egyptian people can never progress or reach the level of other peoples."[51] A return to Turkish imperial rule at this point was unthinkable as a political goal. But after all, the sultan was still a focus of Islamic solidarity, which could only enhance the unity sought by Kamil's party. The French Enlightenment thinkers were still considered brilliant; the French Revolution, a model to be emulated. But there was a sincere conviction that its principles of freedom and equality were indeed the true values of Islam. This belief in the power of Islam to strengthen the nation is perhaps best expressed in an episode reported at the time Japan defeated the Western imperial giant, Russia (1905), an event that caused sympathetic euphoria in Egypt. It was widely rumored that the reason the Japanese had been able to slay the giant was that they had become Muslim. One of 'Abduh's disciples recalls a conversation held at 'Abduh's house when the victory was announced:

We were at the home of the Imam ['Abduh] talking about what we had just heard, namely, that the Japanese wished to adopt Islam. Shaykh Hussein al-Jisr exclaimed, "Islam now has hope to regain its former power and glory!" [Shaykh Salman] answered, "Leave [the Japanese] alone. If they are converted to Islam we will probably corrupt them before they ever have the chance to reform us."[52]

Obviously the rumor was not taken altogether seriously, particularly among the educated elite. But it does indicate the popular level the drive for independence had achieved. For Muslims, political success was a reward for virtuous behavior. Islamic piety may not have been considered sufficient as the sole reason for such reward, but it surely was necessary. Islam was at once the champion of oppressed peoples, their road to victory, *and* at the heart of the sought-after national solidarity that included all Egyptians.

When British policy in Egypt changed, Mustafa Kamil's attitude changed somewhat as well. Following the *khedive's* loss of interest in the National Party once he had been liberated by Gorst, the focus of the National Party turned to constitutional government. Even while praising Muhammad 'Ali's family for having effected the independence of Egypt, Kamil pointed out that they were simply expressing the national will. In so doing they had created a lasting bond with the Egyptian people, all the people—Muslim and non-Muslim alike. But now that popular Egyptian will had to be voiced in a representative government. Mustafa Kamil therefore brought the Islamic reformation in Egypt full circle—from de facto autonomy to demands for real independence and all the attendant changes in the theoretical infrastructure. The former basis of political legitimacy was not abandoned, just repositioned to give its followers strength. The calls for representative government, with its implied limits to political sovereignty, and for Islam to be the center of a pluralistic society bound by shared values— these were the practical steps needed to implement the ideals set out by the early reformers. They were, in fact, a reassertion of the demands for adaptation of Islamic principles to changing political needs, in the finest tradition of Ibn Taymiyya. Ibn Taymiyya's calls had not been heeded, and Islamic society had succumbed to centuries of stifling autocracy. Now the Arabs had reawakened, but the road to self-determination would still be arduous.

Mustafa Kamil did not live to see the first actual representative government in Egypt. He died in 1908. His party was banned by the British and fell into oblivion with its exiled leader, Muhammad Farid. It was the next popular leader of Egypt, Sa'd Zaghlul (d. 1927), who became a candidate in the elections for the legislative assembly established by Britain. Zaghlul had been a friend of both al-Afghani and 'Abduh and was also associated with Lutfi al-Sayyid and Qasim Amin. He shared devotion to the main themes of all their endeavors. He worked as a lawyer and judge to reform Egypt's legal system and as minister of education to nationalize education. But unlike Kamil, Zaghlul believed Ottoman suzerainty was more onerous than British, until England simply dismissed the *khedive* and declared Egypt a protectorate at the outbreak of World War I. This would change Zaghlul's approach to Egyptian independence. But he would not get a chance to express his views again until after the hiatus in Egyptian politics imposed by the war.

Syrian Political Organization

In Syria, on the other hand, events gained urgency following 1908. That was the year 'Abd al-Hamid's tyranny finally spawned a revolution in Turkey. Calling themselves the Committee of Union and Progress (CUP), a group known as the Young Turks—mostly Muslim and some Jewish—determined to end despotism and restore the Constitution of 1876. 'Abd al-Hamid was forced to acquiesce and the CUP ultimately gained virtual control of the government. Among their first acts was allowing Shariff Hussein to return to Mecca and awarding him the title of Servant of the Two Holy Places.

But this was not enough to appease the Arabs. They also wanted fair representation in the reconstituted Chamber of Deputies. As Syrian historian George Antonius notes, although the exact population of the Ottoman empire at the time was unknown, Arabs probably outnumbered Turks three to two.[53] The 60 seats held by Arabs in the 245-seat chamber were hardly sufficient. Of the forty members of the Senate, only three were Arabs.

In the early days of the movement to curb tyranny and undermine the Ottoman regime, the CUP had been joined by many Arab officers from the Ottoman army. But once the Young Turks gained power, their own nationalist interests became apparent. Their concern was the struggle of Turkey, and they were not about to let rebellious provinces weaken it. In short, they did not look favorably on Arab nationalism, whether Egyptian or Syrian. In their effort to curb Arab nationalism, the CUP placed a ban on all non-Turkish organizations. Clearly a blow to the very heart of the Arab nationalist movement—the beloved literary and scientific societies—the measure had the effect of increasing Arab agitation. In the following years new societies appeared and attracted literally thousands of members in chapters throughout Syria and spreading into Iraq.[54] By now the societies had lost all vestiges of religious distinction. They were distinguishable only by their political demands. Some called for decentralization, a reversal of the CUP's centralizing policies. Others called for a dual monarchy, a Turko-Arab empire like Austro-Hungary. Some demanded home rule. The most extreme called for uncompromised independence.

In 1913, one of them, the Committee of Reform (*Jam'iyyat al-Islahiyya*), went public with a demand for home rule in all matters of regional concern to the Arab provinces. The committee was supported in public demonstrations throughout Syria and Iraq. Within two months the CUP closed the Committee of Reform's headquarters in Beirut and arrested its leaders. Following further protests, the government was forced to release the leaders. Despite a few concessions to their demands, the Arab provinces were not satisfied. At the same time that the leaders of the Committee of Reform had been arrested, another group—the Young Arab Society (*Jam'iyyat al-'Arabiyyat al-Fatat*)—was holding an Arab congress in Paris to call for full Arab independence. The Ottoman treatment of the Committee of Reform had so incensed the members of other groups that even those who had previously only called for decentralization now joined the delegates in Paris. The twenty-four delegates—mostly Syrian—issued a list of moderate resolutions that amounted to no more than self-rule on Arab provincial issues and an effective voice in the central government. The CUP again tried to appease the Arabs with apparent concessions, for example, allowing the use of Arabic in primary schools. But once again there were no real concessions. The CUP nominated five Arab senators, but only one of them was an Arab nationalist leader (and when he accepted the nomination under such circumstances, he was considered a traitor to the movement). From then on the Arab nationalists gave up trying to work with the Ottomans.

The following year (1913), Ottoman attempts to suppress Arab nationalism temporarily brought the Egyptian and Syrian movements together. That year 'Aziz 'Ali al-Misri—former inspector general of the Egyptian army, disaffected member of the CUP, and well-known Arab nationalist—formed a new society, *Jam'iyyat al-'Ahd* (Society of the Covenant). Al-'Ahd called for a dual monarchy, reconciling Arab and Ottoman loyalty, and only differed from other societies in that its members were entirely military (mainly Syrian and Iraqi).[55] The Arab nationalist movement was no longer a civilian movement, but had entered the ranks of the Ottoman army. When the CUP had al-Misri arrested, tried, and condemned to death on contrived charges, protests were heard throughout the Arab world and Egypt. Lord Kitchener, the British agent in Cairo, was even moved to intervene on al-Misri's behalf, fearing the ultimate break between Arabs and Turks. His fears were well founded. Even though British pressure finally forced the Ottoman government to set al-Misri free, the Arabs were convinced by the incident that they could not be secure without independence. Al-Misri's military nationalist group would eventually join forces with the civilian nationalists and stage a unified Arab revolt. Their movement needed only the leadership of an Arab whose loyalty transcended national boundaries—Shariff Hussein of Mecca.

CHAPTER FIVE

The Arab Revolt and Its Aftermath

*A*t the end of hostilities in 1918 . . . Britain took the mandates for newly created Palestine, Transjordan, and Iraq, giving it control of a land bridge between the Mediterranean and the Gulf. The terms of the mandate for Palestine, quoting the Balfour Declaration, were drafted by Britain and endorsed by the Conference of San Remo. France was given the mandate for Lebanon and Syria but had to take Damascus by force and remove Emir Faysal from the throne to which he had been elected by the General Syrian Congress in 1920. With this, British wartime promises to support Arab independence in areas liberated from Turkish control were irrevocably broken.
—Alasdair Drysdale and Gerald H. Blake[1]

The events leading up to the Arab Revolt are well known.[2] The revolt came with the outbreak of World War I, which itself marked the explosive intersection of Europe's attempt to consolidate nation-states, begun centuries before, and the Arab Ottoman provinces' incipient attempts to create nation-states. The Balkan states stood at the crossroads of the Christian and Islamic empires. Traditionally perceived as a buffer zone between the two, they finally decided to declare themselves independent of both. That was the ostensible start of the war. But the drama of the Eastern and Western empires played in the Arab lands, too. For the Arab states the involvement of the Ottomans in the war

110

was their opportunity to finally shake off imperial control, and Europe wanted to take over the sultan's role.

European involvement in Arab independence struggles came against the backdrop of the developing Egyptian and Syrian nationalist movements described in the previous chapter. Cairo and Beirut/Damascus were the two centers of nationalist activity in the Ottoman provinces. At this stage Egypt was not generally considered Arab. Although Egyptians were Arabic speakers, Arabs were still considered inhabitants of the Arabian peninsula; Syrians were the inhabitants of the Fertile Crescent, from the Egyptian borders of the Sinai to the Taurus Mountains and from the Mediterranean Sea to the Euphrates River. Iraqis inhabited Mesopotamia. As we have seen, the nationalist movements began with a sort of amorphous Islamic identity. But the incongruity of claiming Islamic independence from an Islamic state had quickly led to a more specifically Arab identity, based on the notion of shared language and culture and including traditional Arabs, Syrians, and Iraqis. Religious legitimacy was the model of the past; linguistic or cultural identity was the trend popular among European thinkers of the time. Both models were therefore familiar. Within the latter context, that of linguistic or cultural identity, were even more localized calls for Egyptian and Syrian (and, later, Iraqi) national unity as a basis for independence.[3] But they lacked a key component—a popular leader. That need was fulfilled by Shariff Hussein of Mecca. He was indeed an Arab, i.e., neither Egyptian nor Syrian nor Iraqi. His leadership was a function of Islamic identity. Only someone of such authority could command the respect of the populace and lead them in such a momentous move against the institutionalized religio-political authority. Only a religiously authorized spokesman could lead the people against the old religious order into a new political form, giving assurance that the cherished religious values would be retained in the process. As it had been in Europe, the progression from religio-political authority to secular democracy was a natural corollary to the process of evolving geographically limited states out of a potentially universal empire. Throughout the process, the values of freedom, equality, and justice remained constant. Therefore, for Shariff Hussein to lead the movement for Syrian, Iraqi, and even Egyptian independence was natural. Had the movement been successful, it is unlikely the development of nationalism in the Arab world would ever have been questioned. But the movement was not successful, thanks to European involvement, and that is what set the stage for the current entanglements of progressive and reactionary processes in the Arab world.

The Nationalists Find a Leader

Shariff Hussein returned to Arabia in 1908 after his involuntary sixteen-year stay in Istanbul and immediately began filling the vacuum of power. There were other powerful leaders in the region, of course. Ibn Sa'ud still commanded the respect of the Wahhabi tribal confederation in the Nejd (central Arabia); Ibn Rashid was his traditional competitor. But none had the standing of the shariff from the Hijaz (west-northwest Arabia), the descendant of the Prophet and servant of the Two Holy Places (Mecca and Medina). He and his sons—Faisal, 'Abdullah, and 'Ali—quickly became privy to the aspirations of Arabs throughout the Ottoman world. 'Abdullah, deputy from Mecca in the Ottoman parliament and a devotee of Arab culture himself, took the first available opportunity to act on those hopes. In 1914 he went directly to the British Agency in Egypt to see how Britain might respond to an Arab move for independence. He pointedly asked Oriental Secretary of the British Agency Ronald Storrs if the agency would help them acquire military equipment. No response was made immediately. But when war broke out in Europe in August, Britain kept the request in mind. They watched with concern Germany's increasing involvement in Ottoman affairs and began to see the strategic value of helping the Arabs. Storrs was therefore directed to elicit a commitment from the shariff: If Turkey came into the war on Germany's side, could Britain count on the Arabs to open a second front against the Ottomans?

Despite their esteemed positions, neither the shariff nor his sons felt they could speak for all Arabs. Nor were they about to declare themselves unilaterally. They therefore responded that an Arab revolt was possible but that before it came about, they would want to know what Britain's position would be. It was not until Turkey joined the war in October of 1914 that Britain promised the shariff they would support the Arab fight for freedom if the Arabs would enter the war effort on the Allies' side. But this was not enough. The shariff wanted to know the kind and extent of Arab freedom in question. What would the borders of the proposed Arab kingdom be? Perhaps more important, he insisted on a commitment to Arab political independence, not just a promise of freedom from Ottoman control. All the while the shariff sought these clarifications from England, he was stalling the Ottoman sultan, who was trying to get him to authorize war against British Egypt. And before any commitments could be made either to Britain or the sultan, the shariff had to consult with the leaders of the nationalist movements in Syria and Iraq, for whom he would be speaking, as well as with the other Arab leaders.

The Arab leaders' responses were mixed. The Sa'udi leader was generally sympathetic. He had heard of the Arab nationalist activities and supported them. After all, the Wahhabi heritage was fiercely independent, recognizing no earthly leadership as ultimate. The Rashidis, on the other hand, were unused to national politics. Their attitudes were tribal and their concern was their competition with the Sa'udis. It was a foregone conclusion that if the Sa'udis sided with the Allies, the Rashidis would support the Ottomans. In any event, they were not a major power. Imam Yahya, the Idrisi leader in 'Asir (southwestern Arabia) was virtually surrounded by Turkish troops in the Yemen and considered it best to maintain neutrality.

The main concern was with the Arab nationalist leaders, and as it turned out, they approached the shariff before he had a chance to contact them. Early in 1915 *Jam'iyyat al-'Arabiyyat al-Fatat* (the Young Arab Society) sent a delegate to the shariff asking him to lead an Arab revolt on behalf of Arab nationalists in Syria and Iraq. By spring 1915 the leaders of al-Fatat and their military counterpart, *Jam'iyyat al-'Ahd,* had outlined their demands in what is called the Damascus Protocol. It states essentially that the Arabs would accept the British offer to coordinate efforts against the Ottomans provided the British would commit themselves to support the independence of a specifically defined Arab region. That region included what are now Iraq, Syria, Lebanon, Israel (including the Occupied Territories), Jordan, and the entire Arabian peninsula except Aden (which was already a British protectorate). Then the leaders of the Arab nationalist groups swore to accept the decisions of Shariff Hussein in the matter (an example of *bai'a,* the early Islamic practice of swearing allegiance to a leader chosen by the majority of tribal representatives). If Shariff Hussein could get Britain to accept the Damascus Protocol, the nationalist leaders would see to it that the Arab troops in the sultan's Syrian divisions—most of whose officers were members of al-'Ahd already—would mutiny on command.

The Arab position was therefore solid, but the question of British support for an Arab revolt was still up in the air as far as the shariff was concerned. The specific clarification he had requested had not yet materialized. In an effort to sort out these strategic questions, the shariff's younger son Faisal visited Damascus in March 1915.

Faisal represented the conservative side of Arab nationalism. As passionate as any for independence from the Turks, he also distrusted the Europeans' intentions in the region. It was natural for the Arabs to distrust the Europeans, especially after the revelation of the Entente Cordiale. The European states even distrusted each other, so much so that in 1912 Britain was forced to promise France that it would never lay claim to Syria. This implied that France was expanding its claims to former Ottoman lands to include Syria as well as Morocco. Faisal, in particular, believed that such French expansion was occurring. He preferred to leave Europe out of the Arab movement and just use Ottoman preoccupation with the war as an opportunity to assert Arab independence. Among the leaders of al-Fatat and al-'Ahd were many who shared his attitude; he was made a member of both groups.

By June of the same year (1915) Britain pledged to support the independence only of the Arabian peninsula. Clearly this was not enough to secure the cooperation of Syrian and Iraqi nationalist leaders, and they were in charge of the troops that really counted in the proposed revolt. So Shariff Hussein's next job was to get a British commitment to the independence of the rest of the territories outlined in the Damascus Protocol. Toward that end he exchanged a series of letters (dated from July 1915 to February 1916) with Sir Henry McMahon, the British high commissioner in Cairo, outlining the extent of the desired British commitment to Arab independence. Because the shariff was speaking for the Arabs primarily on the basis of his religious legitimacy, the British initially tried to get around specific territorial demands and placate him with promises to recognize him as the new caliph. The shariff responded that the caliphate was not a central issue. He said the cooperation of the Arabs depended entirely on Britain accepting the proposed borders for Arab independence.

Eventually Britain accepted the Arab demands. In McMahon's words, "Great Britain is prepared to recognize and uphold the independence of the Arabs in all the regions lying within the frontiers proposed by the Shariff of Mecca," subject only to "certain modifications."[4] The modifications proposed by Britain comprised the exclusion of the northwest sections of Syria from Arab control—because they were only partially Arab, as McMahon put it—and were rejected by the Arabs. They knew the real reason the northwest sections were excluded was that the Europeans had already agreed among themselves that France could exercise its influence in those regions. However, in the interest of expediting the movement and taking advantage of Ottoman weakness at the appropriate time, the Arabs were willing to suspend discussion of that issue until after the war. Nor did they quibble about McMahon's further stipulations that the future Arab state should accept only British advisers and that Britain be granted some special administrative control in Iraq. Those details could be sorted out after the war. The essential thing was that Britain would support Arab independence in virtually the entire territory designated in the Damascus Protocol. The Arabs were now ready to act.

The Arab Revolt

Meanwhile, the commander of Turkey's Fourth Army in Syria, Jemal, was pushing Shariff Hussein for recruits in the Ottoman campaign against British-occupied Egypt and becoming increasingly suspicious of the shariff's delaying tactics. Jemal began to react to the reports he was receiving about the Arabs' nationalist activities. Arrests of suspected nationalist leaders increased, stories of their torture and heroism spread, and imprisonment and deportation became common. When these measures proved ineffective in breaking the Arab spirit, Jemal resorted to public hangings. As reports of nationalist sentiment within the military began to circulate, he also started to transfer those divisions led by Arabs out of Syria and replace them with Turks. To make matters worse, famine struck in Syria. Caused by a devastating combination of drought, locust plagues, currency depreciation, and maladministration by a preoccupied Turkish government, the famine would be responsible for the death of tens of thousands within a year.[5]

This was the situation Faisal found when he returned to Damascus in early 1916. His pleas to Jemal for leniency with the suspected nationalists only heightened Jemal's resolve to quash the Arab movement. That spring twenty-two respected leaders—both Christian and Muslim—were hanged publicly. This, in turn, convinced Faisal and his colleagues in al-Fatat and al-'Ahd that the time had come to act. Reports of increasing numbers of Turkish troops being sent to the peninsula under German leadership finally moved the Arabs to end their deliberations about strategy. Without even completing plans to coordinate Syrian and Arab efforts, Faisal returned to Mecca to assist his father in the uprising.

Meanwhile, the shariff had been busy gathering recruits for the Arab revolt and trying to get military equipment from the British in Egypt. In June 1916 the shariff's sons declared the Arabs independent. Leading the shariff's troops, they attacked the Turkish garrisons throughout the Arabian peninsula. By the end of September they had secured the surrender of the Turkish troops everywhere but Medina and had captured the Ottoman governor-general of the Hijaz.

The Ottomans still did not comprehend the depth of Arab nationalist sentiment. With the memory of Muhammad 'Ali and Isma'il still fresh in their minds, they considered the shariff's rebellion just another attempt to consolidate personal power at Turkish expense. They tried to dismiss the shariff and replace him as the leader of Mecca, but his replacement was not accepted by the people and eventually had to leave Arabia. They also attempted to control the damage in Syria, publishing stories of British intrigue and heavy rebel losses. The three sons—Faisal, 'Abdullah, and 'Ali—were variously described as defeated, in hiding on a British warship, and wandering lost in the desert. More significant, imprisonment, torture, and deportation of suspects increased once again. And condemnations of the shariff began to circulate. In Muslim India, for instance, which considered British-held Iraq its eminent domain, he was called a traitor to Islam and accused of using his position to consolidate personal gain. Such accusations, of course, were inevitable. Just as European nationalist leaders had been excommunicated for going against the religiously legitimated imperial government, the shariff and his sons were opposed by a system that did not recognize limited political claims. The Ottoman sultan, though undeniably effete and irreversibly limited, still held theoretically unlimited power. He was the caliph of Islam, and Islam was a universal religion; therefore, his reign was at least potentially unlimited. Even if he was prohibited from exercising power over non-Muslim regions, there was certainly no theoretical justification for Muslim regions to reject his leadership. And under no circumstances could a Muslim leader challenge his political role without challenging his religious position. Thus, even a limited claim such as the shariff's was perceived in the Ottoman capital as a challenge to the entire caliphal institution.

European Treachery

Had the shariff's uprising been successful in gaining the independence of the Arabs, his position no doubt would have been vindicated. He and his family commanded immense respect in the Arab world, among both Muslims and non-Muslims. At first, it appeared the revolt had been successful. More and more key Syrian and Iraqi leaders joined the uprising. By November 1916 sufficient support had been expressed for the shariff to openly declare himself king of the Arabs and ask for European recognition. Britain and France, in a foreshadowing of things to come, acknowledged him only as king of the Hijaz. But the revolt continued to make gains. Turkish troops were driven out of one Arab town after another. By July 1917 Arab troops had advanced northward into Syria, isolated Ibn Rashid from his Turkish suppliers, and, with the help of the flamboyant Thomas Edward Lawrence (Lawrence "of Arabia"), disrupted the Hijaz Railway so effectively that Turkey lost reliable communications with its southern forces.

Success breeds success, and the Arabs' reputation was growing. Faisal spent months consolidating support, arbitrating long-standing tribal disputes so as to forge a unified Arab force for the assault on Damascus. Messages sent to leaders throughout Syria were favorably received. Tribal and urban leaders from Palestine to Anatolia prepared to welcome the Arab troops. Arab soldiers deserted the Turkish army in droves. The

Germans became so alarmed at Arab success that they established a special Arab Bureau in Damascus manned by German experts in Arab affairs. At their urging Jemal changed his oppressive tactics and offered amnesty to any Arabs who would return to the Turkish fold, all to no avail. The Arab Revolt had passed the point of no return.

Meanwhile, British troops began their advance on Jerusalem. Gaza, Hebron, Jaffa, and Bethlehem all fell, as the shariff's forces continued their rout of Turkish troops in the Hijaz and southern Syria. By October the British and Arab troops met outside Damascus and entered the city triumphantly together. Then they split up again; the British advanced up the coast, taking Tyre, Sidon, Beirut, and Tripoli, while the Arabs went inland through Homs, Hama, and Aleppo. Everywhere along the way they were welcomed as liberators. The rejoicing with which they were received was limited only by the devastation of the famine, which had continued unabated throughout the war. By the end of October the Ottomans were a thing of the past. They were the Turks now, and they had no alternative but to sign an armistice. The Arab Revolt had been a success, it seemed.

But no sooner had Arab rejoicing abated than the Europeans began claiming their booty. The missionaries and traders had established cultural and economic beachheads that, since the Entente Cordiale (1904), had been recognized officially as bases of European influence. Now that the final demise of the Ottomans was in sight, the European colonial powers began dividing up their spheres of influence in earnest. As early as 1915 they began their negotiations—held in secret from the people whose land they were discussing, of course. In total disregard of the agreements reached between McMahon and Shariff Hussein, Charles François-Georges Picot (former French consul-general in Beirut), Sir Mark Sykes (a British Arabist), and representatives of the Russian government held a series of meetings to determine the fate of the soon-to-be-liberated Arab lands.

The upshot of their dealings was the Sykes-Picot Agreement of 1916. Russia's claim to Istanbul and other portions of non-Arab Anatolia need not concern us here. But France's claim to southern Anatolia, most of Syria, and the part of Iraq surrounding Mosul and the British claim to southern Syria and Iraq, including Baghdad and Basra, were of utmost concern to the Arabs, as were the claims of all three European empires to that part of Syria known as Palestine. France had been working its claim to Syria for three centuries. Now Britain's self-concern prompted it to try to block France's claim to Palestine. Russia, which also claimed Palestine on the basis of religious affinity, had established extensive Orthodox missions in the region and therefore wanted a Russian protectorate over the "Holy Land." In a semblance of compromise, the

Sykes-Picot Agreement designated for Palestine a special "international" administration.

Initial Arab Responses and British Reassurance

This agreement—secret, illegal, and made feasible only by the superior military power of the European nations—had a staggering effect on the Arab world. For one thing, in betraying the promises made to the Arabs, on the basis of which they had entered into an agreement with non-Muslims against Muslim authorities, the British and French set the stage for a severe backlash against the West—in particular, against Western political forms. It would take some time for the reaction to register, however, again largely due to European deceit. The Arabs did not even find out about the Sykes-Picot Agreement until the Bolshevik Revolution. When the Russian revolutionaries overthrew the czarist government in November 1917, they discovered the agreement in the government files and took it directly to the Turkish authorities. The Turks, in turn, sent it to Shariff Hussein. They hoped the news of the European betrayal would provoke him to abandon his partnership with Britain and make a separate peace with Turkey. There was still hope at that point that the tide of the war could be turned. The Turks were willing to forgive and forget, if only the Arabs would abandon their plan to revolt and establish an independent entity. If the Arabs had agreed with the Turks' reasoning, the outcome of World War I could indeed have been very different.

But the Arabs had lived under Turkish domination too long to trust them, even in this apparent moment of truth. And the shariff had staked his entire reputation and that of his family on his judgment of British sincerity. Armed with the responsibility and respect afforded by the shariffian birthright, Hussein and his sons had worked hard to overcome the protests of those Arab nationalists who distrusted the Europeans from the start. They had convinced the Arab nationalists to follow them in an unprecedented policy: alliance with non-Muslims against Muslims. Only a family of such standing could have led the Muslim world in such a venture. Its failure meant not only a lost chance for Arab independence, but also the loss of the shariff's reputation and that of his family and the failure of his policy of cooperation with the West. This was indeed the moment of truth and the shariff could not risk too light a response.

The shariff therefore sought immediate clarification from the British. In early 1918 the Foreign Office offered an explanation, claiming the reports of the agreement were distorted and outdated. They said there had been no actual agreement, only discussions; that the discussions had provided for popular consent to whatever plans would be made; and that, in any case, the success of the Arab Revolt had changed the situation so that the discussions were no longer even applicable. The message concluded, "His Majesty's government reaffirm their former pledge in regard to the liberation of the Arab peoples."[6]

Arab experience with the Ottomans, and especially the shariff's sixteen years in Istanbul, gave the Arabs no reason to believe the Turks would suddenly change their policy and allow Arab independence. The British, on the other hand, despite suspected imperialist designs, were at least respected for their honesty. After all, freedom, dignity, and equality, the principles at the base of Arab aspirations, were encompassed in England's own governmental structure. The shariff therefore once again chose to trust the British, with what would be disastrous results. Personally, he would lose his position and spend his waning years exiled in Cyprus, and the Arabs would be placed under European control.

Europe's Blueprint for Arab Instability

A subtler but just as devastating aspect of the Sykes-Picot Agreement was its division of the Arab lands. France and Britain agreed that each would divide its holdings into two areas, one directly administered by the occupying power and the other semi-autonomous but controlled economically by the occupying power, which would be the sole resource for administrative and technological expertise. Beyond the fact that this assumption of control was totally against the will of the inhabitants of the land, the respective divisions themselves were brilliantly designed to keep the regions fragmented and therefore weak. In both the French and British areas, the more sophisticated urban centers were placed under foreign administration, while the less-populated areas not accustomed to modern political forms were granted virtual autonomy. The effect was to frustrate the politically advanced areas and, eventually, to radicalize them. Furthermore, this system upset the established power structure. The emasculation of traditional political centers and their leaders allowed those who had until then remained outside the power structure—recalcitrant tribal leaders, minorities, etc.—to gain a kind of prestige and independent base of potential power. Even when independence was eventually gained throughout the Arab world under indigenous leadership, those groups that had been inadvertently empowered by the European settlement were naturally unwilling to accept exogenous domination. They were generally protective of their power, however ill-gotten, and distrustful of the traditional leaders, who had been discredited solely because they had trusted the Europeans.

At the same time, the Sykes-Picot Agreement utterly ignored many of the natural ethnic borders. In the cases of Syria and Iraq, for instance, the borders cut right through Kurdish and Armenian territories, splitting those regions among Iraq, Syria, Turkey, and Iran. The 1920 Treaty of Sevres (between the Allies and the Ottomans) recommended the creation of a Kurdish state and the assignment of the Armenian regions of western Turkey to the Armenian Republic. These recommendations were ignored, however, leaving the Kurds and many Armenians stateless and divided. Similarly, the designation of Palestine as an international zone and a homeland for Jews was the first step in the creation of the Zionist state and the ultimate exclusion of non-Jewish Palestinians from full rights in their homeland. Overall, therefore, the Sykes-Picot Agreement left the Arab world robbed of its traditional leadership and divided against itself in political competition, fragmented and in need of new leadership. Not only that, the new leadership would have neither traditional bases of power nor administrative forms to rely on. Lacking the former it would be forced to rely on autocracy; lacking the latter, it would be forced to experiment with untried political forms or to revert to outmoded forms. Both strategies would be tried in their turn, and neither would be suitable. Both were encumbered by two very difficult requirements: They had to avoid the appearance of the treacherous "Westernism" that had betrayed the Arabs and, at the same time, come to grips with the very circumstances that had led to the evolution of so-called "Western" political forms: the emergence of geographically limited nation-states.

The Palestine Problem

These were the monumental challenges created by the Sykes-Picot Agreement, Europe's answer to the problems of Turkish tyranny over the Arabs. European duplicity and the complexity of the problems it caused are staggering in retrospect. These problems were more significant even than those caused by the other agreement Britain forged, again in secret from the Arabs—the Balfour Declaration, which came two years after the agreement to support Arab sovereignty and a year and a half after the Sykes-Picot Agreement:

His Majesty's Government view with favor the establishment in Palestine of a national home for the Jewish people and will use their best endeavors to facilitate the achievement of this object, it being clearly understood that nothing shall be done which may prejudice the civil and religious rights of existing non-Jewish communities in Palestine, or the rights and political status enjoyed by Jews in any other country.[7]

Having claimed Palestine as an international protectorate as well as pledged it to the independent Arab state, Britain was now pledging Palestine to yet another party, at the same time assuring its previous partners that their respective agreements still stood firm.

The reasoning behind the Balfour Declaration has been thoroughly discussed, as has the development of the Zionist movement and its intentions in Palestine.[8] Briefly, the Zionist movement had been founded at the end of the nineteenth century in eastern Europe. It grew out of centuries of prejudice and persecution by Christian Europe against Jews. In that age of heightened social consciousness, two trends challenged Jewish thinkers. First, the reforms following the French Revolution had for many Jews resulted in liberation from the prejudices against non-Christians that had characterized Europe since the rise of the Holy Roman Empire. There was a noticeable trend toward "assimilationism," a process by which Jews entered the social and political mainstream of European states on an equal footing with the Christians. Though this was no doubt a welcome development for most, it did raise questions about the nature of Judaism. Throughout the centuries of institutionalized inequality, Jews had developed an ethos of divinely inspired separateness from Christian society. The new liberalism therefore called into question the very essence of Jewish identity. If they no longer kept separate from non-Jewish society, then what was the basis of their Jewish identity? Second, the liberation of Jews was far from universal. Persecution persisted, especially in Russia, and despite periods of respite it seemed to return with predictable regularity. And each time it returned, it was more virulent. This was the case, for instance, during the economic recession experienced by eastern Europe in the last quarter of the nineteenth century. Under the influence of Darwinism, anti-Judaism was transformed into anti-Semitism, a pseudoscientific theory of irreversible Jewish racial inequality in addition to cultural and moral inferiority.

Zionism was born in response to these two very different challenges. The first phenomenon inspired what was known as "spiritual" Zionism.[9] Spiritual Zionism was the belief that Jews form a distinct religious and cultural identity informed by the "prophetic imperative," the responsibility to work toward human equality and social justice throughout the world. The second phenomenon, by contrast, inspired political Zionism, according to which Jews would forever be outcasts in non-Jewish society and as such would be prevented from accomplishing the prophetic imperative. Religious duty therefore required the establishment of a national state in which Jews would be free to live truly Jewish lives. Both spiritual and political Zionism looked to Palestine. The former saw it as a cultural center that could revive the spirit of

Judaism throughout the world, and the latter saw it as the locus of the state their faith demanded they establish.

The acknowledged "father of Zionism," Theodor Herzl (d. 1904), was himself a pragmatist. He considered Zionism a political movement pure and simple, necessitated by anti-Semitism. He believed Jews had to establish their own state. Palestine was not a very good place for it, he thought. Argentina was his first choice, with its vast natural resources and relatively low population. But he knew that only Palestine had the kind of popular appeal he would need to accomplish his goals. He also knew the plan could only be successful with the support of the European powers. When World War I broke out, eastern European Jews were so bitter toward Russia that they were reluctant to work with the Allies. Zionist leadership in London, however, persisted in Herzl's efforts to obtain the Great Powers' support for their plan. At first the British rejected the Zionist plan as totally unworkable. This view was shared by the Anglo-Jewish Association as well as the Board of Deputies of British Jews. Both groups believed political Zionism would cause even more problems for world Jewry, laying Jews open to criticism for having taken land that rightfully belonged to others and making any Jews who chose not to go to Palestine foreigners wherever they decided to settle.[10]

However, British Prime Minister David Lloyd George was more concerned with protecting the British Empire's southern flank than with the logic of Zionism. He saw only the strategic value of what he thought would be a grateful and compliant population protecting the Suez Canal and the route to India. He wanted to keep out the French and apparently assumed the Arabs would be too independent to accept British rule. He therefore put Mark Sykes to work again, this time to assure Zionist compliance with British aspirations. It was when Sykes got the Zionists to declare they would officially oppose the internationalization of Palestine and support a British protectorate that the Balfour Declaration was issued. Obviously, the Zionists did not know about the Sykes-Picot Agreement, and the French were not consulted about the Balfour Declaration.

Again Shariff Hussein found out about British counter-pledges despite attempts to keep the information out of Syria. And again he sought clarification from the British. He was assured that the Balfour Declaration implied no threat, either to the civil and religious rights of the indigenous Palestinian population or to its political and economic freedom. It was only a humanitarian move to rescue suffering Jews, Britain told him. Again trusting his allies, the shariff responded that so long as it meant no compromise of Arab sovereignty, the Jews would be welcomed. He then published an article reminding all Arabs of their duty of hospitality and the Muslims in particular that Jews were their brothers in religion, respected and protected throughout Islamic history.[11]

More European Assurances

Concern over the wisdom of the shariff's judgment was growing among Arab nationalists, however. In the spring of 1918 a group of nationalists anonymously requested that the Arab Bureau in Cairo clarify the British government's plans for the future of Syria, including Palestine and Iraq. That summer the Foreign Office responded with the so-called Declaration to the Seven. Britain promised that it would recognize the "complete and sovereign independence of the Arabs" in the Arabian peninsula; that it would see to the establishment of a government "based upon the principle of the consent of the governed" in Iraq and Palestine; and that it would continue to work for the "freedom and independence" of those Arab territories still under Turkish rule (at that time, most of Syria and Iraqi Mosul).[12]

The Europeans went even further in their promises to satisfy Arab concerns. In November 1918 they published the Anglo-French Declaration in every Arab newspaper, posted it on bulletin boards where there were no newspapers, and hired agents to read it aloud to illiterate communities. The purpose of the declaration was to assure the nationalists that the French and British were working together for exactly the same goals the Arabs had in mind. "The goal envisaged by France and Great Britain is . . . the complete and final liberation of the peoples who have for so long been oppressed by the Turks, and the setting up of national governments and administrations that shall derive their authority from the free exercise of the initiative and choice of the indigenous populations."[13]

Despite the Arabs' continued misgivings regarding European intentions, the Balfour Declaration itself, therefore, was not considered a major problem. The Arabs' major concern was their future independence. At the time of the declaration, roughly eight percent of the population was Jewish. Some had lived in the region for centuries (the "oriental" Jews, or Sephardim), and some had recently immigrated to escape suffering in Europe (the "Western" or Ashkenazi Jews). Although the latter population was growing, the Arabs certainly did not foresee the massive influx European fascism would foster. Nor did they envision the loss of Palestine through the creation of a Zionist state in their midst. This happened, not so much because of the Balfour Declaration, but because of the crippling effects of the Sykes-Picot Agreement, which made the Arabs incapable of dealing effectively with Zionist nationalist aspirations. For despite all assurances, as soon as the war was over the

Europeans abandoned their pledges and went right back to their imperialist claims as presented in the Sykes-Picot Agreement, pursuing their plan to separate the Arabs into competing regional or sectarian factions—the Balkanization of the Middle East, as it is often called.

"The Counterfeit Peace"

In the disposition of Arab land devised by the Allies following the end of World War I (January 1919), only the Arabian peninsula escaped European control. The Hijaz was considered an independent Arab state with Shariff Hussein as king, although southern Arabia remained under the control of the Idrisis and Imam Yahya, central Arabia remained under Sa'udi control, and the region northward from Sa'udi territory to Iraq was still controlled by the Rashidis. Iraq, on the other hand, including oil-rich Mosul, which Lloyd George had wrested from French control, was placed under direct British administration. Syria was divided into three territories. Palestine, which Britain also had to finagle from French claims (the Russians having dropped out of the race following the Bolshevik Revolution) was placed under British control, Lebanon was granted to France, and interior Syria (from Aqaba to Aleppo) was Arab. Faisal, who had been sent to London by his father to oversee the settlements, naturally protested immediately. Britain assured him that these measures were only temporary and that in the final peace conference the consent of the indigenous population would be the determining factor. Meanwhile, Lawrence—no longer "of Arabia"—was back in London working with Zionist leader Chaim Weizmann to convince Faisal that Britain would make good on the McMahon pledges as soon as it had secured a safe refuge for Jews in Palestine.

Under no circumstances could Faisal consent to the dismemberment of Syria. As representative of the Arab people he had neither the inclination nor the authority to do so. But he did believe strongly in the duty to offer hospitality to the suffering Jews. He had met with Weizmann in Aqaba the previous year, and Weizmann had assured him the Zionists had no intention of setting up a government that would prejudice Arab rights. In fact, Weizmann had emphasized the advantages of welcoming the Zionists: As Europeans, the Zionists would bring modern technology and learning and would therefore aid in developing the region. Faisal had no reason to doubt Weizmann's sincerity. He signed an agreement with Weizmann to promote Arab cooperation with the Zionists and, at the same time, guarantee Arab sovereignty. Dated January 4, 1919, the Faisal-Weizmann Agreement pledged mutual cooperation and goodwill in Palestine; promised Arab help in encouraging immigration of Jews into Palestine; provided that the rights of Arab inhabitants would be protected and that "no religious test shall ever be required for the exercise of civil or political rights"; and left the matter of determining boundaries between Arab and Zionist areas until after the impending peace conference, naming Britain as arbiter in case of dispute. Faisal then added a proviso stating that the agreement was valid only provided the Arabs obtained their independence as demanded in his memorandum dated January 4, 1919.

With that Faisal submitted his official statement of Arab demands to the Paris Peace Conference. Speaking for "the Arabic-speaking peoples of Asia, from the line Alexandretta-Diarbekr southward to the Indian Ocean," he demanded independence and sovereignty guaranteed by the League of Nations. Establishment and adjustment of boundaries between existing states and the creation of any new states "are matters of arrangement among us, after the wishes of their respective inhabitants have been ascertained." He concluded with a plea to the honor and decency of the Western powers: "I base my request on the principles enunciated by President Wilson [i.e., the principle of self-determination] and am confident that the Powers will attach more importance to the bodies and souls of the Arabic-speaking peoples than to their own material interests."[14]

The Will of the Population

Despite the anxieties caused by the Allies' duplicitous agreements, the Arabs' confidence that they had finally won their independence continued. The formerly secret nationalist societies began to surface as political parties. The Syrian section of Jam'iyyat al-'Arabiyyat al-Fatat became the Hizb al-Istiqlal al-'Arabi, the Arab Independence Party, and began to prepare for a constitutional government. With the support of Faisal they held elections throughout Syria—including French-occupied Lebanon and British-occupied Palestine—and thus established the General Syrian Congress in Damascus in the summer of 1919. The congress consisted of eighty-five delegates and included Jews, Christians, and Muslims. Although France prevented sixteen designated representatives from attending the opening session, the congress passed a set of resolutions that can fairly be described as the "will of the indigenous populace," in British terminology, which was supposed to guide Syria's ultimate disposition. The set of ten resolutions demanded the unity, independence, and sovereignty of all of Syria as well as Iraq. The government of Syria was to be a constitutional monarchy with Faisal as king. The resolutions rejected both French and Zionist claims to any portion of Syria, although the measures guaranteed that "our Jewish fellow-citizens shall continue to enjoy the rights and to bear the responsibilities which are ours in common."[15] Later, at the urging of U.S. President Woodrow Wilson, another survey was made of Syrian popular will, known as the King-Crane Commission, which confirmed the sentiments expressed by the General Syrian Congress.[16] Nevertheless, in total disregard of the King-Crane report, as well as of the resolutions of the General Syrian Congress and the persistent protests of Faisal, France and Britain continued haggling over who would get what in Syria. Even as French and British occupation began, the General Syrian Congress met and proclaimed Syria a unified and independent constitutional monarchy with Faisal at its head. France and Britain publicly announced that they considered the congress and its resolutions invalid. And when the Allies finally met at San Remo, the mandates envisioned in the Sykes-Picot Agreement were institutionalized, modified only for the subsequent French and British trade-offs and the Balfour Declaration. Thus, Lebanon and Syria were given to France, Iraq and Palestine were given to Britain, and Palestine was established as a national home for world Jewry under British mandate.

Tentative Formation of Arab States

Thus began the next phase of the Arabs' fight for independence. There were attacks on French garrisons in Lebanon, which France used as an excuse to expand military occupation. As French troops advanced on Damascus, riots broke out in the city. Faisal's attempts to maintain order resulted in the deaths of his own citizens. That combined with the anger and resentment over Europe's betrayal of Arab trust had a cumulative effect, the burden of which was borne by the Hashemites (the shariff's family). When France occupied the capital, Faisal was forced to leave. The guerrilla attacks increased and spread throughout Syria and Iraq, where Britain continued its administrative control without significant Arab participation. Attempts to suppress nationalist activities resulted in general rebellion throughout Mesopotamia, with casualties on both sides numbering in the thousands.

Britain eventually decided it had to grant some form of administrative control to the Iraqis and formed the Council of State, with Iraqi ministers advised by British officers. When Winston Churchill was appointed secretary of state for the colonies, advised by Lawrence, he decided to go even further. In the spring of 1921 arrangements were made to return Iraq to Arab government and compensate Faisal for his ouster from Damascus by making him constitutional monarch in Iraq. His brother 'Abdullah was to be king in the region of Syria east of the Jordan River, which France had not occupied and had agreed to include in the British mandate. That area was known as Transjordan and is now called Jordan. 'Abdullah agreed to the plan as the first step in returning all of Syria to Arab rule. Churchill had already refused 'Abdullah's request to reunite the Palestinian and Transjordanian portions of Syria and join Transjordan to Iraq. But promising to work with France to restore Syrian unity and independence, Churchill convinced 'Abdullah to accept sovereignty in Transjordan.

Thus, having installed Shariff Hussein's sons Faisal and 'Abdullah as monarchs in states designated sovereign and soon-to-be independent, and with the shariff himself as king of the Hijaz, Britain assumed it had fulfilled its pledges to the Arabs. The Arabs, of course—their land divided and under various degrees of European control—believed just the opposite. The arbitrariness of the boundaries and the lack of Arab input into their own administration would form the backdrop of the problems that continue to plague the Arab world. But, again, the first to bear the brunt of British and French duplicity was the shariff, who had trusted them in the first place. His domain in the Hijaz was strictly limited and was subject to border disputes with the Sa'udi domain in the Nejd and with the southern regions of the Idrisi Muhammad and Imam Yahya. In the early days of the disputes, Britain supported the shariff against the incursions of the militarily superior Sa'udis. But when Ibn Sa'ud annexed the Rashidi territory up to the Iraqi border in 1921, the Sa'udis became undeniably dominant in the peninsula. The British turned against Hussein when he refused to recognize the British mandate in Palestine based on the Balfour Declaration. Though he continued to support limited Jewish colonization on humanitarian grounds, he insisted that Britain include safeguards of the political and economic rights of the native Palestinians. His final downfall came when his supporters declared him caliph in 1924, upon Turkey's abolition of that institution. His detractors, who claimed he had failed both the Arabs and Islam by leading them into the Anglo-Arab partnership, took their opportunity. The Sa'udis marched into the Hijaz. The shariff abdicated in favor of his son 'Ali and went into exile in Cyprus. 'Ali eventually surrendered and took refuge in Baghdad. Ibn Sa'ud consolidated his regime, establishing its borders in the northwest with the French mandate authority, in the northeast with the British mandate authority, and in the south with the 'Asir and Yemen. Britain formally recognized Ibn Sa'ud as king of the Hijaz and of Nejd and its Dependencies in 1927. And Ibn Sa'ud, vindicated in his anti-Westernism, set out to establish an Islamic regime on the grounds laid by none other than Ibn Taymiyya in the fourteenth century.

Faisal was proclaimed king of Iraq in 1921 over the dissent of his detractors and set about the enormous task of coordinating Iraq's disparate social, religious, and ethnic groups into a single administrative unit. The boundaries devised for Iraq by Europe included Sunni Muslims, Shi'i Muslims, a significant urban Jewish population, at least six Christian minorities, non-Arab Sunni Muslim Kurds, non-Arab Nestorian Christian Assyrians, and fiercely independent Shi'i tribal confederations. Faisal was successful in establishing at least a rudimentary parliamentary system and in gaining Iraq's admission to the League of Nations by the time of his death in 1933. However, the nationalist aspirations of the Kurds, the Assyrians, and some Shi'is continued and, in fact, have yet to be addressed by the Iraqi government.

Syria's problems were even worse. Instead of the British tactic of grouping strange bedfellows (as in Iraq and Palestine), France continued with her policy of dividing groups that naturally belonged together. To safeguard its carefully nurtured base of influence among the Maronite Christians, France kept the Lebanon separate from predominantly Muslim interior Syria. This was the policy that had already been imposed on the area following the disturbances in 1860. Its effect was not only the division of Syria into competitive parts on the basis of religion, each of whose autocratic leaders had good reason to try to maintain the status quo, but also the separation of Damascus and Beirut, the two centers of Syrian nationalism. Unable to work in concert toward transcending religious differences for the sake of national unity, Syrian nationalist strength, it was hoped, would dissipate. But France went even further. Lebanon was enlarged in 1920 to incorporate territories adjacent to the traditional Lebanon (the region around Mount Lebanon), including the key port cities of Tripoli, Beirut, Sidon, and Tyre as well as the fertile Beqaa Valley. However, many of these regions were largely Muslim and were oriented toward Damascus (rather than Beirut), thus diminishing the credibility of the Maronites' leadership claims and increasing central Syria's resentment. France then further subdivided Syria, creating four separate administrative districts: the Druze region along the Syrian-Transjordanian border; Alexandretta, which was actually Turkish; Latakia, which included the northern coastal region occupied by yet another Muslim minority sect, the Alawis; and the rest of Syria, with its capital, Damascus. With that, Syria was hopelessly divided along sectarian lines. To top it all off, a new currency was introduced based on the French franc, and French language and culture were promoted in the schools—at the expense of Arabic.

Meanwhile, conditions in Palestine were steadily worsening. By 1922 the Jewish population had risen to 11 percent of the total. In May 1925 it was officially estimated at 108,000; by the end of 1935 it was around 300,000. By the end of 1936, Jews made up 28 percent of Palestine's population. The amount of land owned by Jews was 177 square miles in 1914. By 1935 it had risen to some 500 square miles. Most of this land was purchased, with funds supplied from outside Palestine and in the name of the National Fund (*Keren Kayemeth*), as the perpetual and inalienable property of the Jewish people. The Arabs had no such outside funding or sophisticated legal devices. Urban growth was even more dramatic. Tel Aviv was founded in 1909 as a suburb of Jaffa. By 1935 its population exceeded 100,000. It had become a center of industrial development, again made possible by the influx of foreign capital. Throughout this phenomenal growth of Zionist presence in the region, Chaim Weizmann (who had assumed control of the Zionist movement upon Theodor Herzl's death) maintained Herzl's policy of "present[ing] the entire affair in as inoffensive a way as possible."[17] As Arab suspicions grew, still no mention was made of ultimate plans for a sovereign Zionist state in Palestine.

The Zionist leaders also kept their nationalist goals from Britain. They asked only for settlement facilities and open immigration (i.e., the dropping of immigration quotas). They also expressed full support for British mandatory government, to the extent that they opposed the creation of a representative body of government. The Arabs were still in the majority and a representative assembly would not have been in Jewish interest yet. Only British support could sustain the extent of immigration required to establish population sufficient to uphold statehood demands.

The Arabs were therefore feeling increasingly threatened. By the time of the mandates it was quite clear that they had been deliberately misled and sorely ill-advised. Instead of the great united and independent Arab state that had been promised, Arab territory had been divided into protectorates controlled by European powers, in which even Arabs' right to determine their own affairs was severely restricted. And a significant portion of Arab (now a designation referring to those who had followed Shariff Hussein's leadership, i.e., including Syrians and Iraqis) territory had been given away to foreign immigrants, whose rights were being put ahead of Arab rights. At the same time, Arabs were losing faith in their leaders, who, having accepted nominal positions of kingship (a notion foreign to Islamic tradition) seemed to be acquiescing to the status quo. Thus Arab frustration grew and erupted in major uprisings against the Zionists in 1929, 1936, and 1939.

Egyptian Developments

Egypt, of course, was already under British occupation when World War I began. Egyptian nationalist leaders continued their efforts, despite the interruptions caused by the war. The leadership of Lutfi al-Sayyid's People's Party had been assumed by Sa'd Zaghlul. As noted in Chapter

Four, Zaghlul combined traditional Islamic education with modern education. In his early years Zaghlul had been imprisoned by the British for suspected nationalist activities. But later on, again in the path of earlier leaders, he worked with the colonial establishment to modernize Egyptian institutions.[18]

Egypt was far better off than Syria and Iraq under occupation. Egyptians were able to participate in the government—Zaghlul became a judge and, later, minister of education. What was more, the boundaries of Egypt were not an issue for arbitrary decisions.[19] Since the time of Muhammad 'Ali, and especially with the British occupation, Egypt had been recognized as an autonomous—if not totally independent—entity. Her independence was, of course, the overall goal for which nationalists worked, but despite continued British presence, nationalists tended to work toward strengthening Egypt internally so that occupation would no longer be possible.

Zaghlul had originally thought the partnership with Britain would be an effective means of limiting the Ottoman governor's power. In 1913 he even ran for a position in the legislative assembly Britain established. He was elected and held the position throughout the war. Once the Ottomans had been defeated, Zaghlul proceeded to use his position to work against British occupation. He and other nationalists formed a delegation (in Arabic, *wafd*) to demand independence at the Paris Conference. When Britain refused to allow the delegation to attend the Paris Conference, riots broke out around the country and Britain was forced to acquiesce. At first the British offered a constitutional monarchy that was nominally independent but was really linked with Britain, because they wanted to maintain troops in Egypt. Zaghlul's delegation refused. Britain responded by arresting and deporting Zaghlul. In 1922 Britain officially declared Egypt independent, although it claimed the right to control certain aspects of Egypt's affairs, such as defense, communications, foreign policy, and the Suez Canal. The British chose Fu'ad, a descendant of Muhammad 'Ali, to be king and drew up a constitution for him.

The following year, Zaghlul was allowed to return to Egypt. It was then that he set to work on the vestiges of British control over Egypt. He and his supporters formed a political party, the Wafd, and swept the early postwar elections.[20] Zaghlul, as prime minister, pushed Britain for complete independence. Tensions mounted as Britain stalled. Eventually the British commander of the Egyptian army was assassinated, and Zaghlul resigned in the controversy.

Throughout his career, Zaghlul's goal was limiting autocratic government, whether Turkish, British, or native Egyptian. Democracy was naturally chosen as the antidote to autocracy, and, for Zaghlul, this led to an emphasis on individual freedom. Zaghlul worked diligently to reform Islamic institutions accordingly. Justice, he said, "should be decided in the light of *maslaha,* public interest, and public interest should be defined in terms of the sum of private interests."²¹ As minister of justice under British occupation, he established a special school to train Islamic judges in modern jurisprudence, based on the principle that the government should serve "social and individual welfare." Instead of fearing the government as a bird fears a hunter, Zaghlul said, the people should be able to look with trust to the government as equal members of the nation.²² His democracy, again quite naturally, led him to champion the rights of religious minorities, particularly the Copts. The Wafd, following the lead of Qasim Amin, even included women among the equal citizens of the nation. (Considering the fact that women were still not allowed to vote in the United States, this was indeed a progressive view.)

Another approach was that taken by 'Ali 'Abd al-Raziq (d. 1966). A religious leader with a contemporary European education as well (he studied at al-Azhar and Oxford University), 'Abd al-Raziq concentrated on the need for developing a coherent political theory in Islam. In 1925 he published a book, *Al-Islam wa Usul al-Hukm* (*Islam and the Foundations of Government*), in which he claimed that Islam had *never* developed a political theory. In 1924 the new Turkish National Assembly had abolished the caliphate, and 'Abd al-Raziq thought the time was right to develop a political theory. Al-Azhar held a conference in 1926 about the caliphate, which essentially confirmed the findings of the Turkish National Assembly, although in an indirect way. These religious scholars could hardly deny the legitimacy of the institutions that had produced them. Rather than delegitimize the caliphate, which might have led to questions about other Islamic institutions, they simply declared that the caliphate was a legitimate and necessary institution, but that it could only exist under the proper circumstances. Its future, they hoped, would be brighter, but for the time being nothing could be done about it. 'Abd al-Raziq disagreed. He questioned the very legitimacy of the caliphate. He said the Qur'an and Sunna require obedience to those in authority but do not even mention the institution of the caliphate. Instead, he said, the legitimacy of the caliphate had really always been based on force. No one had ever truly been allowed to question it and, as a result, there was no legitimate consensus of Islamic scholars about it. In fact, he said, the lack of freedom to discuss the caliphal institution was the reason there was no developed political theory in Islam.²³

Just as Ibn Taymiyya had said, some form of political order was necessary, but Islam does not specify what kind. And just as Ibn

Taymiyya had been censured, 'Ali 'Abd al-Raziq was condemned by his colleagues at al-Azhar and fired. They interpreted his analyses as denials of the virility of Islam. In making Islamic unity spiritual, they believed he weakened it. They thought he was trying to make Islam like Christianity—a step short of the kind of order the Prophet was sent to create, the kind of political reality required to implement God's call for the equality of all people on earth. Nevertheless, 'Abd al-Raziq's calls for representative, democratic government continued to ring throughout Egypt. 'Abd al-Raziq's critics, even while upholding the validity of "the caliph and universal imam," spoke of his authority as vested in "a democratic, free, consultative government," thereby logically limiting that authority.[24]

'Abd al-Raziq's chief critic was Muhammad Rashid Rida (d. 1935), an expatriate Syrian from Tripoli trained in Qur'anic school and the National Islamic School. He had come to Cairo to study with 'Abduh and remained there, styling himself as 'Abduh's spiritual heir. Utterly devoted to Islam as the basis of political life, he was horrified by 'Abd al-Raziq's views. He said 'Abd al-Raziq had been influenced by the enemies of Islam, who were trying to fragment the Muslim world and make it "prey to the wild beasts of imperialism." Rashid Rida asserted that there was indeed a truly Islamic political system that was based on the Qur'anic principles of *shura* (consultation) and *bai'a* (popular ratification). And it was crowned by the institution of the caliphate, which must be restored. This would take a while, however. First Muslims had to establish a "caliphate of necessity," which was what he had called the Ottoman caliphate when it still existed. It was a substandard caliphate—not least because the Turkish caliph possessed no skill in Arabic, the minimum prerequisite for a legitimate caliph—but it was sufficient to hold the Muslim world together against external threats. Meanwhile, Muslims must work toward producing candidates for the real caliphate.

Thus, despite the opprobrium heaped upon 'Abd al-Raziq's call for recognition of the necessarily limited nature of modern political states and the incongruity of limited political claims with universal religious claims, even his detractors assimilated his basic principles. Rashid Rida knew very well there could no longer be a single, unified Islamic state. In fact, he had started his career as a Syrian nationalist. Early on he joined with a group of other mainly Syrian Arabs living in Cairo to form the Ottoman Party of Administrative Decentralization (1912). They wanted Arabic to be recognized as an official language in the provinces, worked toward the establishment of Arab provincial governments with wider powers, and envisioned eventual autonomy for Syria on the Egyptian model. The group even organized the 1913 Arab Congress in

Paris to ask European governments for help in achieving their aims. Rashid Rida therefore spoke of cooperation among the political units within the Islamic community, rather than of a single Islamic state. However, he seemed oblivious to the incongruity of basing states' limited political claims on a universal religion. The only kind of solidarity he could imagine was religious. He claimed that national solidarity based on anything other than religion would be a regression to pre-Islamic days, the days of *jahiliyya,* or "ignorance." National solidarity was necessary, but the basis of Arab solidarity was Islam. That, in fact, required that Arabic be revived, for the only language of Islam is Arabic. And, even more important, it also required that the caliphate be revived and that the caliph be an Arab.[25]

What we see in a figure such as Rashid Rida is the kind of living anachronism characteristic of any revolutionary movement. Like the pre–Thirty Years' War Europeans who had continued to press their convictions on others while demanding the right to formulate their own ideas in freedom, he had not yet grasped the essential elements of the very forces that drove him. Despite his position and erudition, his assertions reflected no intellectual understanding of the historical processes in which he was involved. He remained active in Syrian politics; he was made president of the Syrian Congress of 1920, which called for the complete independence of Syria and declared Faisal the Syrian king. He also participated in the delegation of Syrians who went to Geneva in 1921 to call for Syrian unity and independence. His Syrian sympathies remained with him, even in his writings on the caliphate. When he discussed possible candidates for a revived caliphate he immediately ruled out the Hashemites—despite his previous support for them—for they had colluded with the non-Muslim enemies who had so callously betrayed Syria. (In fact, he welcomed the ouster of Shariff Hussein by Ibn Sa'ud, even though he had also criticized the Wahhabis for what he called their innovative practices.)[26] Instead, he said the caliph would have to be some other member of the Prophet's family and then made sure everyone knew he himself happened to belong to that august lineage.[27] But he did not see the incongruity of calls for an independent Syria and a pan-Islamic, nonsecular caliphate. In attempting to reform politically, then, he had actually reverted to the principles of the empire that he hoped to replace.

In a way, Rashid Rida's Islamic-Arab nationalism was more authentic than that of some of his more sophisticated colleagues. Even when he was trying not to be, he was a nationalist. He said there was nothing wrong with Islam; it was just that the non-Arabs—in particular, the Persians (who had influenced the 'Abbasids) and the Turks—had changed it. Even when he was trying to assert the loyalty of Arab subjects to the Turks, he could not disguise his Arab nationalism. Before he decided it would be a good idea to work with Britain against indigenous tyranny in the provinces, he had advocated cooperation with Turks against European encroachments. He said that until the Europeans had come in, it was only a few Christians who had advocated Arab independence, although he himself had been a member of the group of seven Syrians who had petitioned Britain in 1918 regarding the independence of Syria and Iraq after the war.[28] Islamic solidarity had replaced Arab solidarity, he said; the Turks were therefore considered brothers. But if there was any problem between Arabs and Turks, it was the Turks' fault, he said. They were the ones who were neglecting the Arabs for their own selfish interests. And in the process, the Turks only stood to lose because, after all, the Arabs were more intelligent, they had more potential military strength, and their language was the language of the official religion. After the war and the defeat of the Ottomans, Rashid Rida's hostility was turned toward the Europeans. He praised the Bolshevik Revolution and expressed solidarity with its motives. Muslims too were an oppressed proletariat, he said, oppressed by European capitalism. Socialism, because it aims at the liberation of the oppressed, encompasses Islamic ideals and therefore must be supported.[29] And in this last about-face, the unpredictable Rashid Rida inadvertently predicted the direction interwar politics would take in the Arab world.

CHAPTER SIX

The Legacy of
Interwar Political
Developments

*f*irst, from its infamy [Western-style liberalism] was
challenged by another doctrine (socialism) which
had more vitality. . . . A main reason for the weakness
of [our] nationalist call at its initiation was its primary concern
with the achievement of independence and unity without a reform
program aimed at unlocking the internal shackles, combating
social and economic tyranny, and working to give all citizens
equal opportunitites. This factor worked to the advantage of
socialist thought.

—Constantine Zurayq[1]

Following the betrayal of Arab aspirations for independence, there was,
quite naturally, a reaction against the European nations responsible for
it. But turning against Europe at that time did not mean turning against
Europeans or rejecting Western political forms as foreign to Islam, as
Islamic anti-Westernism has now come to mean. Instead, the most
visible reaction was a rejection of that aspect of European culture that
many Europeans themselves criticized as the root cause of imperialist
oppression: capitalism. This was closely related to a rejection of the
leaders who had led the Arabs into the disastrous alliance with the
Europeans. The early leaders had been drawn mainly from traditional
elites, both urban and rural tribal. It was they who had negotiated
with the Europeans, they who had led the Arab Revolt, and they who

were placed in nominal positions of national leadership by European mandate.

Two factors led to the demise of the traditional Arab elites' reputation during the period between the world wars. First, European tutelage, despite promises of autonomy or independence, dragged on. Even in the areas that achieved official independence—Iraq, Egypt, and Jordan, for instance—Britain maintained control over significant issues, such as military and foreign policy. In Syria and Lebanon, France held on to direct control until Nazi occupation forced its retreat. In none of these areas were large-scale reforms undertaken. Communications were improved, and Western education retained its pride of place, but the kind of development that would lead to economic self-sufficiency in an industrialized world, let alone to competitiveness in the international market—the kind of development that would allow real independence— clearly would not have been in the interests of the occupying powers. Instead, the Western presence tended to strengthen most the positions of the traditional elites who accommodated it. These traditional elites therefore had to share the resentment engendered by their European patrons.

Second, the situation in Palestine continued to deteriorate. As per-secuted European Jews streamed into Palestine in unprecedented num-bers, clashes with indigenous inhabitants became more frequent. Vio-lence spawned violence, and terrorist organizations formed on both sides. Zionist terrorist organizations had originally formed with the idea of establishing a Jewish state militarily, rather than through political means as Chaim Weizmann (Theodor Herzl's successor as leader of the Zionist movement) advocated. Vladimir Jabotinsky's Revisionist Party, founded in the early 1930s, demanded the open declaration of a Jewish state on both sides of the Jordan River as soon as possible and threatened to declare war against anyone who opposed establishing such a Jewish state. But Weizmann's policy remained dominant until 1939. It was then that Britain issued its infamous White Paper (May 19, 1939) proposing an independent Palestinian state in which Jews would constitute no more than one-third of the population. With that in mind the mandate government in Palestine established Jewish immigration quotas and limitations on the sale of land to Jews. However, by that time the massacre of Jews in Europe had made the immigration quotas intolerable, and the Revisionists' program finally achieved popular appeal. Although the terrorists were by far the minority of Zionists, their attacks finally convinced the British to withdraw from Palestine (1948). This left the Zionists face to face with the native Palestinians, against whom Zionist attacks were next turned with the overall goal of driving the Palestinians off their land. As is well known, Zionist policy against the native

Palestinians—a combination of expropriation of land, discriminatory economic policies, intimidation, and terrorism—was largely effective. By 1947 the immigrant population roughly equalled that of the natives. In 1948 the Zionists declared themselves a state. By 1949, native Palestinians were a minority in Israel, while some 750,000 to 800,000 were living as refugees in neighboring lands.[2]

Coming on the heels of the Arab humiliation by Europe in World War I and in the context of continued European occupation of Arab lands, the problem of Palestine came to represent the ultimate failure of Arab leadership. Traditional leaders were variously criticized as incompetent, self-seeking, or impotent. They were condemned for accepting the status quo—the division of the Arab world into arbitrarily drawn states.

Among the reasons elucidated for the failure of the Arab leaders was their lack of proper organization. They had failed to nurture popular participation in politics. Relying on traditional forms—consultations among tribal leaders and conferences among Muslim elites—even their beloved rhetoric and mighty pronouncements were powerless in the face of modern political realities. Fresh, sophisticated leadership was needed, and that had to come from the newly awakened populace. Thus populism and the call for new leadership joined anticapitalism as the theme of interwar Arab politics. Only the goal of Arab unity remained to mark continuity with the old generation.

Indeed, the call for new leadership was predicated on the call for Arab unity. "Pan-Arab nationalism," as it is often called, became all the more cherished for its elusiveness. It became the gauge by which Arab leadership was judged. Naturally, therefore, contenders for the new leadership would rely on its heady appeal. Yet, paradoxically, in the very process of changing the Arab guard the traditional distinctions among the Arab regions and even among the newly created states became entrenched realities. Arabia, the least developed and politically mature of Arab lands, had achieved independence far in advance of its more sophisticated neighbors. Iraq and Egypt, both under British domination, were granted greater degrees of independence earlier and with much less trouble than Syria. This in itself intensified the traditional distinctions among those areas. But French and British control in Syria created further political distinctions where none had existed before. Modern Lebanon, Syria, Transjordan, and Palestine had comprised geographic Syria from time immemorial; now Lebanon and Palestine were separated along religious and sectarian lines, and Transjordan was isolated under British tutelage, while interior Syria remained under French control. The new leadership would thus hold out the reunification of Arabs in some nebulous form as an overall goal. But it was a goal born in contradiction. For Arab unity in this fragmented postwar context could only be achieved once each "counterfeit" state attained its independence. And that could only be done by developing the social and economic bases of the particulate states, a process that inevitably created vested interests in the survival of the newly developed entities.

Traditional Calls for Arab Unity

The traditional leaders of the interwar period made attempts at Arab unity. The Syrian Congress of 1920 called for the reunification of Syria as a first step in the reunion of Syria, Iraq, and the peninsula. Rashid Rida's biographer reports that Rashid Rida was involved in secret negotiations with France in the early 1930s to try to unite Syria and Iraq under King Faisal.[3] As soon as Iraq became independent it signed the Treaty of Arab Brotherhood with Saudi Arabia (1936), on the basis of shared Islam and other national links. The ambitious Arab Muslim Inter-Parliamentary Conference held in Cairo in 1938 spoke of Arab unity and the threat of Zionism. Faisal's trusted aid Nuri al-Sa'id came up with a plan for reuniting Syria, Lebanon (with a special place for the Maronites), Transjordan, and Palestine (with a special place for the Jews). Then all the Arab states could join an Arab league.[4]

Perhaps the best known of the advocates of Arab unity working within the traditional elite structure was Sati' al-Husri (d. 1968). Al-Husri's family was among the religious elite of Aleppo, although he grew up in Istanbul, was given a modern Turkish education, and became involved in the Ottoman establishment.[5] It was only after the collapse of the Ottomans that al-Husri became a dedicated pan-Arabist. He attached himself to Amir (an Arabic honorific term for leader) Faisal's entourage, holding key positions first in his Syrian government and then in Faisal's Iraqi regime. In al-Husri's view, it really was not terribly important what administration one worked for in the fragmented Arab world, because all Arabs formed one nation. He had observed that in European states the bases of nationalism were language and shared history. Therefore, he figured, because all Arabs share the same language and history they must be a single nation. Astutely recognizing that universal religions cannot be the basis of nationalism, which is by definition limited, al-Husri said all religious groups in the region— Muslim, Christian, and Jewish—sharing a language and history are Arab. For that reason al-Husri was a major proponent of including Egypt among Arabs—at the time a novel idea. And he worked tirelessly to convince the various regimes of his views. He argued against Lutfi al-Sayyid's Egyptian nationalism, for instance, hoping to persuade Egypt to institutionalize his own theories.

Ironically, al-Husri was more successful convincing Egyptians they were Arabs—as Nasser and Sadat would demonstrate—than he was at realizing nationalist goals for his own regime in Iraq. The Iraqi regime was interrupted by a coup in 1941.[6] It was led by Rashid 'Ali al-Gailani, who shared al-Husri's goal of Arab unity and sought help from the German and Italian fascist regimes to achieve it, since they were the enemies of the occupying British and French. The success of the coup was short-lived; after one month the British helped reinstate the Hashemite regent 'Abd al-Ilah (Faisal had died in 1933 and his son was still too young to assume the throne). Al-Husri's role in the coup was unclear but he was nonetheless deported to Syria. He continued to work toward his goals there, in Egypt, and, at the end of his life, again in Iraq. There is no question of the popularity of al-Husri's ideas regarding Arab unity. He is frequently revered as the father of Arab nationalism (meaning pan-Arabism), and he inspired many other popularizers of Arab nationalism. The Iraqi 'Abd al-Rahman al-Bazzaz (d. 1973), for instance, also tried to instill a sense of unity in the Arab world. Unlike al-Husri, he said the basis of Arab unity was essentially Islamic. Nevertheless, he continued, Arab identity existed prior to Islam. Even Islam, he said, was Arabic; it incorporated all the highest ideals of "natural" Arab morality. Therefore, non-Muslim Arabs were just as Arab as anyone else.[7] The real bases of Arab nationalism were language, history, literature, and customs. And of those, al-Bazzaz said, returning to al-Husri's position, language was the most important, for it fostered a sense of communal identity essential to Arab nationalism.

The Syrian Christian Constantine Zurayq also became famous for his essays on what he called Arab nationalism and what would be required to realize it. He said Arabs needed a sense of collective responsibility. It had to be inspired by Islam, since Islam is at the core of the Arab experience. But it was not limited to the Muslims alone. Zurayq believed all religions contain the same core of truth. Their differences are only cultural variations. So it did not make any difference to Arabness whether one was Muslim or Christian or even Jewish.[8] In fact, state institutions had to be kept separate from religious institutions, simply because religion could not limit itself to national concerns, while the state had to.

Such ideas reflected a growing understanding on the part of Arabs of the needs of a new political order and the Arabs' continuing efforts to formulate governments that would coincide with changed or changing socioeconomic reality. As such, these ideas were in keeping with those of the early modernists, who similarly sought ways to transcend the ambiguities of a religiously legitimated government within a given state. Like the early European Protestants, the Arabs recognized the incongruity of legitimating a limited national entity by means of a universal ideology. Unfortunately, however, that was no longer enough. In the transition from Arab provinces/Ottoman subjects to Arab states/European colonial subjects, the nature of the problems had changed. As a result of the European betrayal, the budding Egyptian and Syrian nationalism of al-Tahtawi and al-Bustani became submerged in pan-Arab nationalism. Egyptian and Syrian nationalism had been a reflection of political-economic reality: the emergence of geopolitically limited states from a crumbling empire. By contrast, pan-Arab nationalism was a reflection of neither social, economic, nor political developments, but an attempt to create them. It was really no more than a recognition that some new source of strength had to be found to resist continued imperialism.

Pan-Arab nationalism was not a pragmatic movement. It was utterly idealist. Its advocates believed their cherished Arab nationalism was a feeling that could be induced or willed. They frequently condemned Arabs' lack of commitment to Arab unity and spoke repeatedly of the need to foster that unity. Yet, in the very states used as models for nationalism, whether British or French or German, nationalism was not based *primarily* on such cultural ties as shared language. As described in Chapter One, the phenomenon called nationalism appeared in Europe only as regional economies had developed sufficiently—on new mercantile and then industrial bases—to make the old feudal, transnational, tributory political-economic system obsolete. Language became the identifying feature of units that shared politico-economic interests. Loyalty was not given to the group simply because they shared a language or even a historic heritage. (After all, virtually all of Europe had been under Holy Roman imperial sovereignty; surely that was a shared heritage.) The kind of "national" loyalty sought by these pan-Arab nationalists was something that had to develop on its own within a group with common interests. It would evolve only within units in which people felt they had a stake. And the stake most basic to any human being is the ability to make a decent living in relative peace and privacy. The cohesiveness of the Arab world therefore could not just be summoned up on command, particularly in this postwar context.

If the Arabs had indeed been granted their independence—if Europe had not betrayed their trust by imposing the mandate system—it is perfectly reasonable to assume Egyptian and Syrian nationalism would have continued to develop in accord with their respective economic and political systems; Arabia probably would have maintained its anomalous position within the Arab world.[9] But whatever the reality may have been under other circumstances, the outcome of World War I changed it. The new reality, however ill-conceived, was individual states under various degrees of foreign control. That new reality had to be dealt with before any others could be created. And for that to happen, somehow control of the political apparatus of each entity had to be seized. That is why pan-Arab nationalism as envisioned by the likes of Sati' al-Husri was a failure. It was an anachronism in the making. Even as it articulated romantic notions of pan-Arab unity, however "objective" the reality of shared language may be, the ideal was becoming outmoded by political-economic reality. The pan-Arabists were working within the old elite structure and failed to take control of the actual administrative mechanisms that could make their goals a reality.

Those who rejected the failed elitist structure, on the other hand, gradually did organize sufficiently to implement their aims on a state-by-state basis. And in doing so, although they continued to base their appeal on the ideology of Arab unity, they in fact entrenched the divisions among Arab states.

The Socialist Reaction

The new leadership—nontraditional, populist in appeal, and pragmatic—was to emerge chiefly through political parties. There had been early attempts at popular political organization through parties, such as the Ottoman Party of Administrative Decentralization. The next generation of political parties, those active after Turkey was no longer a threat, was concerned mainly with Arab independence. The Wafd, for instance, and the Liberal Constitutional Party had worked for autonomy within the Ottoman domain and then concentrated on independence from European colonial powers. Their strategy was to work with the occupiers, building up sufficient infrastructure to convince the Europeans Egypt could handle independence. Similarly, the National Bloc in Syria worked with France for independence. But none of these parties had a particularly profound effect on Arab sociopolitical organization. They were still dominated by the traditional elites whose power bases were in the semi-feudal, land-based economy, the capitalist economic system of the Europeans. The opposition, therefore, naturally gravitated toward an alternate system, socialism.

Yet it was not only the economic aspect of socialist thought that appealed to the new Arab leaders, nor did this economic approach appear particularly revolutionary. Socialism itself was relatively familiar in the Arab world, having been first introduced on the popular level by Shibli Shumayyil (d. 1917). Shumayyil believed above all that state control had to be limited. He proposed the formation of a party to establish the duties and limitations of state control. The state should only be allowed to interfere in society to prohibit oppression of one group by another and to facilitate individual development. Thus, its responsibilities include providing work for the unemployed, ensuring fair wages, preventing monopolization of public resources, and disbanding institutions that emphasize discord among social groups and replacing them with enlightened ones based on modern science and human equality.[10] This was what he called socialism.

Shumayyil was a member of the older generation; he had worked within the Ottoman Party of Administrative Decentralization. By the time of al-Bazzaz, anticapitalism had become an accepted component of pan-Arabist thought. As he described it, the Arab people wanted "a happy medium between the absolute individualism that gave rise to capitalism and Marxist-inspired communism."[11] Similarly, Shakib Arslan (d. 1946) articulated the "great socialist principles" incorporated into the Shari'a and therefore far superior to European socialism.[12] Yet these were not economic programs. They were explications of ideals, part of the more general ideals of social justice and solidarity.

It was not until the 1940s that socialist parties as such were formed in the Arab world. By that time socialism had come to be seen as a necessary element in Arab development. For one thing, it could provide a rationale for the seizure of the state machinery in order to oust imperialists and their clients.[13] More importantly, by the 1940s the need for economic change as an essential step toward Arab independence had been recognized. The economies were underdeveloped, having been under semi-feudal and semicolonial control for centuries. As described in Chapter Three, the capitulations had granted Christians, both European and indigenous, special privileges in Syria and Egypt. Naturally, they took advantage of the situation, exploiting the trade opportunities in each region. Among the effects of this policy was the creation of a new economically elite group, because the Christians were able to outstrip the traditional native elites in economic competition. More significantly, however, it created a situation in which those natives who did enter the economic competition had to do so on terms created by the needs of international trade. Specifically, that meant their wealth was put into those things they could trade on the European market. While some indigenous products (such as Damascus silk) fit into that category, in general it was raw materials that were valuable to the increasingly industrialized Europeans. Therefore, indigenous wealth was invested in land rather than industrial development. This underdevelopment had been exacerbated by famine, warfare, and continued revolution. Reform of the crippled economy was therefore included in the goals of the Arab political parties that formed in the 1940s.

Yet socialist organizations were formed primarily in response to the failure of traditional leadership. This questioning of traditional leadership, and not opposition to capitalism, was the most revolutionary aspect of the new political organization. In the Western models of socialist revolution, traditional leadership was overthrown because of its capitalism. Capitalism was blamed for the exploitation of the working classes by a class of owners. In the Arab case, capitalism would be overthrown because of the failure of traditional leaders—themselves victims of European duplicity. This had two major implications. First, it meant that the strictly economic implications of socialism were never taken very seriously in the region.[14] In Syria and Egypt both, socialism would be used to weaken the traditional semi-feudal elite by breaking up large estates and redistributing the land. But economic reform never came to dominate the politics of the region. The second and more important implication was that the new generation of leaders would inherit an unexamined criterion of success: Arab unity. The net effect of the European betrayal on the Arab populace was rising pan-Arabist sentiment, and the new leadership—despite its apparently progressive revolutionary approach—would have to work within that very idealistic framework. They would be born handicapped by the need to work for the elusive goal of Arab unity. This was indeed the heritage of perhaps the most tenacious party in Arab politics, Hizb al-Ba'th al-'Arabi al-Ishtiraki, the Socialist Arab Ba'th Party.

The Ba'th

The Ba'th Party had its origins among Syrian university students in the early 1940s. From various areas throughout greater Syria (Syria, Lebanon, Jordan, and Palestine), the students had concerns typical of the time—freedom from foreign domination and reunification of Arab society. The first ideologue of the group was Michel Aflaq, who outlined its platform in his bid for the Syrian parliament in 1943. Because he had been greatly influenced by al-Husri, Aflaq's formulation reflected no questioning of the goal of Arab unity, just a more pragmatic approach to politics, starting with Syria. In addition to Arab freedom and unity, it specified an end to factionalism and localism and condemned materialism.[15] By 1947 the appeal of the platform and the leadership of Aflaq had attracted enough educated Syrians to hold a conference. In Damascus that spring, some two hundred delegates devised a party constitution, created an executive committee, designated a leader, and officially announced the birth of the party.

The Ba'th constitution was a significant advance in organizational sophistication over the previous generation of political groupings. It set out a series of thirteen general principles of party organization and thirty-five articles detailing the party's internal policy; foreign policy; and economic, social, and educational policies. It even established specific mechanisms for amendment of the constitution. The Socialist Arab Ba'th Party, says its constitution, is a comprehensive party concerned with overall Arab interests. It condemns colonialism; asserts that sovereignty derives from the people; calls for freedom of speech, assembly, belief, and art; proclaims that Arab women shall enjoy full citizenship rights; and mandates that primary and secondary education be free and compulsory. What is more, the Ba'th Party believes socialism is "the ideal social order through which the Arab people may realize its potentialities and achieve the fullest flowering of its genius"— although the party safeguards the "natural rights" of acquisition of property and inheritance—and stipulates that ownership of means of production shall be by the workers, who shall also share in profits.[16] As well, the constitution guarantees free unions and labor tribunals made up of state representatives, workers, and peasants for the settlement of any disputes.

However, from the very first statement, the constitution tied itself to the goal of Arab unity: "The Arabs are one nation which has a natural right to live in one state and be free in directing its destinies. . . . The Arab homeland is an indivisible political and economic unity." Again, the term *nationalism* means pan-Arabism, i.e., *trans*nationalism. Article Six says the Arab Ba'th Socialist Party is a revolutionary party whose aim is the "resurrection" (in Arabic, *ba'ath*) of Arab nationalism, "to bring together all Arabs in a single Arab state" stretching from Turkey to Iran to Ethiopia and including North Africa. The constitution gives no hint as to how this monumental task is to be accomplished, but goes on to describe the system of government in the proposed state. It will be "a constitutional representative system, and the executive power will be responsible to the legislative power, which will be directly elected by the people" (Article Fourteen). In a note of realism, Article Sixteen admits that "The system of administration in the Arab state will be decentralized." But the Ba'th constitution does not address exactly how the party is going to unite at least a dozen states—under various degrees of foreign occupation, at differing stages of physical and political underdevelopment, and plagued by widespread illiteracy— into a single, decentralized, constitutional democracy.

The most practical thing the Ba'th constitution establishes is that the headquarters of the party is in Damascus (Article Two). And from there begins the tale of the unravelling of party unity—indeed, of pan-Arab unity itself. Damascus consistently and fiercely protected itself not just from non-Ba'th Arab unionists, but from non-Syrian Ba'thists as well. The same article provides that the party headquarters "may be transferred to any other Arab city if the national interest requires it," but to this day there are effectively two Ba'thist party headquarters—Damascus and Baghdad, the capital of the other Ba'thist regime—and the two are mortal enemies. For the Ba'thist pan-Arabism was strictly idealist and, like their socialism, primarily reactionary. The framers of the constitution were not thinking far enough into the future to recognize that no Arab leader—including themselves—would relish the idea of dissolving his borders and therefore having to relinquish his position. Instead, they were appealing to wounded Arab pride. Together the Arabs would oust European imperialism; surely, the Ba'thists thought, such magnanimity, such an outpouring of Arab solidarity would transcend any individual's sense of loss of personal position that the grand scheme might require. On this basis the Ba'thist leaders were successful at exploiting the Arabs' discontent with the humiliating status quo and their enthusiasm for the cause of Arab unity.

One of the most interesting examples of a more pragmatic party platform was that of Antun Sa'ada's al-Hizb al-Qawmi al-Ijtima'i al-Suri, the Syrian Social Nationalist Party (SSNP, also known by its French name, the Parti Populaire Syrien or PPS). Sa'ada, a Syrian Christian, formed the party in 1932 with a small number of students at American University of Beirut, where he taught German. The organization remained secret until 1935, when the French exposed it and arrested and imprisoned Sa'ada for his opposition to their administration. When he was released a year later, he revived his organization on stricter grounds of secrecy.

Sa'ada outlined his theories in his book *Nushu' al-Umam* (*The Development of Nations,* 1938).[17] Interestingly, his rhetoric was even more idealistic than that of the Ba'thists. Sounding like a nineteenth-century European, he said a nation is created by common interest and will, not by religion or language. As such, it is an autonomous unit, the basic unit of human history. And that is what Syria is, he said, traditional Syria, which existed long before Islam and, indeed, before the rest of the Arabic-speaking world that pan-Arabists included in the Arab nation. (In the first edition of *The Development of Nations,* Sa'ada included Syria, Lebanon, and Palestine, as well as Cyprus, in traditional Syria; in the 1951 edition, he expanded it to include Iraq as well.) Therefore Syria should be unified (dissolving the borders and governments of Lebanon, Palestine, and Jordan) and totally independent. And to maintain its social solidarity, sectarian religious considerations should be kept out of politics. The people of Syria should work together for social and economic reform to ensure Syria's strength and longevity. Syrian nationalism must be kept independent of all other national questions, Arab or otherwise (whether they be European imperialist or communist internationalist). And he insisted on the separation of religion and state—since religion cannot be geographically bounded—including the prohibition of clerical interference in politics or the judiciary and equal treatment for all religions. He also called for the dissolution of feudalism and the creation of a nationally autonomous economy as well as a strong national army to sustain and defend this radically Syrian entity.

But Sa'ada's emphasis on Syria ran counter to the popular appeal of Arab unity. Therefore, even the SSNP's meticulous hierarchical organization (modeled on that of the German and Italian fascists) could not create a widespread following. Its membership remained small, and although the party still survives, it does so legally only in Lebanon, having been banned in Syria since 1955 and in Jordan since 1966. Its realistic approach to statism just could not compete with Ba'th pan-Arabist rhetoric—even when it later modified its Syrian absolutism to accommodate Arabism, claiming Syrian independence was only the first step in the establishment of an Arab state. The Ba'th Party, on the other hand, proliferated. Aflaq, as dean of the party, participated in Syrian politics in both parliament and cabinet positions. Branches of the party were established in Jordan (1948), in Lebanon (1949), and in Iraq (1950).

The added shock to the Arab sense of reality created by Israel's declaration of statehood in 1948 further enhanced Ba'th popularity. Indeed, all Arab political parties gained membership. The Ba'th in particular, with its insistence on Arab strength through unity against foreign attempts to destroy Arab society, gained credibility. Yet the more successful the idea was politically, the more Arab unity receded from the realm of the possible.

The United Arab Republic

By 1956, following nearly a decade of post-independence military rule in Syria, the Ba'th Party was well represented in Syrian government. In 1958 they made their first attempt at Arab unity. By that time a revolutionary group within Egypt's military, known as the Free Officers, had overthrown the British-dominated government of King Faruq (1952; see Chapter Seven). Gamal 'Abd al-Nasser had emerged as the popular hero of Egypt—indeed of the entire Arab world. For it was Nasser who took credit for the first (and still the only) Arab victory against Western powers. In 1956 Britain, France, and Israel had invaded Egypt, and Israel occupied the Sinai. It was really international outrage that forced Israel to withdraw from Egyptian territory after four months' occupation.

The United Nations placed a special Emergency Force (UNEF) along the Egyptian-Israeli border and the United States threatened to cut off aid if Israel did not comply with international law. Nevertheless, it was considered a triumph for Egypt and its outspoken leader. Having already taken credit for ridding Egypt of Britain, Nasser had become a leading figure throughout the third world. In 1955 he joined with other third world leaders—including Nehru of India and Sukarno of Indonesia—at the Afro-Asian Conference in Bandung to form the Non-Aligned Movement. With the outcome of the 1956 crisis, then, Nasser began to appear as the only leader capable of confronting the imperialists and the last colonial presence in the Arab world, the Zionists.

Nasser, like the Ba'thists, was a socialist and called for new leadership, new social organization, and realignment of international politics. But, also like the Ba'th, he consolidated his popularity largely through the appeal of Arab unity. The constitution drawn up by the Free Officers following the 1952 revolution stated that Egypt "consciously perceives of its existence as a part of the great Arab whole, and correctly acknowledges its responsibility and duty within the common Arab struggle for victory and glory of the Arab nation."[18] So the stage was set. When the Ba'thists proposed that Egypt and Syria unite, Nasser could not refuse. In 1958 the United Arab Republic was proclaimed—a united Syrian-Egyptian state. But no sooner had the papers been signed than the reality of statist nationalism (as opposed to Arab transnationalist nationalism) became apparent. This was the first hard evidence that Arab unity, if interpreted as a single Arab state, was not going to be achievable.

In the first place, the union of the two states was not motivated merely by the magnanimity of Arab leaders. It was, among other things, an attempt by Syria and Egypt to counter the growing power of Hashemite Iraq. In 1953 Iraq had entered the Baghdad Pact (1953), a formidable alliance with Turkey, Pakistan, and Iran that was backed by Britain. When Iraqi King Faisal's Hashemite cousin Hussein ascended the Jordanian throne (1952), it was rumored that he planned to bring Jordan into the pact, too. The events immediately following World War I under the Hashemite shariff of Mecca and his son 'Abdullah's provisional acceptance of the throne in Transjordan—as a first step in the reclamation of Arab sovereignty—were still fresh in Arab memory. More specifically, Syria, which considered Jordan a part of its natural domain, saw the proposed union as a direct threat. Nor had Nasser ever been well disposed toward the Hashemites, frequently referring to them as sycophantic Western puppets. In addition, the Jordanian king was a known opponent of Nasserism. This had become clear in 1956 when the Nasserist opposition party gained significant representation in the Jordanian parliamentary elections and signed an agreement with its Egyptian and Syrian counterparts. A plot to overthrow the Hashemite monarch was revealed, implicating the complicity of the Nasserists, and Hussein took the opportunity to dismiss the government and impose martial law. The idea of a Hashemite Iraqi-Jordanian union, therefore, loomed as a threat to Nasserist power, and the proposed union of Egypt and Syria seemed an effective counterweight. (Indeed, ten days after the formation of the United Arab Republic, Jordan and Iraq did federate to form the Arab Union, which enjoyed even less success than the United Arab Republic. Within six months Iraqi King Faisal had been assassinated and Iraq severed its ties with Jordan.)

Overall, Nasser saw the union as a chance to strengthen his own position throughout the Arab world. Instead of being an isolated bastion of anti-imperialism in Africa, Egypt could become the center of a massive struggle against colonialism throughout the third world. Indeed, the basis of his appeal was Arab unity and the failure of traditional Arab leadership to achieve it. But Egypt's claim to being Arab was still rather tenuous; the union of Egypt and Syria could therefore consolidate his centrality to the Arab world, he thought. The Charter of the United Arab Republic, drawn up by Nasser himself, stated: "The Arab states were divided among the imperialist states to satisfy their ambitions. Moreover, the imperialist statesmen coined humiliating words such as Mandate and Trusteeship to cover up their crimes."[19] To further strengthen his claim to Arab leadership, Nasser went on to emphasize the plight of Palestine and blamed its loss on the Hashemites. This subtle shift from the nebulous "Arab unity" to the more specific question of Palestine would become more common as the impossibility of Arab political unity became more obvious. But here it demonstrates Nasser's commitment to Arabism as the basis of his legitimacy. That was what made it essential for Nasser to accept Syria's offer. His plan was to develop a strong Egypt as the center of the Arab world.

Unfortunately for Arab unity, Syria's Ba'thist leadership also tended to see the United Arab Republic as a chance to strengthen its position. So when Nasser demanded as a condition of unity that the Ba'th Party dissolve in favor of his National Union umbrella party, an unmistakable imbalance between the two power centers emerged. Soon after the Ba'th's decision to dissolve the party and replace it with a Syrian National Union along Nasserist lines (1959), opposition began to appear. To Syrian party members the decision seemed to come from nowhere, and the United Arab Republic was perceived as undemocratic and unrepresentative. Immediately after the formal dissolution of the Ba'th Party, its members began to call for its reestablishment. The Jordanian branch, working in conscious opposition to the non-Ba'th King Hussein, broke with Syrian Ba'thism and affirmed its loyalty to the Egyptian leader. But in Syria there was greater loyalty to both the state and the party. In 1960 the Fourth National Ba'th Conference tried to revive the party as a political movement separate from any state mechanism. Similar to the Christian Reformation leaders' attitude toward the church, party members wanted the Ba'th movement to remain aloof from the niggling considerations of power politics, so that Ba'thists could be free to influence and guide through moral persuasion in branches reestablished throughout the Arab world. Many Ba'th leaders took more direct measures, however: They threw their support behind the 1961 Syrian coup that effectively ended the United Arab Republic.

The attempts to suppress Syrian nationalism, therefore, had effectively strengthened it. The threat of losing Syria through assimilation into Egypt actually heightened Syrian nationalism, so much so that when the Fifth National Ba'th Conference called for reestablishment of the United Arab Republic the party lost many influential supporters. Realistic Syrian nationalism—i.e., concern for Syria within the undeniably real, if truncated, geographic boundaries separating one political regime from another—began to gain acceptance.

What is more, the tenacity of the pan-Arab unionists tended to exonerate the pragmatic nationalists. When the SSNP, for instance, had advocated strictly Syrian nationalism, they had been disparagingly labeled "regionalists" (*iqlimiyyun*), traitors to the pan-Arab cause. But under the pressure of Nasserism, "Syrianism" became an accepted, if not articulated, motivator. Nasser had tried to mitigate the influence of those Ba'thists who fought for the survival of an autonomous Syria, particularly in the military (the only portion of the population he could effectively control). Those with high positions were appointed either to posts that put them under Nasser's direct command or to diplomatic posts that took them out of the country. Others were transferred to service in Egypt. But the effort failed. As Munif al-Razzaz, then general secretary of the Ba'th Party, reports, Syrian nationalist elements posted in the Egyptian military formed a highly organized underground group bent on the resurrection of the Syrian state.[20] When the Ba'thists were allowed to return to Syria in 1961, they retained both their intensified Syrian nationalism and their clandestine organization. The Ba'thist military officers returned to Syria espousing a regionalism like that of the SSNP. It appeared to the old-guard Ba'thist pan-Arabists, in fact, that these "neo-Ba'thists" had abandoned their most basic Ba'thist principles. Michel Aflaq, co-founder and leading Ba'th ideologue, said at this point, "I no longer recognize my party!"[21] Not only was regionalism gaining precedence over pan-Arabism, but also the party was effectively split into military and civilian factions.

Iraq

The 1961 coup that brought the United Arab Republic (UAR) to an end represented the rejection of Nasser's attempts to run Syria and a victory of Syrian nationalism. A 1963 pro-Nasser Ba'thist military coup set out to reunite Syria and Egypt and this time to include Iraq. A Charter of Unity was agreed upon, but discarded before it was ever implemented, by Nasser himself, who recognized the practical impossibility of the union. Then a 1966 coup put into power some of those anti-Nasserist Ba'thist officers who had been part of the Syrian underground in Egypt. After purging the military of the Nasserists, they further contravened previous Ba'thist policy by determining to cooperate with the Syrian communists and other leftist nationalists. Earlier Ba'th leaders had excluded the communists, fearing Soviet influence and expansionist goals. This group recognized instead the strategic advantage that communist support could afford. They even followed Nasser's lead and established ties with Eastern Bloc nations. At the same time, in opposition to the very essence of Ba'thism, they remained aloof of Arab countries that threatened their Syrian autonomy, in particular, Iraq and Egypt. As noted above, the Iraqi Hashemite regime was brutally overthrown by 'Abd al-Hamid Qasim in 1958. In 1963 a Nasserist and pro-Egyptian Ba'thist coup overthrew Qasim and then proceeded to rid the country of contending political alternatives, especially communists and supporters of the previous regimes. Soon thereafter, the Ba'thist General Amin al-Hafiz gained control in Syria. With Ba'thists in the ascendancy in both Syria and Iraq, then, the party challenged both states to honor their supposed commitment to Arab unity. With that, the Iraqi president dismissed the Ba'thists from his government. The union, of course, never materialized.

Meanwhile, Nasser continued to speak of Arab unity. But as far as the Syrian leaders were concerned, Nasser's rhetoric obscured what was no more than an attempt to take over Syria. The Syrian leaders, in turn, continued to talk of "greater Syria," *al-Surya al-kubra*—Lebanon, Syria, Jordan, and Palestine. The regionalist position was becoming standard. In particular, it gained credibility among the Syrian populace following Israel's defeat of the Arabs in 1967. Nasser had been the undisputed Arab patriarch in the 1967 war. But this time he not only failed to defeat the Israelis and reclaim that part of Palestine they had occupied prior to 1967, he also lost even more of Palestine (those parts known as the West Bank and the Gaza Strip), along with the Golan Heights—which was Syrian territory—and Egypt's Sinai Desert. Nasser remained a charismatic figure on the popular level, but this latest defeat for Arabs showed the weakness of rhetorical Arab unity.

By 1969, Hafiz al-Assad gained control of the Syrian military. Like Amin al-Hafiz, Assad was one of the military officers who had been posted in Egypt during the United Arab Republic and thus harbored distinctly anti-Nasserist sentiments. He had himself elected secretary general of the Ba'th Party—effectively declaring the party synonymous with Syria. No longer worried about Egypt, he began to consider Iraqi Ba'thism the major threat to Syrian autonomy. Iraq had already demonstrated that it had no intention of dissolving itself into Syria. Now Assad wanted to make sure no one expected Syria to merge into Iraq. After all, Ba'thism was still the vehicle of legitimacy, and its popular rhetoric still traded in pan-Arabism. Therefore, Assad set about strengthening his position vis-à-vis Iraqi Ba'thists by demonstrating his fidelity to Ba'thist principles. He led Syria into a reunion with Egypt and this time included Libya, too: the Union of Arab Republics (1971). Assad had no intention of abandoning Syrian autonomy. But by this time Nasser was obviously too weak to implement unity and Libya's young colonel, Mu'ammar al-Qadhafi, hardly seemed a threat to Syria's real autonomy.

Meanwhile, Iraqi Ba'thists in the military joined forces with Iraqi nationalists and overthrew 'Abd al-Rahman 'Aref's Nasserist regime (1968). Once again, Syria and Iraq had Ba'thist military regimes, but this time no pretense of unity was made. The two regimes finally recognized the reality of geographic nationalism. They were distinct entities and refused even basic cooperation.

Pragmatic Nationalism

Thus pan-Arabism gradually receded into the ideological past, while pragmatic concerns occupied the regional states. But contrary to the opinions of the pan-Arabists, those pragmatic concerns were not simply the product of wrong thinking and could not simply be willed away. They were part of the very process of rising to power in any given geopolitical unit. No matter how magnanimous one's plans for a state or a nation, one first had to obtain power in order to implement those plans. The "catch-22" of the ideal of Arab unity—an idea predicated on the belief that the extant geopolitical units in the region were counterfeit or arbitrary—was that in the process of assuming a position from which one could expose the alleged falseness, one actually created an infrastructure where none was supposed to have been.

Consider, for instance, Assad's rise to power. As Syria scholar Yahya Sadowski observes, it was made possible in the first place by the sociopolitical structure of Syria.[22] Syria's traditional elites consisted of semi-feudal landowners and merchants and often included or were closely allied with the Sunni Islamic religious hierarchy. When interwar reformist groups such as the Ba'th began to organize, they did so in conscious and declared opposition to the ruling elites. Obviously, then, their membership was going to come from minority groups who had been excluded from the elite. In Syria, the Christians, Druze, Isma'ilis, and Alawis (the last three are all sects of Shi'i Islam) fell into that category. As is commonly the case, the military was among the few options for upward mobility for these groups. For the Alawis, it was the preferred option. Rural social patterns in the region being what they were, it was very common for entire extended families and even whole villages to follow the same path. By the time the Ba'th took power, the Alawis already comprised a high percentage of noncommissioned officers in the army. Their *outré* status, furthermore, tended to create strong cohesiveness within those groups. So when the Ba'th began to recruit from the underclass, they found a ready pool of willing and cooperative Alawis, well entrenched in the military. As Hafiz al-Assad became active within the Ba'th, particularly in the Secret Military Committee he helped to establish while stationed in Egypt under the UAR, he found Alawi cohesiveness very effective, naturally, and fostered it. He worked to restructure the "old Ba'th" into the neo-Ba'th, gaining his major support from friends and relatives within the Alawite cadre. It was that base of power that allowed him to ultimately take control of the party from its civilian founders, Michel Aflaq and Salah Bitar. Within ten years of Assad's assumption of control in Syria, Alawis commanded half of all army divisions.[23]

Assad consolidated his power by giving Alawis key positions in the military. Absolute loyalty was demanded in return, and it was received. Outside Assad's Ba'th, there was no room for Alawis. Other minorities were also included in his clique, but the most sensitive positions went to close relatives. Elite defense units were awarded to Assad's brothers, and most of the positions in the Presidential Security Council went to members of Assad's own tribe; his native village, Qardaha; and his wife's family.[24] And virtually all sensitive intelligence positions were kept in the family.

Rising to power in what one scholar describes as Syria's "cauldron of counteracting forces," Assad actually had no other way to ensure success. He had to protect himself from the traditional Sunni elite, from the Kurdish minority who had assumed dominance in the military in the early 1950s, from the pan-Arab Ba'thists, and from the Nasserists.[25] And once he had thus gained control of the state machinery, there was too much at stake to give it up. After all, by the time Assad assumed leadership, after the socialism of previous Ba'thist and Nasserist regimes, the state was the largest landowner in Syria. Thus—in the name of Arab unity—a self-protective and self-perpetuating state machinery was created, with very little likelihood and even less incentive to self-destruct.

The Failure of Pan-Arabism

The final attempt at Arab unity (the 1971 Union of Arab Republics) decisively demonstrated the shallowness of the pan-Arabist notion in the first place. Literal unity of the existing geographically drawn states was virtually impossible. If the Syrian state had begun in European artifice, by the time Hafiz al-Assad achieved control it was as much a state as any other. It had a massive and complex infrastructure in which its citizens had a vested, if not totally satisfactory, interest. Yet the regime still had to establish itself among its Arab neighbors somehow. It could not altogether abandon the vocabulary of Arab unity. To this day it makes periodic overtures of unity toward Iraq. In September of 1986, for instance, Assad offered "total and immediate unity" with Iraq as a way to end the Gulf war.[26] Of course, Syria was well aware Iraq would not and could not accept such an offer, especially in light of Syria's continued assistance to Iran, Iraq's enemy in that same war. (When the war started, Iran made exporting oil through the Gulf impossible, thus shutting off Iraq's main economic lifeline. In 1982, Syria sealed Iraq's only alternative, its overland pipelines to the Mediterranean. In return, Iran agreed to supply Syria with affordable oil for five years.) But Hafiz al-Assad can make no pretense of adhering to principles of Arab unity. Instead, he emphasizes Greater Syria. That is the only vestige of Ba'thist legitimacy Assad's Alawi regime can claim. As recently as February 1986, in a speech celebrating the Ba'th rise to power in Syria, Assad promised to regain the Golan Heights and to make it the center of Greater Syria.[27] This is certainly not the way to foster regional cooperation, especially among the rulers of Lebanon and Jordan, not to mention Palestine—whether under the Israelis or the PLO. It is likewise a threat to Egyptian leaders, who inherited Nasser's emphasis on reclaiming Palestine as their measure of legitimacy.

Insistence on Arab unity as the goal of leadership in Egypt, Syria, and Iraq, therefore, actually keeps the Arab leaders in a condition of constant turmoil. They must walk a tightrope, pursuing the pragmatic politics required to achieve and maintain control of economic, military, and political machinery in their geopolitically limited states, but at the same time speaking of Arab unity for fear of censure among their peers and their respective populaces. Pan-Arabism, the popular reaction to the European betrayal that was intensified by Arab defeats in Palestine, made limited nationalism anathema. Nationalism was seen as regionalism, and regionalism was seen as self-seeking and beneath the dignity of a true Arab leader. In the finest spirit of Arab solidarity, they were to pull together against the invaders. Egypt was even redefined as Arab, lest it be left to fend for itself or, worse yet, lest it seek its own settlement and leave its Arab neighbors on their own. The Syrian, Iraqi, and Egyptian nationalisms that had been developing so naturally and relatively unself-consciously before World War I were thus mutated into the ideal of pan-Arab nationalism expressed as Ba'thism and Nasserism. But the real forces of nationalism did not die. Regardless of what people are told their national identity is, they will continue to define as "other" anyone perceived as a threat to their basic economic self-interest and will define themselves accordingly. Thus when Nasser and the Ba'thists tried to implement their shared pan-Arabist ideal, they foundered in seas of self-interest, as did the Iraqi and Syrian Ba'thist regimes. National self-interest is certainly not a bad thing, as such. It is the stuff of legendary heroism, in the proper context. But the post–World War I Middle East was not such a context.

As those regimes that based their legitimacy on claims of Arab unity continued to confound attempts to achieve such goals, Palestine achieved greater focus. Palestine, of course, is part of Greater Syria; Syria's focusing on that issue therefore seems quite natural. But that is not the case with Egypt. When Anwar al-Sadat consolidated his claim in Egypt, following Nasser's death in 1970, he inherited Nasser's focus on Palestine. There was a great deal of competition for Nasser's position, and Sadat worked assiduously to undo the Nasserist socioeconomic infrastructure in order to replace it with one of his own making, which he could control. But he could not renege on the goal of Arab unity. It was in his own best interest to present himself as the one leader who could regain territory lost to the Israelis. That was no doubt at the root of his historic decision to deal unilaterally with Israel. This policy approach was called unilateral—even though there were two sides: Egypt and Israel—because Sadat's action was Egyptian, rather than Arab. The other Arab leaders were not even consulted about the decision. And as will be discussed in Chapter Eight, Sadat received nothing but censure for his fruitless venture. It is certainly not that Palestine should not receive Arab attention; indeed, it should receive full Arab attention. But it needs more than just attention. It needs cooperation, which the phantasm of Arab unity—when placed in the political arena—seems to preclude.

There are some Arab leaders who do work on practical levels for Arab cooperation, of course. Most notably, Jordan's King Hussein, with Sa'udi support, makes periodic efforts to reconcile Iraq, Egypt, and even Syria. But he is the leader of a state over which Syria claims eminent domain; there is little he can do to change the course of Syrian politics, especially in light of Syria's economic and vast military superiority over his own resources. King Hussein is also the only Arab leader who has made significant concessions to Palestinian sovereignty. While both the Syrian Ba'thists and Sadat continued to try to finesse regional leadership by reclaiming Palestine, King Hussein publicly pronounced the Palestinians' chosen leadership, the PLO, the only legitimate spokespeople for Palestine in 1973 and reiterated the decision in 1988. Yet so long as pan-Arab unity remains the language of Arab politics, such realistic efforts to recognize limited geopolitical claims are unlikely to succeed.

The Arab Nationalist Movement

The Ba'thists and the Nasserists are not the only groups that failed to achieve practical Arab unity. Consider the case of the elusive Arab Nationalist Movement (ANM). The Arab Nationalist Movement was officially organized in 1954 at the American University of Beirut, uniting a number of student groups.[28] Its members were from all over the Arab world. They espoused no particular ideology at first, other than the vague pan-Arabism made fashionable by Nasser and the anticommunism that was to be expected from the level of society that could afford to send its sons to universities in the Middle East in the 1950s. As Nasser became more anti-West, so did the Arab Nationalist Movement, but inevitably these followers of Nasser encountered the same organizational difficulties as the Ba'thists, and factions began to appear in the early 1960s. When Nasser declared that all Arabists should join his Arab Socialist Union (ASU), for example, George Habash led a group that preferred organizational cooperation, but not necessarily union. Muhsin Ibrahim, on the other hand, led a faction that considered Nasser's assimilation of all distinct political organizations an effective means to create Arab unity. By 1965 the merger of his group was virtually complete, and the ANM branches in Iraq and Syria disappeared into Nasser's umbrella party.

In Lebanon, by contrast, the Arab Nationalist Movement branch sought union with the Lebanese Communist Party. The latter had flourished owing to support from the United Arab Republic to support its anti-government stance. This merger produced the Front of National and Progressive Parties, Institutions, and Personalities in Lebanon (FNPPIPL), a title as ungainly as the organization it was supposed to represent. The FNPPIPL included the Arab Nationalist Movement, the Lebanese Communist Party, and the Progressive Socialist Party of the Druze leader Kamal Jumblat, among others. Clearly this ambitious attempt was doomed from the outset. It included groups and individuals ranging from the romantic socialist idealists who envisioned all Arabs working together in the spirit of Islamic solidarity to Marxist-Leninist secularists who believed only a vanguard of enlightened revolutionaries could lead a benighted populace in the overthrow of entrenched feudal reaction-aries. It lasted only until the Arab defeat in 1967 discredited every ideology that had been represented among the defeated Arab leaders. Eventually, Ibrahim's group declared itself Marxist-Leninist, condemning any cooperation with the bourgeoisie as counterproductive.

Meanwhile, those groups most affected by the Arab failures lost faith in pan-Arab cooperation and began to organize independently. The Popular Front for the Liberation of Palestine emerged, as scholar of Arab politics Tareq Ismael puts it, as "the armed wing of the Arab Nationalist Movement after June 1967."[29] And the Palestinian Popular Democratic Front formed under the leadership of Nayif Hawatmeh, while Ibrahim became the leader of the Organization of Lebanese Socialists (OLS).

The OLS claimed it was the only true representative of the proletariat and concentrated its efforts trying to convince other leftist organizations of that fact. Eventually, they merged with former Ba'thist leftists to create the Organization of Communist Action in Lebanon (1971), as well as a great deal of animosity between itself and the Lebanese Communist Party. And George Habash formed the Arab Socialist Action Party, dedicated to transforming what was left of the ANM into a Marxist-Leninist front. Thus the Arab Nationalist Movement as such ceased to exist, as the goal of Arab unity once again was eclipsed by practical concerns.

The War in Lebanon

It is in this context—the competition for claim to true Arab leadership imposed by the ideal of Arab unity—that the war in Lebanon must be understood: Lebanon is the Arab version of the Thirty Years' War, where virtually all Arab regimes back various factions in efforts to keep their rivals from gaining the upper hand. Because of Israel's military su-periority and international backing, the Arabs cannot fight their battles on Israeli soil. Nor are all the battles with Israel. Despite the fact that regaining Palestine has been designated as the measure of successful Arab leadership, the issues of Israeli legitimacy and Palestinian home-lessness are actually quite separate from the inter-Arab rivalries under discussion. Although no one could have planned it, Lebanon became the arena of Arab competition.

The Lebanon war has its origins in the factionalism fostered, first, by competition between the British and French to coopt various elements of the population and thus thwart each other's attempts at Syrian hegemony (see Chapter Four) and, later, by French efforts to keep Syria divided and therefore weak. As we saw in Chapter Five, following World War I Britain took control of the Palestinian and Transjordanian regions of Syria, and France took the rest. Under French control, the Maronites— French clients for centuries—were given autonomy in that region called the Lebanon. The Lebanon included (roughly in order of relative population) Maronite Christians; Shi'i, Sunni, and Druze Muslims; and Greek Orthodox, Catholic, and Protestant communities. The French were forced to depart from Syria in 1943. But before they left, they made the Lebanon a country separate from the rest of Syria. Syria was ruled (at the outset) by representatives of its majority, Sunni Muslim nationalists. But Lebanon was ruled by the Maronites, with secondary positions going to Sunnis and Shi'is. The Druze were virtually ignored.

The first big crisis after the war came when Israel, France, and Britain invaded Egypt in 1956, the Suez Crisis. The Maronites, in an effort to disprove suspicions of European rather than Arab sympathies when the state was first created, had professed their solidarity with the Arab world. But when the Arab states cut their ties with Britain and France following the invasion of Egypt, the Maronite president of Lebanon, Camille Chamoun, refused to follow suit. His prime minister and cabinet resigned in protest. Sunni and Druze factions formed their own front and in 1958 threatened to lead Lebanon into reunion with Syria by joining the United Arab Republic. President Chamoun asked the United States to intervene, whereupon U.S. President Dwight Eisenhower sent in 14,000 Marines. Civil war was avoided, but the Maronites were persuaded to promise to follow Arab policy in the future.

Then when Israel occupied the West Bank in 1967, thousands more Palestinian refugees began pouring over the Lebanese border. Many were Christian but the majority were Sunni Muslim, which vastly upset the state's delicate sectarian balance. A series of confrontations led to a brief war between the Palestinians and the Lebanese army in 1969. It ended with a peace agreement, but the Maronites were still not happy, especially when the 1972 parliamentary elections reflected a significant increase in Sunni Muslim representation. Thus, when Israel invaded Lebanon in 1973 in pursuit of PLO commandos, the Lebanese army refused to offer the Palestinians assistance. This led to the Palestinian decision to arm themselves for their own security, which, in turn, brought an increase in Israeli attacks on Palestinian bases in Lebanon.

The heaviest burden of these attacks was borne by Lebanese civilians (in addition to the Palestinians, of course), particularly the Shi'i communities of southern Lebanon. The Shi'i then began developing their own political front, Amal, while the Palestinians joined with the Druze front led by the Jumblatts. This National Movement was nominally a leftist alliance, but it included dozens of often feuding organizations— including Sunni, Druze, and Shi'i—united by nothing if not opposition to the Maronites. The Sunnis eventually formed their own socialist movement, the Murabitun. Meanwhile, to counter what appeared to be growing Muslim influence, the Maronites continued to refuse to fight Israeli raids, further consolidating their multifarious opposition. The Shi'i began to identify more and more with the Palestinians and the Druze.

All this instability suited the Syrian regime, which had always wanted to reclaim Lebanon. Syria knew neither Israel nor the United States would allow a direct takeover, but it could exacerbate Lebanese instability to keep Lebanon from being able to survive independently. The Syrian Ba'thists therefore gave more and more assistance to the Muslims, at the time the Maronites' greatest threat. That prompted the Maronite Gemayyil family to call for closer relations with Israel, which brought it into confrontation with other leading Christian families who remained pro-Arab. In 1975, the Gemayyils assassinated the leader of the opposition Christians, Suleiman Franjiyya. In the ensuing mayhem, the Franjiyya's Muslim allies were called in for support. The prospect of a Sunni victory in Lebanon, much less a leftist-Palestinian alliance, so horrified the Alawis in Syria that they then sent in 30,000 troops to help the Maronites. This is generally considered the start of the Lebanon war.

Immediately, Israel, the United States, and other Arab regimes began to send in help to various factions. Those Lebanese with sufficient means tended to leave the country, taking along with them much of the state's economic resources. Foreign- and black market–supported militias became the most viable means of economic survival for many of those who remained. In that context, militias proliferated. Almost anyone who could muster a gang of fighters could find a financial backer and arms suppliers. Some of the forces were sectarian in ethos; some were ideological. The Maronites, for instance, developed three main militias: one fascist, one liberal, one pro-Arab. There were pro-Syrian Ba'thists, which naturally led the Iraqis to support an anti-Syrian Ba'thist faction. The Sa'udis, Egyptians, Jordanians, Libyans, Iranians, and Israelis each sent in millions of dollars a year to support their proxy battles in Lebanon.

By 1983 there were sixteen foreign-supported armies and 60,000 foreign troops. Syria continued to switch sides whenever its current client appeared to be gaining too much strength. The situation remains virtually the same today—through repeated Israeli invasions and outright occupation; innumerable alliances made and broken; more than 200 ceasefires; assassinations; the rise and fall of governments; and now, with Lebanon either under two governments, one Maronite and one Muslim, or under no government, depending upon one's point of view.

Indeed, it has gotten worse, for the continued failure of the Arab leaders has spawned yet another reaction. The pan-Arab ideal was a counterfeit criterion of political success, predisposed to breed failure. It imposed a standard of political legitimacy unsuitable for the means required to achieve it. It called for geopolitically limited states to work with geopolitically unlimited leadership. The competition among regional leaders for that position was bound to breed instability. And the more those leaders failed, the more their people suffered. Involvement in Lebanon and the fruitless endeavors to best one another in the international arena kept Arab leaders from working effectively on the real problems of the region: economic development and Palestinian homelessness. The main actors in this drama had been the Ba'thist and Nasserist politicians, who had themselves developed in reaction against so-called Western capitalist models. Their continued failure— so explicitly demonstrated in the 1967 defeat in Palestine—led to a broadening of the definition of "Western." Since then, both capitalist and socialist models have been rejected on the popular level. Indeed, almost anything foreign has been defined as un-Islamic and secularist and therefore has been rejected, as we saw at the beginning of Chapter One. The new reaction: Instead of retreating into Arabism, now the Arab world retreated into Islam. The European betrayal had spawned leaders who followed alien models of all sorts. Islam, it seemed, was the only thing that had not been tried. The Islamic activist groups— to be described in the next chapter—proliferated and joined in the Lebanese conflagration.

CHAPTER SEVEN

The Legacy of Interwar Religious Developments

*S*ince *the suppression of the Muslim Brethren in Egypt and the demise of the Islamic constitution of Pakistan, there has ceased to be any visible likelihood that Islamic legal and constitutional principles would be made to serve as the operative basis of a modern state in any Muslim country.*

—Malcolm H. Kerr[1]

The late Malcolm Kerr could write that in 1966. At that time, Nasser had secured his position as Egypt's first independent leader since the sixteenth century. On the strength of that feat alone he was revered throughout the Arab world. His charismatic personality and skillful appeal to the Arabs' foresaken unity only enhanced his position—so much so that the policy of uniting the Arab world in a socialist state unaligned with either of the great powers in the East-West struggle came to bear his name: Nasserism. However, the bubble was soon to burst. The crushing defeat of the Arabs by the Israelis in 1967 sent shock waves throughout the Middle East. It called into question virtually all the principles previously relied upon and resulted in the current reactionary trend that totally confounds Kerr's prediction.

Impact of the 1967 Defeat

Indeed, the 1967 defeat is often referred to as the turning point (*nuqtat al-tahawwul*), the time when Arabs realized they had to either change their tactics or surrender their autonomy and their very identity to the monolithically perceived West. Actually, however, the reaction to the defeat was a continuation of that begun in the aftermath of World War I. At that time "Western" meant European; European models, with all their attendant liberalism, nationalism, and capitalism, were seen as the source of Arab problems. As we saw in Chapter Six, Egypt, Syria, and Iraq—the centers of political activity in the region—each waged revolutions yielding socialist and transnational or pan-Arabist regimes. Yet we also saw that none of them was able to implement the much-touted Arab unity. Neither Nasser nor the Ba'thist leaders in Damascus and Baghdad was willing to abdicate in favor of any others.

We also saw how the emphasis on Arab unity gradually became focused on the Palestinian issue. The respective leaders vied with each other in the vehemence of their denunciation of Israel and expressions of solidarity with the displaced Palestinians. The plight of the Palestinians was and remains, certainly, a valid issue; all the regimes earned gratitude from the Palestinians for recognizing that this group were actually the greatest losers in the post–World War I settlements. Nevertheless, focusing attention on the Palestinian issue also conveniently sidestepped the failed attempts at general Arab unity. Thus, when Israel defeated the combined Arab forces and occupied what remained of Palestine in 1967, as well as Egypt's Sinai Peninsula and Syria's Golan Heights, the credulous Arab masses found themselves again betrayed by their leaders. They had trusted their traditional leaders who led them into the Arab Revolt, only to find themselves subjected to European colonial control. Now they had been led to defeat by a new generation of leaders, those who had promised to revive the strength of the Arab world on a new, "progressive" basis.

Granted, the Europeans had been chased out, but they had left behind a fragmented Arab world, cut into competitive and frequently contentious states. There were some vestiges of the first stage—Saudi Arabia and Jordan, for instance. Neither of these states had witnessed the socialist revolutions of the postwar period, for several reasons. For one thing, neither had ever been a center of political activity. Arabia, the vast *rub' al-khali*—the "Empty Quarter"—of pre-oil days, had been left to its tribal organizations from the time of the first Islamic dynasty (the Umayyads, 661–750). Since the days of Muhammad until the rise of the Wahhabi confederation at the turn of the nineteenth century, Arabia's politics had not been a concern even to the empires that claimed to control it. Even the Wahabbi movement was considered a threat only when it began to encroach on Syrian and Iraqi territory; thanks to Muhammad 'Ali of Egypt, it had been easily confined. Furthermore, Arabia had never been the object of colonial oppression.

As a result, it did not harbor the resentment against the West upon which the socialist revolutions turned. Indeed, the Wahabbi movement saw laxity and duplicity among Muslims, rather than in the West, as the cause of the Islamic world's stagnation. Interaction with the West, which proved so important to developing and maintaining the Sa'udi regime's oil wealth, seemed only sensible—hardly threatening.

The other notable exception to the socialist trend was Jordan, continuously ruled by Hashemite monarchs since 1921. Until that time it had never existed as an independent political entity. It was created as such only by the British and French, who had no concern with regional precedent. Traditionally a part of Syria, Transjordan as a state was separated from its traditional political centers, Jerusalem and Damascus. Its population, sparse and largely rural or nomadic, was lacking in either political sophistication or aspirations and could scarcely have been expected to repel European imperial machinations.[2] Furthermore, from the beginning Jordan's economic viability had depended on aid from Western states, first Britain and then the United States and Western-oriented Saudi Arabia. The lack of a developed political culture, then, made it unlikely that Jordan would deviate from its liberal, capitalist, and basically pro-Western stance.

Nevertheless, neither the traditional pro-Western states nor the "progressive" anti-West states had been able to rescue the Arabs from their plight. The traditional leaders had been discredited thanks to the British and French disposition of the Arab world following World War I. The next phase—nontraditional, socialist leadership—had failed to make good on promises of populist leadership and, even more importantly, of Arab unity. The loss of the 1967 war and the further dismantling of Arab lands therefore cast these leaders in an equally dubious light.

In effect, this amounted to the discrediting of all foreign models of leadership, since both stages of Arab leadership had adopted nonindigenous political forms. The traditional elites who retained positions in the post–World War I Middle East assumed positions of kingship. Monarchies—a non-Islamic political form—had been established in Egypt, Transjordan, Syria, and Iraq. (The Sa'udi regime, not a traditional monarchy, will be discussed in Chapter Nine.) And as it turned out, the nontraditional elites had been able to oust the traditional elites only through the vehicle of the military. Party organization was involved, but as we saw in Egypt, Syria, and eventually Iraq, it was ultimately through gaining control of the appropriate military apparatus that the new leadership was able to exercise and maintain its control. Military dictatorship, even under the guise of parliamentary rule, is likewise without Islamic sanction. It is considered *sultan*, raw "power," i.e., lacking in moral authority. While there had been those in the Islamic world who had ruled on the basis of coercion—indeed, as Ibn Taymiyya believed, since the seventh century—they were considered to have deviated from the Islamic standard.

The defeat of 1967 therefore resulted in a popular reaction against foreign models, whether those models were considered Western in the limited sense of European capitalism or in the expanded sense that included socialism and communism. Both were seen as godless and materialistic. They were judged to be the result of removing religion from politics, which was believed to be the thrust of secularism. And both, it was felt, had to be rejected in favor of truly Islamic life.

It is essential to recognize that neither of the "Western" models had received popular support based on an evaluation of strategic merits. Indeed, neither had actually been chosen by the populaces they represented. Despite parliamentary structure in Syria, Iraq, Egypt, Jordan, and even Lebanon, for instance, none of the governments was truly democratic. In the first place, the entire region bore a characteristic element of third world underdevelopment—widespread illiteracy. Even when elections were held, the proportion of the populace involved was too low to qualify as representative. Besides that, as we saw in the case of the Nasserist efforts in Jordan, for instance, when the parliament did something that was not to the liking of the government, it was the latter that prevailed. It was the leaders themselves, not their socioeconomic or political philosophies, who gained what popular support they had, whether through hereditary claim, personal charisma, or, as in the case of Nasser and the Ba'thists, the emotional appeal of Arab unity. Like their traditionalist predecessors, these so-called progressives also failed to develop populist political participation. Instead, they relied on the same rhetoric of Arab unity that had been motivating politics in the region since the time of al-Afghani and 'Abduh. When they, too, failed so demonstrably in 1967, their system, like that of their predecessors, was condemned.

Roots of Islamic Resurgence

There had, of course, been beacons of Islamic resurgence long before 1967. As we saw in Chapter Two, Ibn Taymiyya had warned against deviation from the true path. That, he said, was the reason the original unity of the Islamic community had dissolved. Outside the Arab world, in North Africa and India, Islamic revivalist movements had appeared in the eighteenth century. In the nineteenth and early twentieth centuries, Jamal al-Din al-Afghani had again called for religious revival as a source of social and political solidarity sufficient to drive out foreign adventurists. Muhammad 'Abduh and his disciples had done likewise. But none of their warnings had been heeded. The states established by the European powers were controlled by leaders who implemented political orders alien to Islamic tradition. It was in this context that Ibn Taymiyya was resurrected. When he had been named as inspiration for the Wahhabi movement in eighteenth- and nineteenth-century Arabia, his influence was considered reactionary. But under the post-1967 Islamic resurgence, he became known as the father of Islamic resurgence. Actually, this trend began in the same era that produced the more Western-oriented political movements in the Arab world. Best represented in the famed Jama't al-Ikhwan al-Muslimin or al-Ikhwan al-Muslimun (the Society of Muslim Brothers or the Muslim Brotherhood), the revivalist founders were contemporaries and, in some cases, admirers of the work of the early modernists, particularly Rashid Rida's interpretation of Muhammad 'Abduh. But unlike the monarchists and political parties who assumed control in the interwar period, this was a populist movement. There are two significant implications here. First, because it was a populist movement, it would take a great deal longer to mature. It had no coercive power to impose its solutions on society. Its strength was only in numbers, which were drawn largely from among non-elites. Indeed, it was the elites' failures that fuelled the Islamic movements' success on the popular level. And second, as with most popular movements, a good deal of intellectual sophistication would be lost in the popularizing process.

The Society of Muslim Brothers

The Society of Muslim Brothers or the Muslim Brotherhood was begun by Hasan al-Banna (d. 1949), appropriately enough, in a village nearly one hundred miles northeast of Cairo. From its inception in 1928 through the rise of Nasser, the Brotherhood gradually accumulated a widespread popular following. By 1948 it had at least half a million members and an equal number of sympathizers.[3] As a result, it became instrumental in providing the popular support necessary for Nasser's overthrow of King Faruq and establishment of the government by his Revolutionary Command Council (RCC). An examination of the Brotherhood's ideology and development reveals the reasons for its popular growth, as well as its utility to Nasser's nationalist movement, but at the same time explains its inability to achieve its own goals.

In the first place, the Brotherhood was at its most basic level a nationalist movement. As one Muslim Brother put it, "Nationalism (*qawmiyya*) in our minds attains the status of sacredness."[4] Egyptians felt the foreigners who had controlled Egypt for nearly fifty years had robbed them of their very identity. They felt alienated, lost, and wanted nothing so much as to feel a part of their own culture again. According to al-Banna, the original impetus for formation of the group was a conversation he had with some laborers employed by the British near Isma'iliyya:

> We have heard and we have become aware and we have been affected. We know not the practical way to reach the glory of Islam and [to serve] the welfare of Muslims. We are weary of this life of humiliation and restriction. . . . [W]e see that the Arabs and the Muslims have no status and no dignity. They are no more than mere hirelings belonging to the foreigners. We possess nothing but this blood . . . and these souls . . . and these few coins. . . . We are unable to perceive the road to action as you perceive it, or to know the path to the service of the fatherland [*watan*], the religion and the *umma* as you know it. All that we desire now is to present you with all that we possess, to be acquitted by God of the responsibility, and for you to be responsible before him for us and for what we must do. If a group contracts with God sincerely that it live for his religion and die in his service, seeking only his satisfaction, then its worthiness will assure its success however small its numbers or weak its means.[5]

But this nationalism was not acknowledged as such. In the 1920s nationalism was an alien feature in Islamic terrain. Just as the postwar ideologues (discussed in Chapter Six) had condemned nationalism as regionalism and replaced it with a call to Arab unity, the Islamic activists (as I will call the participants in this phase of Islamic reaction against the West) likewise condemned nationalism. But they saw it as godless—"secular" in their terminology—and so replaced it with a call for *Islamic* unity. Thus, it was in the language of Islam now, rather than that of Arab unity, that al-Banna rationalized patriotism. Loyalty to Egypt, he said, was a *religious* duty. Why? Because Egypt was the center of the Islamic world. Egypt "is a part of the general Arab nation, and . . . when we act for Egypt, we act for Arabism, the East, and for Islam."[6] He claimed that only Egypt had remained truly Islamic while the rest of the Arab world fell to the Christians and the Mongols. And conversely, "Egypt cannot be reformed except by and through Islam." For at the core of the Egyptian "conscience and emotions" was Islam— its "faith, its language and its civilization."[7] Therefore, Egypt had a unique role to play in returning the Arab world to Islam.

The contrived nature of this argument is obvious. Egypt was never the center of a regime claiming, much less exercising, legitimacy throughout the Islamic world. As noted in Chapter Six, it was not until the twentieth century that Egypt was even considered Arab. Another revealing inconsistency in Brotherhood lore was the fact that Muhammad

Ali was praised as the "leader of Egypt," the "great man who rejuvenated a great people."[8] But, as we saw, in fact Muhammad 'Ali was neither ethnically Egyptian nor particularly Islamic; his cultural orientation was distinctly secular and European. He did wrest control of Egypt from the Ottomans, however, and set Egypt on a path of modern development, and that was what appealed to Egyptians.

Brotherhood spokesmen tried to address any appearance of inconsistency by distinguishing this "sacred nationalism" from the decadent nationalism of the West. In the latter case, they held, the narrow, materialistic interests of the state are worshipped as if they were divine. By contrast, the nationalism advocated by the Brothers is a "nationalism of divine principles," decreed by God.[9] "So long as nationalism is loyalty to the nation, then religion is its gate, for no loyalty is possible for him who has no religion."[10] Thus the Brotherhood's ideologues condemned the forms of nationalism that had reference to pre-Islamic Egypt and that expressed devotion to Syria for Syria's sake rather than for the sake of Islam, such as that of the Syrian Social Nationalist Party (SSNP; see Chapter Six). They also condemned pan-Arabism of a type that was not motivated by Islam alone, such as that of Sati' al-Husri. It was in this context that the Brotherhood condemned secularism, which it described as nationalism not motivated by Islam. Instead, religion had to be the legitimator of political movements. But, in fact, when al-Banna tried to clarify the moral standing of nationalism, he actually revealed that the thrust of the movement was exactly the same as that of its predecessors: independence for Egypt. He said that love of one's country as a place of residence is acceptable because the Prophet himself expressed affection for Mecca, his home. The desire to restore the dignity and independence of one's country is likewise an honorable pursuit, as is the pursuit of social solidarity or cooperation.[11]

Indeed, what the Brotherhood was offering was a revived cultural identity. Just as in the work of al-Banna's mentor, Rashid Rida, the backwardness of Arab culture in the face of foreign occupation was a major factor. The Arabs discovered that the Europeans had made enormous advances since their early encounters in the crusades. At that time, the Islamic world had been far in advance of European civilization. And the greatness of the Islamic world had been created solely on the inspiration of Islam. Before Islam—in the Age of Ignorance or *al-jahiliyya*—the Arab world was splintered into competing tribal factions, racked with injustice and corruption. The message of Islam had created the moral strength and social solidarity to build the most advanced and widespread civilization the Western world had known. Surely, such a civilization could be created again, al-Banna said, if only Muslims would return to a truly Islamic life.

For al-Banna, a return to a truly Islamic life meant a return to the Qur'an and the Sunna and rejection of Western innovations. It did not mean that the technical advances introduced by the Western world should be rejected. But technology was something that could be achieved in a number of ways. Europe had only been able to develop techno-logically because of its social solidarity, moral and intellectual discipline, and sense of self-sacrifice.[12] But the Europeans' motivation was sheer nationalism. The Muslims had something even better: Islam. Islamic solidarity was based on human equality and a system of specific rights and responsibilities, as formulated by pious Muslim ancestors (the *salaf;* hence the name for this overall approach, Salafiyya). Al-Banna taught that Islam was a much better source of social strength than mere nationalism was. National loyalty was arbitrary, but Islam was ultimate truth.[13] For these reasons, Muslims needed only return to the pure and uncontaminated system of Islamic belief and practice to regain their strength and independence.

The search for identity was repeatedly highlighted in the Brother-hood's attempts to distinguish Islamic culture from any other. It is unique, they said, although it combines the best of all other cultures. The West's capitalism has its good points: intellectual advancement, material benefit, and democracy. But it is too materialistic and leads to oppression of the poor by the wealthy. In addition, its excessive individualism breeds personal and class competition, rather than coop-eration.

Besides that, capitalism inspires imperialism, the Brothers believe:

> The West surely seeks to humiliate us, to occupy our lands and begin destroying Islam by annulling its laws and abolishing its traditions. In doing this, the West acts under the guidance of the Church. The power of the Church is operative in orienting the internal and foreign policies of the western bloc, led by England and America. . . . A hundred years ago the situation was one of enmity between the state and Christianity. Today, however, the relationship is obviously a cordial alliance.[14]

Similarly, al-Banna said, communism has its good points: concern with social justice, egalitarianism, social solidarity, and humanitarianism. But it is materialistic, and equality on a merely material basis is meaningless. Atheism, dictatorship, tyranny, and lack of freedom—these are its negative characteristics. Actually the Soviets had not deviated from czarist imperialism, the Brothers taught. "Czarist Russia was one of the most violent in its enmity to Islam and Muslims." It was "a slaughterhouse of religion" for Muslims. Now it is simply "Red barbarism" and the Brothers had no mercy in their condemnation of the Soviet heirs of the czars.[15]

In this attempt to establish a unique cultural identity by condemning the West, both capitalist and socialist, the Brotherhood revealed its distinctly reactionary nature. The rise of Islam was necessary because everything else has failed: "The western world, during [recent] centuries, has been materialistic in tissue and fibre . . . resulting in a deadening of human sentiments and sympathies, and in the extinction of godly endeavors and spiritual values."[16] The entire world is suffering, the Brothers taught. "Revolution is in process everywhere."[17] The Islamic world (the "East") must regain the dominance it once held for the sake of all humanity.

The Brotherhood believes Islam offers everything a society really needs:

> We believe the provisions of Islam and its teachings are all inclusive, encompassing the affairs of the people in this world and the hereafter. And those who think that these teachings are concerned only with the spiritual or ritualistic aspects are mistaken in this belief because Islam is a faith and a ritual, and nation and a nationalism, a religion and a state, spirit and deed, holy text and sword. . . . The glorious Qur'an . . . considers [these things] to be the core of Islam and its essence.[18]

The form of government proffered is vaguely called "the Islamic order." It is described as the implementation of Islamic law as the basis of political life. Just as Ibn Taymiyya had said, some *ijtihad* (creative interpretation of Islamic principles in light of present realities) would be required to make the Shari'a workable again. And the ruler would have to be guided by *maslaha* (i.e., he would have to rethink Islamic law in view of contemporary developments and in accordance with principles of social well-being). Later commentators believed it would be all right to keep the constitutional parliament in Egypt, provided a few Islamic reforms were put in place. Even the legal codes that had been imported into Islamic countries were believed to be in general agreement with the principles of Islamic law. Only a few modifications would have to be made in the areas of criminal and commercial codes, such as stipulations concerning alcohol, pork, gambling, and usury.

This brings to light an interesting ambiguity embedded in Brotherhood teachings. The reason Islamic law is best is that it is revealed by God. Muslims were blessed with this ultimate revelation and should show their gratitude by implementing it. (The very word for heresy in Arabic, *kufr,* means "ingratitude.") Other legal systems are defective precisely because they lack this element of divine revelation. Indeed, it is the Muslims' ultimate duty to spread Islamic law to these deluded ones. However, al-Banna frequently reverted to a naturalist analysis, claiming that Egyptians must follow Islamic law because it is from their own culture. Revealing the influence of French Enlightenment thinkers, no doubt transmitted through Muhammad 'Abduh, al-Banna said, "Law does not serve its function unless it rests on principles accepted by the people and in which individuals and societies have faith."[19] The Shari'a, we are told, plays the same role for Muslims as communism plays for the Soviets and democracy plays for "Anglo-American governments," i.e., it is a function of social integrity and "national pride." Clearly, if the value of Islamic law is in its divine origin, no other justification for its implementation need be given. Likewise, if the Islamic duty is to make Islamic law universal, the condition of national or cultural origins of law loses significance.

This type of ambiguity in Brotherhood ideology does not mitigate the significance of its message. It simply reveals that that message goes much deeper than its literal meaning. It was not logic that made the Brotherhood's teaching so compelling; it was the appeal to national or cultural pride, however that nation or culture was defined. But this national or cultural pride was only partially articulated, for political language was Islamic language, and Islamic language did not deal in national or cultural pride. Similarly, when Germanic princes gained independence from the Holy Roman emperor, it was not in the name of nationalism but in the name of religious freedom. Martin Luther's criticism of papal impiety was the justification for the princes' pursuit of religious freedom. But this did not mean political goals were being disguised as religious goals. The German princes were just using the language of the times—a language that was still politico-religious. The two had not yet been separated. If the German princes had had popularly accepted principles of national autonomy at their disposal, surely they would simply have demanded that the imperial authorities conform with those principles. But such principles had not been developed in Europe even as late as the seventeenth century (see Chapter One). In the twentieth century, principles of national autonomy and the right to self-determination did exist. But appeal had been made to them by Shariff Hussein in the aftermath of World War I, and the various Arab states had also made such appeals repeatedly since then—all to no avail. The Europeans seemed to consider these principles applicable only to themselves. The Arabs were forced, therefore, to turn back to the political language of their own culture, as distinct from that of European culture. And that was the universalist language of Islam. But the goal was still national strength and independence was no less ardently sought.

That goal is again revealed in the Brotherhood's constant appeals to democratic principles. The relationship of democracy to geographic limitation has already been discussed. On a functional level democracy provides a built-in limit of sovereignty. It substitutes geographically limited political authority for potentially universal authority. If a ruler's legitimacy is granted by the people she/he rules, clearly her/his reign is limited to the place those people live. Brotherhood writings are full of references to democratic principles. The phrase "social contract" (*'aqd ijtima'i*) is even used. The ruler is called a laborer or an agent of the people, again, just as in the work of Ibn Taymiyya. "The authority of the ruler must come from the nation."[20]

Furthermore, in a significant departure from Ibn Taymiyya, Brotherhood commentators specifically denied that governments established by sheer force should be obeyed. Ibn Taymiyya's contention that even tyrants should be obeyed was motivated by a horror of anarchy and an abiding belief in the power of Islamic principles to overcome all evil. In the modern context, the focus of responsibility had become more specific: If people do not make sure that Islamic law is obeyed by everyone, including the leaders, then Islamic law will not prevail and it will be the people's fault. People have a right to expect and, in fact, demand satisfaction of their needs. If the leader does not satisfy the needs of the people, they have both the right and the responsibility to replace him.[21] Accepting the authority of the people is the ruler's religious duty.

Finally, the proto-secularist principles of separation of institutionalized religion from the state machinery and of religious freedom are also implied in the teachings of the Muslim Brothers. Al-Banna and other Brotherhood commentators were adamant in their condemnation of what they perceived as Western secularism:

> [T]here is no authority in Islam except the authority of the state which protects the teachings of Islam and guides the nations to the fruits of both religion and the world. . . . Islam does not recognize the conflict which occurred in Europe between the spiritual and temporal . . . between the church and the state.[22]

Yet at the same time the Brotherhood calls for the very things that actually characterize secularism as it developed in Europe, i.e., as a function of the limitation of the universal sovereignty of a religiously legitimated government. As the "Islamic order" was described, it was determined that people should elect representatives and then abide by their decisions. Those representatives should include but not be limited to Islamic religious scholars. Ordinary people who happen to have leadership abilities must also be included. Accordingly, if sovereignty comes from the people, then all people within a given country must share in that sovereignty. Freedom of religion must be enjoined. And, in fact, it is. Islamic principles must guide society, but all true religions espouse Islamic principles, so there should be no conflict. The Muslim Brothers called for the equality of all citizens in rights and duties.[23]

Indeed, the Brotherhood specifically called for the separation of religious and political movements. Al-Banna began his career criticizing the "civil servant *'ulama'*," those in the employ of the government who could therefore do little besides ratify the government's position.[24] In particular, it is explained, religious scholars could hardly be expected to maintain their objectivity if they tied their fortunes to the government. They should remain independent of government so they can carry out their responsibility to criticize it. This, as we saw in Chapter One, is precisely the origin of secularism as it developed in the West. And the Brotherhood consistently refused to affiliate itself with any government or political party, even those it supported, for fear of compromising its independence. In fact, the only kind of national loyalty explicitly prohibited by the Brotherhood was loyalty to a political party. It was called false nationalism, because people who were loyal to parties ended up engaging in "party strife and the bitter hatred of one's political opponents with all of its destructive consequences. . . . It does not benefit anybody, not even those who practice it."[25] Another revealing element of Brotherhood teaching is the insistence on Arab superiority. As mentioned above, the Brotherhood condemned that kind of nationalism motivated by pre-Islamic national loyalties, calling it the same as racism. Instead, nationalism must be grounded in and motivated by devotion to Islam. But at the same time, they condemned Sati' al-Husri because he failed to understand the unique place of Arabs and Arabism in history. The Arabs were the first Muslims and they must remain the most important Muslims. The Prophet, we are told, said, "If the Arabs are humiliated then so is Islam."[26] Indeed, all Islam's problems—in this context—are attributed to non-Arab leadership: "Persians, Daylamits, Mamlukes and Turks." None of these was able to "taste the real Islam" because they could not perceive its true meanings. And that led inevitably to even more foreign domination—the crusaders, the Tatars, the Carmathians, and then the Europeans. The Turks, in particular, were "enemies of Islam" and had devastated the Islamic world, guaranteeing its "impotence in the face of future encroachments on the peoples of its lands."[27] Clearly, this is another indication of the desperate search for unique identity, a basis of solidarity sufficient to cast off foreign domination.

But these goals—national autonomy limited through democracy and the separation of church and state—remained embedded in Islamic language. And Islamic principles are not easily confined to any given state. Despite the undoubtedly limited nature of their claims, the persistent justification of these claims by appeal to Islam implied far greater ambitions than national autonomy. Indeed, these implications became explicit every so often in Brotherhood publications, which even go so far as to rationalize Islamic imperialism. The desire to conquer the world is ratified in Islam, because it is motivated by the desire to establish "the best system of colonization and conquest, as is indicated by the Qur'an (2:193/189)."[28] A Muslim Brotherhood publication specifically articulated the imperialist principle:

We Muslim Brothers do not recognize geographic boundaries in Islam. Our concern is with the welfare of Islam, and we will engage, in its defense, in battle which includes the Muslim world in its entirety. For example, it may not be to the interest of Islam that a battle begin in the [British-occupied Suez] Canal, but rather . . . in Tunis first. . . . We have our plans, our goals, and our independent commands which address themselves to this spacious field. It is not necessary that their vision be bound by local problems in Egypt.[29]

The Brotherhood's Political Involvement. Followers of al-Banna were inspired by this flexing of Islamic muscle. The Brotherhood's membership soared, and its political involvement became inevitable.[30]

Al-Banna's active political life began when he was "discovered" by the military officers who would eventually overthrow King Faruq. His first contact in the military was Anwar al-Sadat, who was sympathetic with the Brotherhood's message but did not join the society. Through Sadat, al-Banna learned of the existence of revolutionary groups within the military. Al-Banna agreed with the revolutionary officers that, as Sadat would later recall, "the salvation of the country could be assured only by a coup at the hands of the military."[31] It was this pooling of resources that made the future overthrow of King Faruq possible. For although the disgruntled "Free Officers" had been planning some sort of revolution and had the tactical means to carry it out, they needed to know there would be popular support in order to make a success of it. In discovering the Society of Muslim Brothers, with its devoted and increasing membership, the military found the missing element for their successful revolution.

In the early years of King Faruq's reign, the Brotherhood had expressed support for him. He seemed pious, having trained under Islamic scholars, and was an opponent of the dominant Wafd Party (see Chapter Four).

King Faruq was opposed to the Wafd because of its efforts to limit his power, but the Brothers preferred to see this opposition as anti-secularism. However, by 1942 the Brotherhood found they could no longer place their faith in the government of King Faruq. It was his police who carried out the orders to intimidate and arrest those the British deemed enemies of the regime, including, on occasion, Hasan al-Banna. The palace faithfully followed orders to dismiss the Wafdist government in 1944, when it became too vociferous in its demands for British evacuation, and replaced it with minority party governments that lacked the organization and popular support to effect real changes. It was then that another Muslim Brother in the military, al-Banna's personal assistant in the Palestine war, met with Gamal 'Abd al-Nasser—who was by then a member of the Free Officers—and expressed the Brotherhood's support for revolution. The Brother told Nasser, "Begin to organize in the army groups which have faith in what we believe so that when the time comes, we will be organized in one rank, making it impossible for our enemies to crush us."[32]

Egypt's worsening economic condition hastened the Brotherhood's political debut. The Egyptian economy, as we have seen, was far from developed. The plight of Egyptian laborers was made worse by postwar developments. Britain's war effort and the presence of Allied troops in Egypt had led to the employment of over 250,000 people. The sudden release of this work force following the war led to massive unemployment problems not revealed in the numbers alone. Most of these workers were unskilled or semiskilled, and many of them had been drawn only recently to urban centers from villages. The limited industrialization Egypt was experiencing, largely in the hands of elites, was not sufficient to absorb the numbers of people seeking new opportunities. As well, postwar inflation was rampant, exacerbating the difficulty of their situations.[33] Remote from their traditional family and cultural environments, these newly urbanized masses readily gravitated toward the kind of "family" organization offered by the Muslim Brotherhood. A growing trade union movement did offer an alternative, as did the communist parties. But overall the Brotherhood, with its full complement of activities and its intense indoctrination in a traditional cultural component, attracted the most members. In the Brotherhood "family" cells (the basic organizational units of the society, limited to five members), not only did members find a substitute for the support structures they had left behind when they came to the cities, but they also found that they were not alone in their discontent. And they found hope that the system would change and the promise that simple devotion to their Islamic leadership would solve their problems. They were largely uneducated and unable to articulate the nature let alone the source or solution for their discontent. They had little understanding of national or international politics; sophisticated economic theories left them largely unaffected. In the Brotherhood they found formulations they could understand.

It soon became apparent that the Wafd and the Brotherhood were the two strongest antigovernment forces in Egypt. Their competition for popular allegiance raged in the universities, which have always been at the center of political life in Egypt. Each held conferences, and they vied with each other in their lists of demands that the government jettison the British. They worked together when it was of mutual benefit against the government. But tension between the two groups was far more common, often erupting into violence. Efforts were made at rapprochement in the fall of 1946, so that a united front could be formed to impose demands on the British government. These efforts were successful. Anti-British riots broke out, and the government responded by shutting down universities and newspapers and arresting key figures from all the opposition parties. The crisis eventually brought down the government. But when the next government followed the Muslim Brotherhood's recommendation of bringing Egyptian demands for autonomy before the United Nations and sent a high-ranking member of the Brotherhood to New York to assist with the negotiations, Wafd antipathy toward the society was revived.

The mission was a failure anyway; the United Nations reached no decision on the case. The organization was too busy trying to sort out the Palestine problem. The British were under intense pressure from Zionist terrorist groups and were doing their best to get out from under the burden of the mandate. Soon after its failure to resolve the Egyptian case, the United Nations passed the fateful Palestine Partition Plan of 1947. Egypt, like the rest of the Arab world, was incensed by the plan to split Palestine into two states, one for Zionists and one for Arabs, and to put Jerusalem under a UN trusteeship.[34] Though it represented a tremendous gain for the Zionist immigrants from Europe, clearly the Arabs had little incentive to accept a plan—initiated and executed by foreign governments—to cede a significant portion of their land to an alien population. For them, therefore, the UN partition plan represented one more example of European treachery. Newspapers at the time reported continual public protests in the major cities throughout the region. And the Brotherhood was eager to play its part in the defense of Palestine, which it did through its paramilitary cells, the Secret Apparatus.[35]

The participation of the Muslim Brothers' Secret Apparatus suited the initial strategy of the Arab League perfectly. It was generally agreed among Arab leaders that governments should not become directly involved in the Palestinian conflict. Financial and political support was expected, of course, but Arab leaders wanted to avoid the internationalization of the conflict. It was felt the Western powers had already inflicted enough damage in the area; Arab leaders did not want to give them an excuse to reenter the region. The Brotherhood's involvement in Palestine also underscored the centrality the Palestinian issue had assumed in the Muslim and Arab world. Just as it had been for the pan-Arabists, for the Islamic activists Palestine was the preeminent symbol of Arab effeteness. Perhaps most importantly, however, the Brotherhood's involvement in Palestine demonstrated the high degree of organization and effective structure it had achieved by this time. The Brothers' dedication to the cause of liberation seemed to give positive direction to all the recruits who volunteered for service on the Palestinian front. The military felt frustrated and alienated at home, but in Palestine, under the leadership of the Brothers, they were able to vent their frustrations. The Palestine war was, of course, a failure for the Arabs, but that blame was placed on inept and indifferent Arab government leadership. By contrast, it was believed that the Brothers fought and died with valor and inspired others to do the same.

As far as the Egyptian government was concerned, however, the Brotherhood's performance in Palestine revealed something more ominous. Following the war, attacks on the government continued; indeed, they escalated. The Muslim Brothers were not the only Egyptians involved in assassinations, attempted assassinations, and other terrorist activities, but they were frequently the most visible. Therefore, when the commander of the Cairo police was killed during a riot, the government immediately blamed the Brotherhood and took decisive action. On December 9, 1948, the Society of Muslim Brothers was ordered to disband. Those Brothers who were fighting in Palestine were rounded up and ordered either to submit to army rule or return to Egypt. Arrests were made, the society's newspaper was closed, and the Brotherhood's property was confiscated and placed under the control of the Ministry of Social Affairs. According to a contemporary observer: "[The government] had done with a society that could be regarded as its strongest opponent. This was not just a party but rather resembled a state with its armies, hospitals, schools, factories, and companies."[36] The government's case against the Brotherhood included "the overthrow of political order," "terrorism," arming and training paramilitary groups, "the manufacture of bombs and explosives," raising funds by demanding protection money from businesses, and even embezzling. Predictably, the government's action sparked a reprisal. On December 28, 1948, the prime minister was assassinated by a member of the Brotherhood. Less than two months after that, al-Banna was assassinated, most probably under orders from the government.[37]

The next government continued to enforce strict measures against not only the Brotherhood, but all other opposition groups as well. Stories of torture of political prisoners became legendary. Arrests and confiscation of properties increased. And again, such measures effectively united the otherwise contentious groups in their opposition to the government. In May 1949 a failed attempt by a group of Muslim Brothers to assassinate the new prime minister initiated a new wave of arrests. The Brotherhood remained outlawed, but in the summer of 1949 it began to reconnoiter. Given the Arab failure in Palestine and the continued influence of Western imperialism throughout the region, the tribulations of the Brotherhood in Egypt had served, in fact, to strengthen the appeal of the organization. The incarceration of the members solidified their relationships, as they maintained their organization even in prison cells, and strengthened their resolve. What was more, the tales of their trials in Egypt, against the backdrop of their valiant efforts in Palestine, made them celebrities throughout the Arab world. It was at this time that the branches in Syria, Jordan, and Pakistan were formed by those who had fled Egypt to escape arrest.[38] In May 1951 members of the Brotherhood sued the government for their constitutional right to form a private society. After a sustained trial, the verdict came in favor of the Brotherhood. Their confiscated properties, their press, and their right to organize were all reinstated in December 1951.

By January 1952 tensions over Britain's continued presence in the Suez Canal zone were at their height. When forty Egyptians were killed in a clash with the British in Isma'iliyya, Cairo erupted into a massive riot as all factions demanded declaration of war on Britain. The king responded by declaring martial law and dismissing the prime minister. A new prime minister was appointed and a new cabinet formed, but elections for a new parliament were put off.

The palace finally signed its own death warrant following the resignation of the last prime minister in June 1952. In July the king attempted to appoint the president of the Army Officers' Club, directing that the officers' own choice for president, General Muhammad Neguib, be stationed outside Cairo. When the king then appointed a new ministry and designated his own brother-in-law as minister of war and navy, General Neguib led the Free Officers in the occupation of Cairo and the overthrow of King Faruq.

The Muslim Brothers were in full support of the revolution, of course, their relationship with the Free Officers having long since been established. Since their interaction in the Palestine war, the association between the two groups had grown considerably. Brotherhood specialist Richard Mitchell reports that in 1950 the palace received information that one out of three army officers was involved with the society.[39]

When the date for the revolution was finally set, the society's leadership was duly consulted and informed. Specific tasks had been assigned to its members, including fighting, encouraging popular support for the revolution, and monitoring foreigners and minorities as well as suspicious Egyptians—anyone who might try to thwart the revolution. Indeed, the Muslim Brothers came to consider the revolution their own doing.

The Muslim Brothers were very gratified by some of the initial acts of the Revolutionary Command Council (RCC), the group that took control of Egypt directly following the revolution. The RCC arranged for the release of political prisoners, most of whom were Brothers; brought the alleged murderers of Hasan al-Banna to trial; and abolished the party-oriented student unions, deeply cutting into the power bases of the Brotherhood's erstwhile enemies, the Wafdists and the communists. But right away problems arose. For one thing, the Brotherhood's insistence on keeping religious and political organizations separate— their condemnation of secularism notwithstanding—prevented them from accepting the RCC's invitation to join the new government being formed by Muhammad Neguib. Yet they wanted to be able to tell the government what to do. They felt they had a great role to play in the new government and set about making their recommendations known. Naturally, the new government considered them a destabilizing factor. But the regime could not yet afford to alienate the society. Especially following the dissolution of other parties (in the fall of 1952), the Society of Muslim Brothers was the sole organized basis of the RCC's popular support. Nasser and Neguib, the two leading members of the RCC, duly paid their respects publicly, even joining the annual pilgrimage to Hasan al-Banna's tomb (February 1953).

Still, the Brotherhood continued to warn the government about excessive reliance on force and pressed for the repeal of martial law and censorship rules. Even more annoying to the RCC, the society indirectly threatened the government over the issue of British presence in Egypt. The RCC had continued in the policy of negotiating with Britain for its withdrawal, while the general populace—at least as reflected in the Brotherhood's attitudes—had long since lost faith in Britain's good intentions. In effect, Hasan al-Hudaybi, who had taken over as general guide for the society following al-Banna's assassination, said that the society would resist any outcome of the negotiations that the society considered inappropriate.[40]

The confrontation between the Muslim Brothers and the RCC began to culminate in the spring of 1953, when a representative of the British Embassy contacted al-Hudaybi to ascertain the Brotherhood's position on the issue of British presence in Egypt. Whatever the conclusion reached—accusations and counter-allegations abound—it was clear that even foreign governments considered the Muslim Brothers the power to be reckoned with in Egypt.[41] The RCC decided that the society—despite the society's claims to the contrary—was a political threat. In early 1954 they demanded its dissolution. Only its humanitarian organizations were allowed to continue functioning.

The Muslim Brothers' Influence on Egyptian Politics. Meanwhile, the RCC was experiencing internal problems of its own, from which the Brotherhood inadvertently helped Nasser emerge victorious. General Neguib, who had become president, and the more radical Nasser had been in contention for some time over the direction of the revolution. Neguib was the more popular of the two; Nasser was considered imperious and irreligious. When demonstrations continued to show support for Neguib as well as the imprisoned Brothers—in the form of demands for an end to military government—Nasser tried a new approach. In March 1954 he acceded to popular demands. In addition to a return to parliamentary rule and the lifting of censorship, the Brothers were all released from prison and their various constituent organizations were fully reinstated, along with all other parties, as the decree of dissolution was rescinded. In return, al-Hudaybi agreed with Nasser to establish a "committee of liaison with the government," whereby the society could show its support for the regime and discuss any differences it might have with the government.

Therefore, despite continued criticism of the government in Brotherhood publications and sporadic demonstrations, the Brotherhood was generally allowed to continue its operations, while the Wafdists and the communists and all other political parties were oppressed. This was due to the influence of Anwar al-Sadat. Sadat, having allied himself with the Free Officers group in the military, joined the revolutionary government. He authored the RCC's press campaign against the Society of Muslim Brothers but believed further oppression would make heroes of these "revolutionaries." It was better to "fight fire with fire." If the strength of the Society of Muslim Brothers lay in the popularity of Islam, Sadat reasoned, the government should begin to demonstrate its own piety. Thus, Sadat's version of true Islam—liberal and in accord with the principles of the RCC—began to appear in a series of articles in the popular press. Even Nasser became a focus of Islamic piety, as his pilgrimages and consultations with other good Muslim leaders received great publicity.

Meanwhile, the condemnations of the Brotherhood's version of Islam by some al-Azhar scholars were promulgated. This sparked rivalries within the Muslim Brotherhood, effectively splitting it into progovernment and antigovernment factions. The Secret Apparatus, always the most militant of the society's members, were in the latter group. They hatched a plan to assassinate Nasser. The attempt was made while Nasser was delivering a speech before a huge crowd in Alexandria. Somehow, all eight shots fired missed their target, and Nasser suddenly became a hero. As the crowd watched stunned with terror, Nasser rose to the height of his charismatic skills, delivering an impassioned speech about struggling even to the death for his beloved people.[42]

The assassination attempt was the excuse the government needed to get rid of the Muslim Brothers. Within one week Hasan al-Hudaybi was arrested and the Brotherhood was accused of conspiracy to overthrow the government, destroy Cairo and Alexandria, and take control of Egypt itself. Al-Azhar condemned the Society of Muslim Brothers for civil war against an Islamic government. Within a month more than one thousand Muslim Brothers were arrested. Trials were conducted by a tribunal that included Anwar al-Sadat. In December sentences were announced, including death by hanging for six members. The society's membership dwindled, and Nasser assumed the widespread popularity he held for the rest of his life (see Chapter Six).

It was not that the appeal of the Brotherhood's message dissipated during this time. It was simply that Nasser appeared to be offering the same things—as Middle East scholar R. Hrair Dekmejian summarizes, "dignity, unity, popular participation, defiance of the West, and a semblance of socio-economic justice."[43] And for a while Nasser seemed unassailable, so much so that he legitimized the society once again in 1964.[44] By that time Sayyid Qutb (d. 1966) had become the undisputed ideological leader of the Brotherhood. He had been in prison since 1954, during which time he composed his famous *Ma'alim fi'l-Tariq* (*Signposts on the Road*). That, along with his commentary on the Qur'an, *Fi Zilal al-Qur'an* (*In the Shade of the Qur'an*), quickly became—as they remain—among the most widely read literature in the Arab world. Qutb was released from prison in 1964 but was arrested again in 1966, tried for leading the Secret Apparatus in another attempt to assassinate Nasser, and executed. But even Qutb could not provide the kind of unified leadership necessary to sustain the society's preeminence in Egypt. That lack, combined with Nasser's growing prestige and apparent success, seemed to render the Brothers superfluous to Egypt's official life. And without the Egyptian Muslim Brotherhood as inspiration, the Brotherhood's branch operations in other Arab countries languished. This condition is described in Malcolm Kerr's statement at the beginning of this chapter.

But the failures of 1967 exonerated the Brotherhood's positions. Indeed, the further humiliation of the Arabs and diminution of their territory elevated—ex post facto—the Brotherhood's condemnation of foreign models of leadership to the level of prophecy. The 1967 defeat became a fulfillment of the predictions made by Ibn Taymiyya and reiterated by 'Abduh, al-Banna, Qutb, and all others that if the Arabs did not return to truly Islamic government, disaster would result. That is why the year 1967 became known as the "turning point": It inspired the rebirth of the Society of Muslim Brothers, as well as the birth of a number of more militant offshoots.[45]

Sadat

Nasser died in 1970. When Anwar al-Sadat took over Nasser's position, the Brotherhood once again became a pawn in the Egyptian power struggle. The society and Sadat already had a long and checkered history. It will be recalled that Sadat was the society's first liaison with the military, until he was arrested in 1942 as a result of his contacts with the German fascists. Sadat was on the tribunal that tried the Brotherhood's leadership in 1954 and condemned six of them to death and Hasan al-Hudaybi to life imprisonment. Now, Sadat chose once again to liberate the beleaguered Brotherhood, just as Nasser had done before him, in order to consolidate his leadership among the contending heirs to Nasser's regime. Again, it was popular support that would allow the leader to dominate his competitors, and the Brotherhood was the acknowledged source of that popularity. Sadat had learned the lessons of Nasser well.

Sadat's strategy at this point was to distance himself from the Nasserist claimants to his position. In a total about-face from Nasser's socialism, Sadat therefore adopted strictly capitalist economic order. This would bring in foreign capital, both in the form of investments and foreign aid, particularly from the United States. And in the process, it would create a prosperous private sector, presumably earning the gratitude and support of the middle class for the system's architect.

But Sadat also knew that he had to accede to the power of Islam. To avoid the destabilizing popular criticism the Brotherhood were so practiced in manipulating, Sadat became perhaps the most conspicuously Muslim leader modern Egypt has known. In 1971 a new constitution was promulgated, making Islam the official religion of Egypt. This did not fully meet the Brotherhood's demand that the Shari'a become the basis of Egyptian law, but it did proclaim that the Shari'a was among those bases. Sadat's press began to refer to him as al-ra'is al-mu'min, "the believer president." He advised the nation that his real name was Muhammad and emphasized his humble—and Islamic—beginnings. He began and ended every speech with a prayer and referred to himself as the head of the Egyptian "family," who should be obeyed as such. And he increased government support for mosques.

In a more aggressive stance, Sadat undertook to prove that he was, as a result of his fervent devotion to Islam, favored by God, by leading Egypt into a war of liberation against Israeli occupation. Ramadan, the Islamic holy month, was chosen for the beginning of the October War, and it was code-named "Badr," the name of the battle at which Prophet Muhammad and his early followers defeated the mighty Meccan infidels. Despite the inconclusive outcome of the 1973 war, Sadat (as well as other Arab leaders) claimed victory—at least they had not lost any more territory—and Sadat again played up his Islamic fidelity, referring to himself as the "hero of Badr."

At the very same time, Sadat was tying Egypt more and more to Western interests. Nasser had been a prime architect of the Non-Aligned Movement. As an official Egyptian publication put it, the purpose of the Non-Aligned Movement was "to mobilize the nationalist forces in the Afro-Asian countries to fight imperialism in all its forms throughout the world."[46] Nasser's socialism, moreover, had been anti-feudal, designed to break the power of the traditional ruling elite (large landowners, both private and religious). Now Sadat wanted to establish a new capitalist elite in order to build up his own power base. Still, he was careful to get Islamic sanction for his policies. In classic form, he saw to the installation of a cooperative rector of al-Azhar who would ratify the government. It was Shaykh 'Abd al-Halim Mahmud who blessed Sadat's system, at least for the first four years.[47] He dutifully condemned communism as religious heresy and lauded Sadat's trip to Jerusalem in 1977, which led to the signing of the Camp David accords. Sadat, al-Azhar claimed, was a *wali al-amr*—according to Islamic law, the national leader who alone has the right to make decisions concerning "the disposition of things."[48]

Through all this the Brotherhood remained technically illegal. That way Sadat could present himself as their protector and, it was hoped, earn their gratitude. He allowed the Brotherhood to publish its journals, although he occasionally forbade their distribution, and in return he gained some Brotherhood support in parliament. But many other Muslim Brothers were not convinced by Sadat's apparent piety. After all, the Egyptian ruler had the right to appoint the rector of al-Azhar. Since 1911, the al-Azhar religious scholars (shaykhs) had been financially dependent upon the government, their property having been appropriated by the state and replaced with government salaries. Furthermore, if a religious scholar "behaved in any manner unworthy of the learned" he could be fired and blackballed from any official position.[49] This did little to inspire confidence in the shaykhs' objectivity.

Indeed, the apparent capitulation of the Brotherhood to Sadat's wiles inspired the growth of more militant groups to fill the role once played by the independent Brotherhood, particularly in its paramilitary operations. One such post-1967 group, the Munazzamat al-Tahrir al-Islami (Islamic Liberation Organization, also known as the Shabab Muhammad or Muhammad's Youth), was led by a Palestinian former Muslim Brother. The group carried out a violent attack on an Egyptian military academy in 1974, for which the group's leader was executed in 1976.

In the mid-1970s Shukri Ahmad Mustafa, a member of the Brotherhood who believed the society had grown effete, formed his own group, al-Takfir wa'l-Hijra. They declared all of Egyptian society, including the Society of Muslim Brothers, infidel (*takfir* means "to declare someone an infidel") and encouraged emigration to a place where they could create a truly Islamic society (*hijra*). In 1977 the group carried out a plan to kidnap the former minister of Islamic properties and al-Azhar affairs, who had been responsible for condemning their group in 1975. When their ransom demand was not met, the former minister was murdered. Members of the group were rounded up, arrested, and executed—as it happened, just after Sadat's visit to Jerusalem. It was again Shaykh 'Abd al-Halim Mahmud who issued the statement condemning the group as heretics who claimed for themselves what only God and the Prophet could do (i.e., judge the piety of other Muslims and perform the *hijra*).[50]

Anti-Sadat members of the society became increasingly active in 1977. Attacks were launched against nightclubs and houses of prostitution, and hostility toward non-Muslims, especially the Copts (a Christian minority of some three million to five million in Egypt), mounted. The Brotherhood's criticism of the regime for supporting un-Islamic elements, both foreign and domestic, proliferated. Sadat's trip to Israel became the signal of his hypocrisy. He was seen as a traitor to the Islamic cause. His fraternization with the Israelis while the Palestinians remained homeless seemed sheer treachery. Both he and the al-Azhar shaykhs who sanctioned his actions were increasingly criticized. The successful Islamic revolution in Iran in 1979 only served to bolster the Islamic activists' confidence and embolden their attacks.

Sadat again attempted to placate the critics, sponsoring social legislation aimed at public drinking and other offenses against Islamic practice. In 1980 the Shari'a was proclaimed the main source of Egyptian law, and the government promised to build one thousand new mosques.[51] Sadat's press increased references to Islamic themes. However, his general policies did not change; repression of the proliferating Islamic activist groups continued. And the Egyptian economy remained precarious, only Sadat's new middle class seeming to benefit. Worse yet, Israel remained in occupation of Palestine, and Sadat became the darling of the degenerate Western world. Much to the chagrin of the Islamic activists (and many secularist Egyptians, as well) Sadat's benefactors rewarded him with the Nobel Peace Prize and the designation "best-dressed man." Islamic activist groups increased their attacks on such apparent hypocrisy but were limited in their ability to express their discontent to intimidation of "Westernized" Egyptians and Copts. During this time, in fact, friction between Muslims and Copts frequently flared into riots.

By 1981 the Islamic activist attacks were severely destabilizing Egyptian society. Sadat finally decided to act decisively. He announced that the government was taking control of all mosques, including the thousands of unregistered mosques run by the Brotherhood and their sympathizers. He then ordered the arrest of some fifteen hundred opponents, including not only Islamic activists, but Copts, Nasserists, and communists as well. Among the detainees was the most outspoken and popular religious critic, Shaykh 'Abd al-Hamid Kishk.

Shaykh Kishk was a powerful and accessible orator. Although his name had previously been banned in the official Egyptian press, his books were numerous and hundreds of his sermons circulated widely via audiocassette tapes. The content of his message was simple: repetitive assertions of Islamic superiority and universality, condemnations of injustice, and demands for Islamic leadership. But his dismissals of the importance of mundane life—reminiscent of Saint Augustine—and his poetic allusions to the glory of the afterlife provided an addictive tonic to the alienated Egyptian masses. He emphasized the sufficiency of true belief and told numerous stories of the miraculous nature of the Qur'an. The only people who needed to fear, he told his eager listeners, were those *lacking* in fear of God. The shaykh's blindness was considered evidence of his elevated status in God's estimation; he frequently thanked God for it because it had been replaced with insight.[52] From his early arrest and release by Nasser in the mid-1960s, Shaykh Kishk's reputation had been been growing; by 1980 he was the most popular Islamic polemicist in Egypt.

The arrest of Shaykh Kishk was the last straw. Sadat was assassinated in October 1981 by an offshoot of the Society of Muslim Brothers known as al-Jihad.[53] The assassins were quickly arrested and brought to trial, for which they seemed grateful. Finally they had a public platform commanding a world audience. In their testimony, they called upon no less an authority than Ibn Taymiyya to justify their actions. Unless something was done about hypocritical Islamic leadership, they claimed, Islam will have failed its divine mission. Unless un-Islamic leadership was replaced—by whatever means possible—the entire Muslim world would be doomed.[54]

The Islamic Activist Reaction Outside Egypt

This Islamic activist reaction to continued political failure was evident throughout the Arab world. In Syria, for instance, the Muslim Brotherhood had been popular since the late 1930s. From 1945 to 1961 the organization was led as a branch of the Egyptian Muslim Brotherhood.[55] The movement was suppressed in 1952 for its continued criticism of the government following the defeat in Palestine in 1948. In 1958, under the United Arab Republic (UAR), the group was dissolved at Nasser's request, although its members survived and reorganized in 1961. When the Ba'thists regained power in 1963, they continued to suppress the society, exiling its leader. Official repression of the society intensified after anti-Ba'th demonstrations in Hama in 1964. The group, therefore, was not as active in Syria as in Egypt until after 1967.[56]

Then the Syrian branch splintered into several smaller groups under leadership of a younger, more militant generation. Among these leaders was Marwan Hadid of Hama. As prisonmate of Sayyid Qutb in 1965, Hadid was a strong proponent of *jihad* (struggle) against the Ba'thists.

The 1967 defeat had also caused a split within the Ba'th Alawi military apparatus. It will be recalled that Hafiz al-Assad was able to prevail in 1971, to become the first non-Sunni president in Syria's history. But, as Assad's leadership became more entrenched and self-protective, the new militant Islamic activist factions found support among those excluded from the central Alawi clique.[57]

It was not so much that Syrian leadership was Alawi rather than Sunni Islam; Assad's government never made an issue of its religious orientation. But Ba'thism is a secularist ideology, and just as it did in Egypt, that appeared to the Islamic activists to be the reason the Arab world was in such disarray. As noted in Chapter Six, Syria, more than other regimes, had tended to focus on the Palestine issue as Arab unity seemed to recede further and further into the background of ideological anachronisms. The 1967 defeat therefore was a particularly severe blow. Palestine was not the only problem, of course. As they did throughout the region, problems of underdevelopment and rapid urbanization, with its attendant social dislocation, plagued Syria. But having made first Arab unity and then Palestine irredentism the gauge of its success, the Syrian regime—like the Egyptian—had inadvertently set itself up for backlash. And as in Egypt, the Islamic activists condemned the non-Islamic leadership. One representative group, the Islamic Revolution in Syria, described the Ba'th Party as "a total disaster," having failed to liberate Palestine, to achieve social justice through socialism, to strengthen the state, or to bring about Arab unity. The Islamic Revolution therefore demanded reversion to the true path of righteousness: reliance on God alone.[58]

The first major manifestation of renewed Islamic militancy came in 1973, when the bazaars of Homs, Hama, and Damascus became the scene of mass protests against the regime's failure to make Islam the state religion in its new constitution. The government dispersed the demonstrators and responded with a watered down amendment to the constitution requiring that Islam be the religion of the head of state. Assad then began following Sadat's example, trying to play to Islamic sentiment, even flaunting his regular attendance at Friday prayers.

The Arab "non-defeat" in the 1973 Arab-Israeli war tended to allay protests temporarily. But economic problems and the unpopularity of Assad's support for the Maronites against the Palestinians in Lebanon (see Chapter Six) soon resurrected open criticism. The Syrian Muslim Brotherhood and its sympathizers were particularly active from 1976 to 1978, carrying out a series of attacks and assassinations of prominent Alawis, including close relatives of Hafiz al-Assad.

The Ba'thists quickly recognized the threat posed by the Brotherhood's renewed criticism. They had already attempted to demonstrate their concurrence with Islamic goals, launching a widely publicized anti-corruption campaign. Arrests were made for "bribery, imposition of influence, embezzlement, exploitation of office, and illegal profit"; people of unquestionable reputation were placed in prominent positions; some exiled political opponents were repatriated.[59] But the Islamic activists were not satisfied. An attack on a predominantly Alawi military school in 1979, in which more than eighty students were reported killed, signalled the escalation of the war between the Brothers and their supporters and the Alawi government. The government, in turn, tightened its control, suspending civil liberties and engaging in virtual civil war with the Brotherhood.

The situation reached crisis proportions with protests in Aleppo, Hama, and Homs in the spring of 1980. The government responded with an all-out campaign against the Brothers, which included—just as it did in Egypt—periodic pronouncements from the *'ulama'* about the government's role in protecting true Islam from the foreign-inspired radicals. In June 1980, for instance, Damascus radio reported President Assad's statement to the *'ulama'*: "The state takes care of religion and calls for adhering to it. Being religious is totally different from killing innocent people and following Zionist and imperialist plans." The report concluded that "the 'ulama' stressed their full support . . . against all conspiracies."[60] The following month, membership in or association with the Muslim Brothers was made a crime punishable by death.

The campaign against the Brotherhood culminated in Hama in February 1982. Mass demonstrations turned into three weeks of riots, to which the government responded ruthlessly. Some two thousand were killed, effectively liquidating the active Brotherhood cells and silencing their supporters.

The pattern was similar in Iraq. The Hizb al-Da'wa al-Islamiyya (the Party of the Islamic Call) was formed in 1958 in Najaf, when political parties were made legal following the overthrow of the Hashemite King Faisal and Ayatollah Ruhollah Khomeini was in exile there from the shah's Iran. Khomeini was expelled from Iraq in 1975, at the shah's request, but the Da'wa Party continued to express the sentiments of the Shi'i majority. The government of Iraq had traditionally been Arab Sunni Muslim, which characterizes only about 20 percent of the population. (Iraq is more than 50 percent Shi'i, and another 20 percent of the Sunnis are Kurds, a non-Semitic ethnic group.)[61] The Iraqi government was therefore leery of Shi'i organizations in the first place, fearing the appeal of Iranian Shi'ism. And like Jordan and Syria, Iraq was equally leery of both the Ba'thist and Nasserist versions of Arab unity, which became dominant after the 1958 revolution, when the monarchy had been overthrown. As we saw in the original break between the Iraqi and Syrian Ba'thist parties, the appeal of Arab unity was effective rhetoric, but none of the leaders who touted it was inclined to abdicate his position of power in favor of the others.

The Da'wa Party does not claim to be sectarian Shi'i. Like the Sunni Muslim Brothers, they see themselves as spokesmen for all Muslims against an un-Islamic government. Indeed, their criticisms are similar to those of Islamic activists in Egypt and Syria: failure to establish social justice and democracy and failure to regain Palestine. As throughout the region, the Islamic activists are not the only critics of the government. The newly urbanized working classes, the Kurdish minority, dissident Ba'thists, as well as communist groups all express discontent with the Iraqi Ba'thist regime. But as in Syria and Egypt, many other dissidents support the Islamic activists, not for their ideological stand but simply in their opposition to the government. Thus the Da'wa consciously attempts to accommodate Sunni Islam in an effort to consolidate opposition. They do, however, add to the list of government offenses failure to cooperate with the Islamic regime in Iran. And they describe the ideal Islamic state in distinctly Shi'i terms.[62]

Following the 1967 defeat, the Da'wa Party was joined by several new and more militant Shi'i activist groups. At the same time, the

Da'wa Party itself became more militant. In 1974 a Shi'i religious festival turned into a series of violent public protests, establishing a pattern that culminated in violent clashes, arrests, and executions in 1977. Then, even more than in Egypt and Syria, the successful Islamic revolution in Iran in 1979 encouraged open activity by the Islamic activist groups. The Iraqi regime responded with a massive crackdown, resulting in the crisis within the government that brought Saddam Hussein to the presidency in July 1979.

Saddam Hussein has systematically attempted to accommodate Islamic activism, both Sunni and Shi'i. He has subsidized shrines, mosques, schools, etc. Conscious of the potential appeal of Iranian Shi'i revolutionaries, especially to the largely Shi'i populace of southern Iraq, Saddam Hussein's regime has emphasized development programs in that area. But at the same time, he has pursued a policy of ruthless repression of Islamic activists, which culminated in the execution of Imam Muhammad Baqir al-Sadr in April 1980 and the outlawing of the Da'wa Party. Al-Sadr was a major Shi'i intellectual, indeed, the chief ideologue of Iraqi/Arab Shi'ism. He was also reputedly in close contact with his Iranian counterpart, Ayatollah Khomeini. When al-Sadr rebuffed Saddam Hussein's attempts to coopt him into the government, the Iraqi president felt he had no choice but to eliminate al-Sadr.

Other, more militant groups formed under the inspiration of the Iranian revolution and after the execution of Imam al-Sadr, such as the Islamic Action Organization. And several new opposition groups formed with the outbreak of the Iran-Iraq war in September 1980, most religiously oriented, some reportedly supported by Syria. Whereas the Syrian government blames the Zionists and other imperialists for using Islamic groups as tools, the Iraqis blame Iranian or U.S. subversion. In reality, due to the enduring antipathy between the two Ba'thist regimes, each encourages the Islamic opposition of the other. Yet, as in Egypt and Syria, despite Islamic language, which is by nature universalist, the concerns of the Islamic activists in Iraq are largely nationalist. Ayatollah Khomeini's persistent efforts to inspire mutiny among Iraq's Shi'i majority were a well-publicized failure.

Conclusion

This chapter is in no way intended as an exhaustive cataloging of Islamic activist groups. As Middle East scholar R. Hrair Dekmejian observes, "Actually, dozens of fundamentalist [*sic*] organizations exist in each Arab country, operating overtly and covertly in pursuit of their political, social, and spiritual objectives. A conservative estimate of the number of active fundamentalist groups in the Arab world would be several hundred."[63] The ideological differences among the groups range from calls to overthrow all non-Islamic governments to moderate attempts to infuse existing governments with Islamic spirituality. The Muslim Brotherhood, however, the oldest and most accessible, is therefore presented as an example of one of the most successful Islamic activist groups. The discontent represented in the rise of these movements was inevitable, just as it had been among the European populace when the Holy Roman Empire disintegrated. As described in Chapter One, it took the Europeans at least two hundred years of internecine warfare to reach a semblance of stability. The Arab world has only recently entered the world of autonomous, geopolitically limited states. It was inevitable that they, too, would take time to develop workable indigenous political structures.

But the Arabs had two added challenges, besides those faced by the Europeans. First, national borders were not allowed to develop naturally, as they had in Europe, but were imposed in radically illogical ways by the vacating imperial overlords. What was more, having been under imperial domination for so long, the Arab world was underdeveloped in a predominantly industrialized world. The Arabs were therefore faced with two monumental tasks at once: to develop an effective and equitable socioeconomic infrastructure to sustain their newly independent status and to either change the borders that had been imposed on them or create bases of political legitimacy within those borders. When experiments with a variety of political forms met with so resounding a defeat as the 1967 war, a reaction was triggered that signified nothing so much as a desire to return to the "good old days." It represented the Arabs' collective frustration at continued humiliation at the hands of imperial powers.

This conclusion is borne out by the fact that, as the ideologies sampled here demonstrate, these groups offer little in the way of specific political or economic plans. They expound on ideals but, like the pan-Arabists before them, they do not take into consideration the practical reality of economically and politically entrenched states. Indeed, in August 1985, at the Muslim Institute's annual meeting, nationalism was again condemned: "[M]odern nationalism is a peculiar product of western political development and has been introduced to the lands and people of Islam through colonialism . . . [and remains] an all-pervasive instrument of colonial and neo-colonial policies of *kufr* [heresy]."[64] The institute's recommendation: Dismantle national boundaries that divide Muslims against themselves. As we have seen in the case of pan-Arabism, this is far easier said than done.

Nor do these groups seem to recognize the intricacies of the one inspiration virtually all of them agree on, the thought of Ibn Taymiyya.

As we saw in Chapter Two, Ibn Taymiyya was also concerned with Arab unity, but he did not define it as political unity. He was well aware that political unity was impossible and said real unity is spiritual. In fact, he laid the foundations for separation of religious from political institutions, as did his early modernist (pre–World War I) followers (see Chapter Four). These thinkers recognized the need for democratically legitimated and therefore geographically limited governments, maintaining the role of Islam as the moral guide of the legitimating populace and the guarantor of Islamic government in whatever state it is implemented. Involving Islamic officials in the government itself, which gave them a vested interest in the status quo, inevitably compromised their objectivity. Perhaps more perniciously, it identified a particular governmental apparatus with Islam and therefore obscured Islamic universality. Unfortunately, therefore, in reverting to outmoded models of Islamic unity, the Islamic activists have inadvertently slowed the natural process of developing suitable political forms in geographically limited states. They have imposed on leaders in the region a political anachronism that, like the transnationalist pan-Arabist thought of the Ba'thists and Nasser, actually contributes to regional instability. Some of the practical results of trying to impose transnational legitimacy in a nationalist context will be discussed in the following chapter.

CHAPTER EIGHT

Straining
Traditional Models

L

*eaving aside the material historical reasons for the
failure of the Salafiyya, we . . . suggest that the inability
of the Salafiyya to come to grips with the inadequacies
of the doctrines they set about to revive constituted an intellectual
failure that contributed to the political failure.*

—Malcolm H. Kerr[1]

As we saw in Chapter Seven, Malcolm Kerr thought the Islamic activist
movements were finished in 1966. The Muslim Brothers had been
outlawed, and secularist governments were in power in most Islamic
states. He was wrong, of course; since 1967 there has been a revival
of the Muslim Brotherhood and a proliferation of other Islamic groups,
generally calling for a rejection of degenerate Western influence and
a return to authentically Islamic order. The success of the Islamic
revolution in Iran in 1979 has given new hope to these movements,
as did the assassination of Sadat in 1981. They are spurred on by
continued instability and underdevelopment in the region and by the
continued dispossession of the Palestinian people. Indeed, the plight
of the Palestinians is a rallying point for popular discontent throughout
the region, standing as a constant reminder of the failure of all Arab
leaders. The leaders' inability to put an end to the humiliation and
suffering of their people is taken as a sign of their moral weakness;

Portions of this chapter were published under the title "Secularism and National Stability
in Islam" in *Arab Studies Quarterly*, Vol. 9, No. 3 (Summer 1985):284–305.

surely such degradation is a punishment from God for religious laxity. The return to pristine Islam is, perhaps more than ever before, popularly believed to be the only hope. Monarchies, parliaments, socialism, capitalism, even the much-vaunted Arab unity have all been tried and none of them has been able to rally the Islamic world to victory.

Nevertheless, the inadequacies of original Salafiyya ideology referred to by Kerr are still evident. As noted in Chapter Seven, many of the Islamic reactionaries seem oblivious to the dynamics of state-building in a postcolonial context. They do not take into consideration the realities of entrenched power and, as a result, actually contribute to their own frustration. Worse yet, they contribute to the conditions that maintain the very instability among Arab rulers that is criticized so relentlessly. Captivation of the popular imagination by visions of a unified Islamic community, as the 1985 conference of the Muslim Institute put it, makes it virtually impossible for a leader to maintain popular appeal on any other basis. Thus, as we saw in Chapter Seven, even the most secularist and nationalist leaders, such as Syria's Hafiz al-Assad and Iraq's Saddam Hussein, give the requisite public attention to Islam. But it is clearly only a veneer. It is what they deem necessary to undermine bases of criticism and thus, hopefully, ward off any Islamic revolutions on their own soil. Meanwhile, behind closed doors, they follow the dictates of nationalist political exigency. What that does all too often is effectively preclude the meaningful participation of the populace in their own government. If they can be mollified by lip service to the Shari'a and support for officially sanctioned mosques, their democratic demands are indeed light. The development of political forms congruent with the sociopolitical and economic realities at hand is all but ignored. By making the Islamic piety of the leader the decisive factor in determining whether or not the society is Islamic, many Islamic activists effectively bypass the need for each individual to contribute to the society's direction.

Ignoring Ibn Taymiyya

Interestingly, that is just what Ibn Taymiyya pointed out in his work, although the implication seems to be ignored in contemporary appeals to his authority. As we saw in Chapter Two, Ibn Taymiyya emphasized that Islamic unity was spiritual, effected by uniform adherence to Islamic principles as established in Islamic law. In fact, Ibn Taymiyya believed that insistence on political unity could be harmful to the Islamic community. He thought the kind of exclusivism that keeps people tied to a tribal or ritual group actually militates against true Islamic unity. If, for instance, one faction—whether ideological or tribal/

ethnic—attains power and then chooses its agents and ministers from within itself, the result is discontent among other, equally qualified members of the community. Islam, he said, was supposed to supersede this sort of solidarity and replace it with moral solidarity, based on shared standards of piety, on shared goals, and on agreement concerning human destiny. Islamic unity, said Ibn Taymiyya, is spiritual unity, unanimous in encouraging goodness and denouncing inequity. The ideal Muslim community is mutually supportive—socially, spiritually, and even physically.

Ibn Taymiyya's was a revolutionary approach to Islamic unity, reorienting the nature of Islamic politics. It turned the tables on the caliphal administration. That administration was no longer the headquarters and arbiters of Muslim unity; the people were. Political unity as such was therefore relegated to a secondary position. For Ibn Taymiyya, political unity was not an essential characteristic of Islamic unity. In fact, it could be dispensed with, provided moral unity remains. Furthermore, if the community is expending its efforts on political unity through force, it may well be doing so at the expense of true Islamic endeavor. It is to the realization of God's will, the creation of a just society, that Muslims should devote their energies. This unity of endeavor was true Islamic solidarity for Ibn Taymiyya.

But the significance of this aspect of Ibn Taymiyya's thought has not yet been realized by many contemporary Islamic activists. Instead, like Pope John Paul II—who refers to the medieval Christian world as a "perfect society," presumably because the church was still the ultimate arbiter of political legitimacy—they tend to eulogize the past. They long for the idyllic time when Islam was the determining factor in political sovereignty. It is true that many Islamic activists recognize the importance of democracy in Islam. Hasan al-Banna, for instance, insisted that Islam is not a theocracy and that ultimate authority lies in the populace, guided by the divinely revealed principles of the Qur'an. That is why he and other ideologues for the Society of Muslim Brothers argue for the creation of truly democratic government. But at the same time, they seek political unity among Islamic states and, in that context, condemn geographically limited "statist" nationalism as part of "secularist" ideology. They continue to regard geographic limitation of political interest (nationalism) as an ideology, rather than a practical reality based in the political-economic structure of a given region.

Nor do they see that geographic limitation of political sovereignty congruent with those limited interests is a function of democracy. As we saw in Chapter One, democracy developed in Europe as a natural outgrowth of the breakup of the Holy Roman Empire. The legitimacy of the empire had been religious. An empire is characterized by fluid boundaries; it extends just as far as it can, which generally determined by its economic and military might. It therefore requires a basis of legitimacy that is also fluid, and a religion claiming universal (or potentially universal) validity fits the bill perfectly. Thus, as we saw, Christianity was the determinant of Holy Roman imperial legitimacy. When the regions of the empire broke free, they had to substitute some limited claim of legitimacy. At first it was the Reformation. The Holy Roman leaders were accused of being not so holy after all. Reformed versions of the religion were substituted for the papal version of Christianity. In the interim stage between the intact Holy Roman Empire and the rise of nation-states with borders recognized as sacrosanct, therefore, the Augsburg formula of *cujus regio, ejus religio* was implemented. Whoever was in political power, regardless of the means he had used to achieve it, was given the right to determine the religion of the realm. Eventually, on the basis of the principles of human dignity and freedom articulated by Reformation and Enlightenment thinkers, institutionalized religion was removed from the political sphere and the right to determine political forms was assumed by the people: democracy. Inherent in democracy was the limitation of political legitimacy to the borders within which the populace resided. Therefore, in the European experience, democracy grew out of religious principles and eventually served to legitimate geographically limited political sovereignty.

But according to Ibn Taymiyya, as well as his contemporary followers, Islam *starts* with democratic principles. The challenge now is to implement them, in order to give social footing to Islamic leadership representative of a responsible populace, regardless of geopolitical limitations. Until that is done, Islamic activist polemics will continue to provide leaders with a rhetorical tool useful for pursuing their own, not necessarily Islamic, ends. And more significantly, in the process, those polemics exacerbate the tensions among regional leaders that so destabilize the Arab world. For just as the Egyptian, Syrian, and Iraqi regimes compete for supremacy in a unified *Arab* state, those regimes that base themselves on Islamic legitimacy compete for supremacy in a unified *Islamic* nation. The result is the same: mutual suspicion precluding real cooperation at virtually any level.

Libya

One of the most interesting examples of these problems is in Libya, technically outside the Arab world but nonetheless involved in the dilemmas of the Salafiyya movement. Libya scholar Lisa Anderson has provided an enlightening review of Libya's traditional appeal to Islam as the basis of national political legitimacy.[2] Anderson points out that Libya as a national entity did not exist until 1934, when Italy consolidated three previously discrete regional entities: Tripolitania, Cyrenaica, and Fezzan. These provinces had traditionally maintained their autonomy, each having different sociocultural and political orientations. It was primarily colonial domination that brought them together in the first place, so they could fight their common enemy from across the Mediterranean. Following the Axis defeat in World War II, the Allies took control of formerly occupied territories and finally granted Libya independence in 1951. But before they left they wanted to appoint an agreeable king. The most obvious thing the three provinces had in common was Islam, so the Allies chose the leader of the Sanusis, a nineteenth-century Islamic brotherhood indigenous to the area. However, the three provinces continued to function autonomously; what legitimacy the king had on a national level was purely religious. As Anderson puts it, "He was widely reputed to be personally pious and his neglect of the day-to-day politics of his realm seemed to suggest . . . that he was attending to the less mundane concerns of the community of the faithful."[3]

It was the discovery of oil in 1959 that made the national bureaucracy in Libya a significant entity; suddenly there was a reason for the state of Libya to exist other than the fact that European powers had said it should. That, combined with the growing influence of Nasser's charismatic appeal to Arab (trans)nationalism, prepared Libya for more self-conscious leadership. The coup that brought Mu'ammar al-Qadhafi to power in 1969, despite its avowed goals of nonalignment and international neutrality, marked the end of Libya's apolitical status, for also among Qadhafi's goals was domestic populism. And the most effective vehicle for to achieve that populism—the only model in Libya's history—was Islamic sentiment. Qadhafi therefore immediately reinstated many elements of Islamic law (expunged when the Italians took over the provinces in 1911) and gave religious scholars positions of prominence in the administration. It was this reliance on Islamic legitimacy that would ultimately embroil Qadhafi in regional disputes.

Despite Qadhafi's inclusion of religious scholars in his government, he still craved independent authority. He did not appreciate criticism of his reforms by the *'ulama'*. In what can be construed as an attempt to secure an independent basis of legitimacy, therefore, he eventually formulated his own ideology, the Third International Theory, contained in the three volumes of his *Green Book.* (Qadhafi ensured that his interpretation of Islam would not be confused with others by initiating a unique calendar for Islamic Libya. Instead of beginning in the year

622 C.E., as the standard Islamic calendar does, Libya's calendar begins in the year 632 C.E., the year the Prophet died.) In the *Green Book* he specifically states that while the Third International Theory is based on both religion and nationalism, it is an "international ideology, not a national movement."[4]

What Qadhafi means is that any national entity has the right to exist free of oppression and colonial domination. He believes the principles he has extracted from Islam are universal. All nations have the right to establish their own political and religious identities. For that reason he supports what he considers liberation movements around the world. Nevertheless, his own claims to Islamic purity are a form of religious legitimacy, understandably considered threatening by other leaders in the Islamic world. If Qadhafi's is true Islamic leadership, then, by implication, theirs is not. The colonel's operations in the Sudan and Chad are therefore taken as evidence of Qadhafi's expansionist plans. Egypt, in particular, feels threatened. A shadowy group known as Egypt's Revolution that operates out of Libya took responsibility for the assassination of several Israelis in Egypt in the mid-1980s. In late 1986 the group publicly threatened terrorist strikes on Americans and Israelis in Cairo, which were taken seriously enough that the authorities stepped up security around the United States and Israeli embassies, even issuing new license plate numbers to protect the identities of diplomatic personnel.[5]

Whether or not Qadhafi is considered capable of actually achieving the regional unity he desires, his appeal to Islamic unity is clearly perceived as a potent force. It is a truism that success is self-legitimating. Inversely, political failures of the Arab leaders under colonialism, military dictatorships, monarchies, and secularist parliamentary forms have militated against the popular adoption of those political forms. As has been noted, the challenges facing the Arab leaders are highly complex: underdevelopment and attendant social problems such as social dislocation, rapid urbanization, and widespread illiteracy; reckoning with geographic borders where previously none existed; nurturing appropriate political forms within those borders; and developing cooperative relationships with neighboring states, themselves engrossed in such monumental challenges. The Arab states' challenges are further complicated by the existence of unprecedented wealth, generated by the export of oil, in an otherwise underdeveloped region. Oil is a source of great power for those few who control it, but only to the extent that they are willing to accommodate a world market. (All the oil in the world will be of little use if it cannot be sold and if the wealth it earns cannot be spent, saved, or otherwise invested in developed economies.) Such enormous challenges will take years—generations, if not centuries—to solve. Success will not be dramatic; it will come in increments. Gradually, equilibrium will be reached and the political form in place at the time will achieve legitimacy. But in the meanwhile, Arab leaders acknowledge the expediency of bowing to the demands of Islamic legitimacy. They have learned through the examples of the shah and Sadat the wages of precipitous action. The best laid plans of economic and social engineers can go awry for failure to consider the sensibilities of those whose futures are being planned. Therefore, Arab leaders vie with each other in "Islamicity."

Unfortunately, however, this is itself part of the problem. In their enthusiasm to present themselves as Islamically legitimate, many even resort to condemnations of others' impiety, a convenient gauge of orthodoxy. In the case of both Iran's and Syria's support of Islamic opposition groups in Iraq, for instance, we saw how competitive regimes can use religious groups to undermine their opponents' national stability. But even without such direct intervention, the requisite language of Islamic orthodoxy feeds regional instability. One can never trust a neighbor who claims that his deed also includes one's own property. That is why Qadhafi's blatant appeal to Islam has led to his virtual isolation among regional leaders. As Anderson concludes in her study, "The importance of Islam in Libya also reflects . . . in its individual way the larger questions of political identity in the Muslim Arab world, where the *raison d'être* of the state remains unresolved."[6]

Iran, Iraq, and Salman Rushdie

Ayatollah Khomeini's war against Iraq was another example of the destabilizing effect of imposing religiously legitimated government in a nationalist context. Iraq and Iran have always been distinct entities, the former being Semitic Arab and the latter an Indo-Aryan culture. Iran had a long and illustrious history of political and self-styled cultural sophistication, even when the Islamic empire arose in the seventh and eighth centuries. The Iranians were therefore determined to distinguish between the *Islamic* hegemony spread through their lands by the Arabs and any presumption of *Arab* hegemony. As noted in Chapter Two, the issue of Persian cultural superiority figured highly in the 'Abbasid revolution of 750. Iran never rejected Islam, but it has jealously guarded its distinct identity within the Islamic world from the very beginning.

The Iranian intellectual tradition is also very different from that of the Arabs. Although there were periods of compromise and cooperation between the Persians and the Arabs, such as in the revolution that brought the 'Abbasids to power, the Persians maintained their cultural solidarity vis-à-vis the Arabs, an identity that often exhibited itself as a Persian superiority complex. From the ninth century, Persian discontent tended to rally around Shi'ism. It is not that political grievances were masquerading as religious protest. Again, just as in medieval Europe, the only model of leadership was combined religious-political authority. The very criterion of criticism was a discrepancy between the values espoused by the legitimating ideology and the effect of the policies implemented in the name of those values. Therefore, questioning the leadership was indistinguishable from questioning its piety or spirituality. It was in this context that Shi'ism, promising closer conformity of Islamic values and practice than exhibited by the Sunni caliphs, became the language of opposition. And just as in Europe, criticism of the government was countered with accusations ranging from religious deviation to heresy.

In their effort to parry the threat posed by the sophisticated Persians, the 'Abbasids, more than any other Arab leaders, fostered the development of a scholarly tradition in Islam. As we saw in Chapter Two, "orthodox" Islam became the ideology on which 'Abbasid legitimacy was based and, at the same time, the tool they would use against those who challenged their position.

Very similar to the conflict in medieval Europe over nominalism, for instance (see Chapter One), the test of orthodoxy came to be the issue of whether or not the Qur'an had been created. Some had said it was co-eternal with God, nothing less than a reflection of divine will. The implication of this position was that only the Qur'an was the arbiter of orthodoxy; even the caliph was subject to its authority. The opponents of this view, applying Greek philosophical principles, distinguished between God's *essence,* eternal and transcendent, and God's *word.* The latter was created, knowable, and therefore, ultimately, open to interpretation. And as such, it needed an interpreter. This position effectively established a basis for the Shi'i opposition to the 'Abbasid caliphate and for the Shi'i theory of leadership. Contrary to the essentially democratic Sunni model, the Shi'is championed the position that direct divine guidance of the *umma* did not end with the Prophet's death. It continued in the person of the *mahdi,* and if there was no *mahdi* around (the last one died—or, according to Shi'i belief, went into "occultation"—in the ninth century), then divine guidance continued through his spokesmen, the religious scholars.

We saw in Chapter Two that the Sunni caliphate eventually had its fill of such rationalism. They tried to stifle further questioning of their legitimacy by stifling intellectualism. The Shi'is, by contrast, encouraged intellectualism. It was their weapon against Arab hegemony. It was under these conditions that Persian culture produced the great philosophical tradition for which the Islamic world is so well known in the West.

Upon the demise of 'Abbasid control, various groups of Turkic tribesmen gained dominance and set up autonomous governments in much of the former 'Abbasid domain. Persian culture was only able to reassert itself in the sixteenth century, following the decline of the Mongols. It was then that Shah ("king" in Persian, i.e., not a religiously legitimated position) Isma'il (r. 1501–1524) established the Persian Safavid dynasty. This was at the same time the Sunni Ottomans were advancing from their Anatolian centers, under the banner of Sunni orthodoxy. To distinguish the two realms once and for all, then, Shah Isma'il proclaimed Persia thenceforth officially Shi'i. The Safavid successors (from whom the Pahlavis took control) followed the same path, declaring their regimes legitimate in the absence of the *mahdi.*

Considering this legacy, therefore, it should not be surprising that of all people in the world who would dispute the claim to Arab dominance within Islam—so pervasive a theme in the Arab Islamic revival—it would be the Iranians. It is, in fact, an egregious error to equate the Islamic resurgence in the Arab world with that in Iran. The issues that gave rise to both movements are quite similar, as are the complications stemming from them. But the Persian and Arab cultures remain unique identities, regardless of ideological similarities.

This is the background of the quarrel Iran and Iraq have carried on over their mutual boundaries at the head of the Gulf. Boundary disputes were the proximate cause of the war. The two countries have been quarrelling over their boundaries for centuries. The traditional boundary is the Shatt al-Arab River, which empties into the Gulf. By the turn of the twentieth century it was fairly well agreed that Iran had sovereignty over Khizr Island (located at the mouth of the Shatt) and that Ottoman Iraq was in control of the waterway itself.[7] However, as Iran's might grew, it tended to treat the entire lower Shatt as its own territory. In 1975, Iraq agreed to legalize that practice; it placed the boundary in the middle of the waterway, giving each nation equal access. In return, Iran was asked to cease its support for Iraq's Kurdish rebels. But Iraq never felt satisfied with the agreement. At that time, Iran, thanks to oil wealth (vastly enhanced by the 1973 oil embargo) and United States patronage, had become a massive military power. Iraq felt it had had little choice but to go along with Iran's terms. The period of disorder following the overthrow of the shah seemed like a good time to redress Iraq's grievances. In 1980, therefore, following a series of border clashes, Iraq revoked the 1975 agreement, and the war was on.

But these border disputes were only the proximate cause of the war. Just as in the case of Libya's isolation, the broader issue is, in Lisa Anderson's words, "the *raison d'être* of the state." Lacking clearly defined criteria for state legitimacy, virtually all leaders in the region rely on Islamic sentiment for what popular support they have. While most of them generally accept the limits of their sovereignty, all must look with suspicion on those who seem to want to take the religious aspect of their legitimacy to its logical—expansive—conclusion. And if the isolation of Qadhafi among Arab leaders is a result of mere suspicions, the Iran-Iraq war is a reflection of articulated expansionist aims. It is, in fact, a paradigm of the inevitable entanglements resulting from using a form of unlimited political legitimacy in a region full of geographically limited political entities.

As we saw in Chapter Seven, more than any other ruler in the region, Saddam Hussein has reason to fear the spread of the Iranian revolution. The close relationship between the dissident Iraqi Da'wa Party and the Iranian regime and the latter's open courting of the Shi'i majority in Sunni-dominated Iraq clearly violate Iraqi sovereignty. And Ayatollah Khomeini's demands for cessation of hostilities went much farther than merely settling border disputes. In fact, as he reiterated throughout the eight years of warfare, nothing short of Saddam Hussein's overthrow would satisfy him.

The cessation of hostilities between the countries, prompted largely by economic pressures on both sides, thus placed Khomeini in a rather uncomfortable situation. He had based his legitimacy on Islamic fidelity. But Islamic law was formulated in the prenationalist context. Just as in 'Abbasid times, it technically recognizes only one legitimate state per religion. Therefore, of course, it lacks extensive legislation regulating relations among multiple Islamic states. What it does is forbid Islamic infighting, calling instead for arbitration. In particular, it forbids revolution against an Islamic leader, even if the leader is perceived to be as impious as Khomeini described Saddam Hussein to be. The only kind of war Islam permits is *jihad,* and *jihad* is only to be waged against nonbelievers. Therefore, Khomeini was forced to perform *takfir*—to declare Saddam Hussein a heretic—in order to justify hostilities. Anyway, territorial disputes are the language of nationalism, and nationalism was anathema to Khomeini's version of Islamic unity. *Takfir,* on the other hand, is the language of *jihad,* and *jihad* is at least Islamic. Indeed, Khomeini repeatedly claimed that the war was not only against Iraq. Baghdad was just a step on the way to Jerusalem, he said. The war was the beginning of the end of all secularist governments and the reestablishment of true Islamic sovereignty. That was why Khomeini could not compromise with Iraq to settle the war.

Having declared Saddam Hussein an infidel in order to justify the war in the first place, he could hardly then sit down with the man and negotiate a settlement. But when the Iran-Iraq war ended and Saddam Hussein had not been overthrown, Baghdad had not been taken, and the Islamic world was no closer to reclaiming Jerusalem, Ayatollah Khomeini found himself in a bind. He was in the awkward position of having to justify negotiating with the wicked Hussein to the millions of citizens who lost sons and brothers in the war. No matter what happened, he could only look like a failure. In fact, the furor over the recent novel *The Satanic Verses*, by Indian expatriate and ex-Muslim Salman Rushdie, was at least partially explained by the ayatollah's quandary. The Islamic sentiment that Khomeini commanded among the masses both within and outside Iran was simply redirected. The threat to Islam posed by Saddam Hussein was eclipsed, we were asked to believe, by the likes of Salman Rushdie. The ayatollah could hardly have been expected to fight two wars at one time. Rushdie, a lone writer in London exploring the plight of marginality shared by so many victims of cultural imperialism, may seem an unlikely substitute for the military dictator of Iran's oil-rich neighbor, Iraq. But when it became apparent Iran could not win the war, the ayatollah needed to focus public attention elsewhere, and Rushdie's work seemed convenient. This is evidenced by the fact that the offending book had been introduced to Iran in the autumn of 1988 with little reaction. At that time *The Satanic Verses* was reviewed in an Iranian religious journal, very negatively, and then ignored. It was not until February 1989, when the Iran-Iraq war was over, that the ayatollah's attention was caught by a violent demonstration against the book in Pakistan. Interestingly, the day before the ayatollah spoke out against Rushdie's work, a political opponent of the ayatollah's son, Ahmad Khomeini, announced that he would run for the presidency in the summer of 1989. The political opponent, then House Speaker Hashemi Rafsanjani, was known for his moderate approach toward the West. In particular, he favored rapprochement at least to the extent of accepting loans in order to rebuild Iran's postwar economy. As one observer put it, "The Rushdie affair gave the Ayatollah the excuse he needed to throw all his weight behind [those who reject cooperation with the West]."[8]

Another revealing aspect of the Rushdie affair was the reaction of other Muslims in the region. Even within Iran noted clerics were reluctant to support the ayatollah's death sentence against the author. At least three of Iran's other ayatollahs are reported to have rejected Khomeini's decision; having never read the book they refused to judge it. More pertinently, the reaction toward the book in the Arab world was noticeably subdued. Because of Arab fears, particularly in the Gulf, that the ayatollah was attempting to exploit Islamic sentiment to his own benefit, they were very cautious in handling the affair. As Nadim Jaber observed:

> The fear in the conservative, Sunni states of the region is that Khomeini's hardline stance on *The Satanic Verses* controversy could, in addition to a domestic political manoeuvre, be an attempt to reassert that extra-territorial role. They see Iran's behavior partly as a bid . . . to rebuild Iran's status as champion of Muslim causes, and to contrast this with the relative inaction of leaders in the conservative Sunni countries.[9]

The Iraqi press therefore downplayed the entire affair, while the Saudis tried to distinguish the Iranian reaction to Rushdie from a "truly" Islamic response. And Egyptian *'ulama'* generally confined their official comments to the inapplicability of Islamic law outside the Muslim world.

Khomeini's response to Rushdie's book therefore appears to fit the pattern imposed by recourse to religious legitimation of his government. That government earned legitimacy through self-proclaimed Islamic orthodoxy; it was, therefore, his duty, he said, to fight disbelief until the entire world submits to the rule of God. That was why he had to overthrow Saddam Hussein. But he did not overthrow Saddam Hussein. Lest anyone draw the implication that he was as vile as he said all the other Muslim leaders were, because they let the Iraqi leader go un-challenged, or, even worse, lest anyone think that perhaps God was not on Iran's side in the holy war, Khomeini tried to distract attention from Iraq and cast Salman Rushdie—"this treacherous man . . . and his blasphemous book"—as an even greater threat to worldwide Islam.[10]

Ideological Acrobatics

These are some of the practical problems resulting from the application of standards of political legitimacy suitable for empires (expansive) to states (limited). Expansive regimes violate other Muslims' territory. But Islamic law does not allow war among Muslims. So the enemies must be declared either non-Muslims or heretics. Then one can declare *jihad*. Indeed, the calls for return to true Islam are almost always made in the name of *jihad*. *Jihad* is the mechanism by which Islam is to be not only spread throughout the world, but also revived in the Islamic world, as a glance at the names of the revivalist groups reveals: Society of Muslims for Takfir, Society of Takfir, al-Jihad, Denouncers of Infidels, Jihad Organization, Takfir and Hijrah, Soldiers of God, Soldiers of al-

Rahman (one of the Islamic names for God), Party of Islamic Revolution, the Fighters of Jihad, Islamic Jihad, etc.[11]

Not surprisingly, this interpretation of *jihad* represents a significant deviation from the path followed by the pre–World War I modernists. As described in Chapter Four, that period was characterized by efforts to develop the political infrastructure required to sustain regional claims for independence from the imperial Ottomans. In that period, *jihad* did not play a major role. It was generally confined to cases of personal piety and self-defense. Military *jihad* was to be fought only as a last resort, in the case of external military attack.[12] Muslims were reminded that although military *jihad* appears to be a thing of the past, they still have the responsibility to use all their energies to create a healthy and stable society. Even Muhammad 'Abduh's disciple Rashid Rida claimed, "Everything mentioned in the Qur'an with regard to the rules of fighting is intended as defense against enemies who fight the Muslims because of their religion."[13] Instead of concentrating on warfare, emphasis was placed on efforts to develop Islamic institutions congruent with the political reality.

But the betrayal of the Arabs by the British and French following the war and the imposition of the mandates fostered a reaction against capitalist powers that led to the rise of socialist regimes in Syria, Iraq, and Egypt. Then, the Arab defeats at the hands of Israel in 1948 and especially in 1967, intensified by the apparent impotence of all the reigning Arab powers, sparked a reactionary movement. It seemed the only form of government that had not been tried was that originally established by Prophet Muhammad. And in Arab memory, that was the only form that had brought them strength and success. Ibn Taymiyya had warned the Muslims more than six hundred years before that if they did not return to truly Islamic government, they would fall into disarray. Indeed, they had; Ibn Taymiyya thus became the prophet of contemporary Islam. But the new generation of activists had considerably narrowed the movement begun with the early modernists. Continued political setbacks in the region had placed primary emphasis on the call to revive Islam and proportionately less emphasis on efforts to reformulate Islamic practice to accommodate modern realities. In the extreme cases there was a tendency, in fact, to reject any nonindigenous form—especially those employed in the West—as un-Islamic.

But because the pious ancestors (the Salaf) did not have to deal with the socioeconomic structures that shape modern society, they did not formulate legislation regulating those structures, much less their political ramifications. To have legislated concerning multiple Islamic states would have implied that the caliph was not, in fact, the imam, the *amir al-mu'minin*, the leader of a unified and potentially universal

Islamic geopolitical entity. Instead, the Islamic jurisprudents—who were, after all, under the authority of the caliph—recognized only one legitimate Islamic ruler. Islamic law therefore forbids both revolution and warfare among Muslims. As a result, contemporary Islamic activists have been forced to subsume the reality of multiple Islamic states and any rivalry among them under the rubric of the only kind of warfare Islamic law permits, *jihad*.

That is why in the contemporary Islamic activist movements—contrary to the Shari'a's strict distinction between *jihad* and revolution—*jihad* is indistinguishable from revolution. Hasan al-Banna, for instance, based his observations on what he considered the revolutionary nature of Islam. Islam, he said, is by its very nature a revolution against socio-economic injustice—as rampant in pre-Islamic Arabia as it is today. He attacked the early modernists' emphasis on *jihad* of the spirit: personal *jihad* or, as it is usually called "greater *jihad*." This notion is based on a hadith report according to which Prophet Muhammad said, upon returning from a raid, "We have now returned from the lesser jihad to the greater jihad." Asked the meaning of this greater *jihad,* he replied that it was the struggle for self-control against temptations to evil. Al-Banna correctly points out that this cannot be considered an authentic hadith because it is not from one of the authoritative collections. But he goes on to claim that it was actually spread deliberately in order to weaken the Muslims' will to fight.[14] Sayyid Qutb, al-Banna's ideological successor, furthers this argument, saying Muslims do not have the leisure to simply keep to themselves unless attacked. Their task, enjoined by the Qur'an, is "establishing the kingdom of God on earth and bringing all humanity from worship of created things to the worship of God alone."[15] Elsewhere Qutb says the primary mission of Islam is "to change the [prevailing unjust] condition and make it better."[16] For as he quotes the Qur'an, "God does not change what is in a people until they change what is in themselves" (13:11).

Furthermore, Muslims will know when they have succeeded. The Qur'an says, "God has promised those of you who believe and do good works that he will make you his viceregents on earth as he has made others before you. He will surely establish for them their religion . . . and will exchange their fear for security" (24:55). Islam is therefore the only basis for political legitimacy. Until truly (not just nominally) Islamic governments are established, Qutb says, Muslims must take up the struggle to change the status quo. In Qutb's words, "Islam . . . has to deliver blows at the political forces that make men the slaves of something that is not Allah, i.e., that do not rule them according to the Shari'a and the authority of Allah, those forces that prevent them from hearing the elucidation and from freely embracing the creed, without being hindered by any authority."[17]

Qutb does not distinguish between Muslim and non-Muslim "political forces." Presumably then, even Muslim leaders, if they do not institutionalize Islamic politics, are also the object of struggle (*jihad*). This, at any rate, is the implication taken by the group responsible for the assassination of Sadat. They claim it is their responsibility to overthrow governments that do not rule according to Islamic law, basing their claim on the Qur'anic verse, "Those who do not judge/govern in accordance with what God has revealed are unbelievers" (5:44). According to this reasoning, even though Sadat claimed to be Muslim, because he did not implement Islamic law, he really was not. It was therefore incumbent on them as Muslims to eliminate him. In the name of *jihad* they say, "To the leaders of Islamic groups today: Kill every leader who looks for fame, wealth, power and social station . . . ," instead of Islamic purity.[18]

This group, like Sayyid Qutb, took inspiration from another leader of anti-Westernism, Abu'l-'A'la Mawdudi (d. 1979). Islam, Mawdudi says, "is an all-embracing order that wants to eliminate and eradicate the other orders which are false and unjust so as to replace them with good order and a moderate program that is considered to be better than [all] others. . . ."[19] Emphasizing the practical rather than the spiritual side of Islam, Mawdudi claims Islamic law has clearly established specific institutions and regulations necessary for the virtuous conduct of human life:

> Islam has a concept and a practical program, especially chosen for the happiness and progress of human society. . . . Its aim is to make this concept victorious, to introduce this program universally, to set up governments that are firmly rooted in this concept and this program, irrespective of who carries the banner of truth and justice or whose flag of aggression and corruption is thereby toppled. Islam wants the whole earth and does not content itself with only a part thereof.[20]

This program is ensconced in Islamic law, he says. Only when the Shari'a is established as the supreme law of the land everywhere can Muslims cease their struggle. This, of course, means that not only must non-Muslim governments be replaced, but so must any Muslim states that do not implement Shari'a. And how is this to be achieved?

> In order to realize this lofty desire, Islam wants to employ all forces and means that can be employed for bringing about a universal, all-embracing revolution. It will spare no efforts for the achievement of this supreme

objective. This far-reaching struggle that continuously exhausts all forces and this employment of all possible means is called *jihad*.[21]

So for Mawdudi, as for Sayyid Qutb, revolution against an Islamic leader deemed impious is as much a part of *jihad* as spreading Islam to non-Muslims. The two terms—*jihad* and *thawra*—are interchangeable for them. They are both enjoined by the same Qur'anic injunction to expend every effort in the way of God.

This was the major theme of Ayatollah Khomeini's program of revolutionary Islam. Expounding at length on the West's plundering of the third world, he called upon all Muslims, and especially religious scholars, to put an end to it. This effort is the "sacred *jihad*." For him, too, *jihad* includes overthrowing Muslim rulers: "Give the people Islam, then, for Islam is the school of *jihad*, the religion of struggle; let them amend their characters and beliefs in accordance with Islam, and transform themselves into a powerful force, so that they may overthrow the tyrannical regime imperialism has imposed on us and set up an Islamic government."[22]

Khomeini frequently cited the example of Shi'i struggles against the Umayyads, for instance, to evoke the aura of Islam-as-revolution. To further support his position, he pronounced a series of legal opinions (fatwas) dealing with revolutionary activities. For example:

If the evil [that is to be forbidden] is of a kind accorded great importance by the Sacred Legislator, one that he in no wise wishes to occur, it is permissible to prevent it by any means possible. If someone wishes to kill another, for example, in the absence of legal justification, he must be prevented. If the killing of the wronged party cannot be prevented except by killing the wrongdoer, then it is permissible, even necessary to do so.[23]

And he specifically included leaders of Muslim countries as prime candidates for this action: "If certain heads of state of Muslim countries . . . permit foreigners to expand their influence . . . they automatically forfeit their posts. . . . Furthermore, it is the duty of the Muslims to punish them by any means possible."[24]

Isolation of Iran and Libya

It is no wonder then that the Arab League recently pronounced Iran the source of instability in the Middle East. At the Amman summit in November 1987, for the first time in the League's history, Palestine was not the focus of attention and Israel was not identified as the major threat in the region.[25] The incitement to revolution emanating from Iran was.

In particular, the summit denounced the "bloody and criminal acts perpetrated by the Iranians" in Mecca the previous summer. In July and August of 1987 Iranian pilgrims had begun a demonstration during the annual *Hajj* pilgrimage that turned into several days of rioting. Despite the Islamic injunction against political activity and violence of any sort during the pilgrimage, as well as the traditional prohibition of religious images, the Iranian pilgrims carried pictures of Khomeini, demonstrated against the United States and Israel, and burned effigies of Ronald Reagan.[26] Violence erupted when Saudi security forces attempted to suppress the demonstration. Operating on an order issued by Ayatollah Khomeini entitled "Charter for Revolution," their "splendid demonstration" resulted in over four hundred deaths and six hundred fifty injuries. When the leaders of the demonstrations were caught, they informed the Saudi security forces that the ayatollah had called upon his followers to rally in unity in Mecca and demonstrate their commitment to "deliverance from the infidels"—the United States and Israel and their allies. Khomeini had told them that pilgrims should "not refrain from giving expression to their hatred of the enemies of God and man." More distressing still to the Arab leaders, the leaders of the demonstration declared that their goal was to make Ayatollah Khomeini the leader of all Muslims.

This was the last straw for the Arabs. Heightened activity by Iranian revolutionaries had been observed throughout the region. Violent incidents involving Islamic activist groups were almost routine in Egypt: fires set at shops selling liquor, attacks on Christian cultural groups, attacks on individuals considered enemies of Islam. The government controls only about a quarter of Egypt's thirty thousand mosques. Its efforts to expand that control became another source of constant conflict between the government and the Islamic activist groups. The government believed these incidents reflected growing Iranian influence in the country. Therefore, in May 1986, Egypt expelled the only Iranian diplomat in Cairo and recalled its own representatives on the grounds "Iran was providing support for clandestine extremist Islamic organizations in Egypt."[27] Saudi Arabia also contributes a good deal of support to Islamic groups in Egypt, but that is generally channelled to those groups, like the Muslim Brothers, which have ceased calls for violent revolution. (See below, Chapter Nine.) The Iran-supported groups, on the other hand, like al-Jihad, call for armed struggle against the "infidel" Arab government.

At the same time, Iran was conspicuously increasing its presence in Lebanon. At least three Lebanese Shi'i factions have become virtual clients of Iran: the antinationalist Shi'i Hizbullah, the Islamic Amal (an offshoot of the Lebanese nationalist Shi'i Amal), and a Lebanese branch of the Shi'i Da'wa Party. The continued failure of Lebanese nationalists to achieve peace has caused a significant increase in the popularity of these Islamic activist groups. This is, of course, enhanced by the relative wealth of these groups. In an economy devastated by nearly fifteen years of civil war—where frequently the only job available is in a militia—infusions of Iranian capital have made it a buyer's market for the Shi'i activist groups. What is more, by 1987 there were reportedly over two thousand Iranian Revolutionary Guards stationed in the Beqaa Valley, and hundreds more in the South.

Indeed, Iran's growing presence in Lebanon was considered such a threat that it prompted significant realignments both within and outside that beleaguered pseudo-state. For example, despite Syria's cooperation with Iran against Syria's Ba'thist competitor, Iraq, Syria began to distance itself from Iran because of the latter's presence in Lebanon. Syria sought reconciliation among several of Lebanon's most important factions, particularly the Druze and the Lebanese nationalist Shi'i majority, Amal, in an effort to offset Iran's growing influence on Syria's doorstep. The United States was so concerned about Iran's influence in Lebanon that it began to soften its attitude toward Syria. Because of the United States' relationship with Israel, which considers Syria its most formidable foe in the region, the Americans have generally opposed Syria's efforts to establish hegemony in Lebanon. However, faced with the possibility of Iranian hegemony instead, it now appears the United States considers Syria the lesser of two evils.

This, unfortunately, left Libya to play the role of America's enemy in the Middle East all by itself. The United States insists on demonstrating its distaste for "state terrorism" in the region. Iran, Iraq and Syria would best qualify for that designation even under America's distinctly biased rubric. But the United States could not "make an example" out of those countries. It considered Iraq the aggrieved party in the Iran-Iraq war, and it wanted to foster Syrian cooperation against Iran. And, in view of the arms sales to Iran revealed in the Iran-Contra affair, the United States does not seem to have known *what* it was doing with Iran. The best evidence indicates that the plan to sell arms to Iran originated in Israel, in line with Israel's traditional policy of supporting the "enemies of its enemies." On at least two levels, this suited U.S. policy; by the Israeli government's assessment, it helped America's ally keep its enemies fragmented and unstable, and it provided a handy source of funds to channel into the United States' undeclared war in Nicaragua. Clearly, however, it was a policy at cross-purposes with the United States' official position, which was in solidarity with the Arab states' support of Iraq in the conflict. In any event, Libya—already isolated in the region owing to Qadhafi's pan-Arabist and Islamic activist rhetoric, and not strong enough to pose a military threat to either the United States or Israel—appeared to the United States the only safe target for its militarist bravado.

Conclusion

Again, the essential differences between the kind of political legitimacy called for in the classical formulations of Islamic law and its contemporary revivalists and that suggested by the early Islamic modernists: In the former, unity required absolute obedience even to an unjust ruler. In the latter, unity required transcendence of religious factionalism and equality for all religions under the law. In the former, the locus of unity was the leader; it was submission to his rule that defined the extent of power. In the latter, it was a geographically limited regional entity. Sovereignty extended only as far as the voices of the people could be heard. Islamic law on political sovereignty was formulated in a prenationalist context. Since political authority was legitimated by religious affiliation, there were laws condemning every sort of dissidence and protest against the central government. But there were no laws regulating interstate relations since only one state per religion was recognized. The early modernists' formulations—like that of Ibn Taymiyya—were attempts to come to grips with the new political reality of multiple Islamic states existing in a non-Muslim world.

The Islamic activists proliferated at a time when the best efforts of the modernists had failed. Their failure was due chiefly to the machinations of European imperial interests, later enhanced by American efforts at maintaining a foothold in the Middle East through unfaltering support for Israel. But the Islamic activists interpreted the failure as a result of deviation from classic Islamic practice. In particular, they focussed on secularism—which they describe as the separation of church and state—as the source of Western immorality and Arab/Islamic decadence. No doubt the contemporary Islamic activists have good reason to condemn the West. They point to the moral bankruptcy of its policies that have led to so much misery in the third world, and take that as evidence of the need for the union of religion and politics. They see secularism as an ideology, designed by the devil himself to destroy the integrity of God's kingdom on earth. But, in fact, an amoral and factionalized society would have been as repugnant to the Reformation thinkers who advocated the separation of church and state as it is to contemporary religious thinkers in the East *and* West. A John Calvin or Martin Luther would never have considered their formulations devoid of religious merit. These men simply claimed that the failure of religiously legitimated sovereigns to conform to well-known principles of morality rendered them no longer eligible to act as intermediaries between God and people. They sought to safeguard morality by making it the responsibility of each believer. Secondarily, removing institutionalized religion from the political arena paved the way for developing forms of limited political legitimacy. But the moral and ethical values involved were no less religiously sanctioned for all that. In fact, some of the early reforms described the new political formation (the state) as a *corpus mysticum,* a "mystical body," just as the church had been called.[28]

Secularism, therefore, is not an ideology. It began as an effort to safeguard the ethical purity of religion, and resulted in the development of mechanisms of political legitimacy other than that accorded by the church. The leader's legitimacy depended upon his/her adherence to those principles agreed upon by the populace, on the basis of their religio-moral training, as conducive to their well-being. Secularism, that is, made possible the development of democratic forms of political legitimacy.

That, in turn, made possible the development of two key elements of states' political stability. First, democratically legitimated government is effectively limited to the territory inhabited by the legitimating population, thus removing the source of competitive interstate legitimacy claims. Secondly, it provides a mechanism for orderly change of government. No longer were rulers sacrosanct, having derived their legitimacy from God or God's representatives. Instead, their legitimacy was a function of their adherence to a given set of directives or ethical principles. Judgement of such adherence was the province of the people governed, and if they found it lacking, it was their right and responsibility to replace the leadership. This was no doubt an improvement over the previous situation; in a religiously legitimated government, criticism of the political authority was indistinguishable from heresy—the legitimating religion being in control of the legislation on such matters. Therefore, the only justification for changing leadership was accusation of heterodoxy, and, provided one claimed ideological purity, even socially destructive programs and ineffective leadership could not merit dismissal.

The indiscriminate opposition to separation of religious from political sovereignty, so common among contemporary Islamic activists, neglects the significance of these developments. Granted, it is an effort to excise the sources of moral corruption and sociopolitical instability; Islam is seen as the ultimate source of social and political strength and therefore the best basis of political legitimacy. Islamic activists reacted against imperialist societies. But secularism, although indeed a component of

Western statecraft, is not the source of moral bankruptcy. The separation of religious from political legitimacy is instead a vital element in nation-building. It is a natural step in the breakdown of empires and the emergence of geographically limited states. In thwarting that step, the antisecularists have inadvertently sown the seeds of yet another source of instability. For they ignore the primary requirements of national stability: a source of political legitimacy logically congruent with the state's geographic boundaries and its corollorary, a means for orderly change of governments. Where Islam is articulated as the sole basis of political legitimacy, ignoring factors of natural social or geographic limitaton, Islamic states find themselves in conflict with other states, both non-Muslim and Muslim. In the former case, their efforts may be justified in classic terms of holy war, but in the latter the only justification can be accusation of infidelity: *jihad* via *takfir*. And as demonstrated in the Iran-Iraq war, such activity exacerbates, rather than alleviates the plight of the people involved.

CHAPTER NINE

Trends and Prospects for the Future

*T*he longer interstate boundaries survive, the more they
become etched into the political and cultural landscape.
. . . As a whole, the boundary system of the [Middle
East] is youthful and in places remains to be allocated or properly
delimited, but it is, nonetheless, far more extensively recognized
and demarcated than is often realized. Although boundaries in the
Arab world may be anathema to some, today they embrace
territories with their own deepening nationalisms and self-interest,
and they are profoundly influencing the economic infrastructure of
individual states.
                    —Alisdair Drysdale and Gerald H. Blake[1]

Fazlur Rahman (d. 1988), the great Pakistani modernist, characterized
the contemporary Islamic resurgence as defensive. He said it was
"spiritual panic" in the face of continued political failures, rather than
a constructive response to new challenges.[2] What he meant is that
while the contemporary call to return to all things Islamic is well
motivated, it is not well thought out, and indeed incorporates elements
ill-suited to contemporary reality. As a result it is bound to cause more
problems than it solves.

Islam is at heart a moral system for guiding human behavior in all
aspects of life. Truly moral behavior, he reasoned, must be chosen;
merit lies in freely choosing the best among various alternatives. The
promise of reward for good choices and punishment for wrongdoing
are meaningless if the individual performing the acts in question is

acting under constraint. For that reason, Rahman insisted that the road to truly Islamic behavior must begin with influencing the minds and hearts of individuals—it must begin with proper Islamic education. Only individuals properly educated in Islamic principles as well as the full range of contemporary sciences (in the broad sense, including the humanities, technological studies, and social sciences) will be able to effectively implement Islamic values. To simply demand that leadership be Muslim or that laws be drawn from the Shari'a does little to advance the cause of Muslim morality, Rahman held.

For that reason, Fazlur Rahman was dedicated to reforming Islamic education. He believed traditional Islamic education was stagnant and that the degenerate condition of the contemporary world was a direct reflection of the failure of Islamic education. He traced the source of Islamic decadence all the way back to the original institutionalization of Islamic law and theology. Those sciences were never based on a comprehensive understanding of the spirit of Islam, but rather were constructed piecemeal, as the need arose during the phenomenal growth of the early Islamic empire. Much of traditional Islamic lore, he claimed, is at best arbitrary and, in many cases, spurious. To truly revive Islam, then, requires a total revamping of Islamic education—isolating the essential principles from the *ad hoc* developments of any given age— to set it on a sure footing and make it applicable in any age.

Nowhere was the lack of careful thinking about true Islamic values and the nature of contemporary reality more evident to Rahman than in the political arena. In particular, he found the implicit universalism in Islamic political rhetoric troublesome. Sayyid Qutb's interminable denunciation of nationalism, for instance, or of any sense of communal identity other than that of the Islamic community, which influenced so many contemporary Islamic activists, was a case in point.

As we saw, Sayyid Qutb was not unconcerned with the independence and well-being of Egypt. But in condemning nationalism as such, he and his followers implied that the truly Islamic endeavor should be directed toward Islamic unity, rather than the practical necessities of Egyptian statecraft. According to Rahman, this was a mistake. Not only did this distract devout Muslims from the essential issues affecting their daily lives—these issues remained beyond their control so long as they refused to participate in the state government—but it profoundly misled those who inferred the priority of Islamic political unity. For the goal of Islamic political unity, according to Rahman, is quite unsuitable for today's world of geographically limited and independent nation-states. In fact, Rahman felt insistence on Islamic political unity never was particularly well reasoned. The political unity of the early Islamic community developed naturally enough, but even by the time of Ibn Taymiyya it was becoming anachronistic. It was Ibn Taymiyya's questioning of the need for political unity that landed him in so much trouble with the caliphal authorities. Then as now, Rahman held, political unity can only be considered truly Islamic if it is conducive to social well-being.

Indeed, the indiscriminate rhetoric of Islamic unity so prevalent among contemporary Islamic activists can be destabilizing and, to that extent, contrary to truly Islamic values. For it has an internal logic that implies, even if it does not articulate it, political unity. That, in turn, implies that some autonomy will be lost—some leaders will lose their jobs in favor of some elusive central Islamic leadership. The insecurity and suspicion engendered among leaders of Islamic states, Rahman felt, was largely responsible for Muslims' inability to achieve true solidarity.

However, this indictment of indiscriminate rhetoric certainly does not mean that a total and unholy disjunction of Islam and politics is the only alternative to a unified Islamic command—as some Islamic activists would have it. Even secularism as such—the removal of institutionalized religion from the political arena—is not essential for stability in geographical limited political entities. Provided some mechanism for limitation of sovereignty is established, as well as some means of orderly change of government, stability can well be achieved within a limited state. Nor is secularism a sufficient condition for national stability. As we saw in Chapter Six, the avowedly secularist Nasserist and Ba'thist systems were a dismal failure in establishing political stability. They replaced religiously based legitimacy with legitimacy based on another expansive ideologly, pan-Arabism, and, as a result, ran into the same problems the antisecularists are now encountering.

What is necessary for stability in the region is the development of political forms consistent with both cultural expectations and geopolitical reality. In lieu of such accepted forms, modern Arab politics has been plagued with instability and interstate rivalry. But there is undeniable evidence that as these states mature, they are gaining senses of self-identity, both geopolitically and religio-culturally. In this chapter we will examine some examples of the successful integration of Islam into a political system of multiple, limited and independent Islamic states. We will see how, in the process, the gradually increasing participation of former opposition groups into national politics contributes to the entrenchment of the multiple state system in the Middle East, an unmistakable indication of the direction of the future.

The Sa'udi Model

While strictly religious legitimation of political authority has expansionist and therefore destabilizing overtones, religious legitimacy can be successfully blended with national or tribal identity to provide natural limits to political sovereignty. This is the story of Saudi Arabia's success.

The establishment of the kingdom in the first place was made possible largely by the betrayal of Shariff Hussein at the hands of the British. The Hashemite leader appeared to have fallen under the evil spell of the treacherous West. They had tricked him into abandoning his Islamic principles and joining with Christians in a war against other Muslims. Although the war had been a victory for the Christians, the Arab allies had been led to defeat. Having led the Arabs into this loss, the prestigious Hashemites were ultimately forced out of the Arabia.

While the shariff had been arranging the Arab Revolt, 'Abd al-'Aziz Ibn Sa'ud—the patriarch of the Sa'udi family—was busy consolidating his control of Arabia's nonaligned nomadic tribes. He had inherited the strict Wahhabi orientation (see Chapter Three) and, in the name of Islamic purity, began establishing communities devoted to emulating Prophet Muhammad's community at Medina. In the process, he established territorial claims in the area, and communities that—having given up their nomadic livelihood—were totally dependent upon him.[3] Each settlement was called a *hijra*, "emigration," the name used to refer to Prophet Muhammad's move from Mecca to Medina in 622 c.e., and consisted of military recruits. Ibn Sa'ud was thus able to raise a large and fiercely loyal fighting force upon command. In this way the Sa'udis, as the Ibn Sa'ud's loyal *ikhwan* ("brotherhood") came to be called, were able to make quick work of their competitors in the Arabian peninsula. They defeated the Rashidis in central Arabia and by 1924 defeated the Hashemites. Islam remains the mainstay of Sa'udi political legitimacy. They are now the patrons of the Hajj (pilgrimage), the central symbol of Islamic unity, and the "servants of the Holy Places" (Mecca and Medina). In keeping with Islamic practice, they have even asked that royal titles be dropped and that the king be referred to simply as "servant of the Holy Places." They claim the Qur'an is the Sa'udi constitution and that they, just like everyone else, are subject to its law. The Hanbali *'ulama'* of the state are on Sa'udi salary, but they are given more wide-ranging responsibilities than religious scholars in other Islamic states. They are largely in control of education, they are in charge of the annual pilgrimage, they are responsible for "public morality"—observance of prayer, prohibitions against alcohol, open mixing of the sexes, dress codes, etc.—and they control religious properties. What is more, they are drawn from elite families themselves; their fortunes are closely allied with those of the Sa'udis. They therefore routinely support those measures that protect the security of the state.

The Sa'udi regime is therefore an effective combination of religious legitimacy with territorial limitation. The kingdom's boundaries have been established over the past fifty years in a series of treaties with its neighbors, and they are relatively stable. The Sa'udis have no expansionist goals; their legitimacy extends only within the tribal affiliations set up by revered ancestors. What is more, the political machinery is based on democratic Sunni Islamic precedents. Granted, leadership is limited to the Sa'udi family, but within that family leaders are chosen by consensus and on the basis of leadership ability. That is interpreted as including not only administrative ability but the ability to command the respect of the populace, as well, by upholding standards of Islamic piety. Thus in 1964, for instance, when 'Abd al-'Aziz's son, Sa'ud, was deemed incompetent to rule, the family sought and received a ruling from the *'ulama'* to replace him with another son, Faisal.

It is not surprising that Sa'udi legitimacy is based specifically on the Hanbali school of law. The entire Wahhabi movement, in fact, took its inspiration from Ibn Taymiyya's Hanbali formulation of Islamic politics. As we saw, Ibn Taymiyya saw Islamic unity as uniform adherence to a set of values. Political leaders and ordinary citizens alike are subject to Islamic law; political forms themselves are of secondary importance. They are considered functional, not ideological or metaphysical concerns. Furthermore, Hanbali law (see Chapter Two) is the most flexible of the four official schools of Sunni law (despite its well-deserved reputation for conservativism, particularly on matters of social legislation). Again on the inspiration of Ibn Taymiyya, the Wahhabi Sa'udis place a great deal of emphasis on *ijtihad,* i.e., the need to use independent reasoning to determine the best way to apply Islamic principles in a given situation. When the Qur'an and the hadith reports of pious precedent are vague or silent on an issue, Hanbali *'ulama'* are expected to use their best judgment. That, no doubt, has provided the Sa'udis with a great deal of flexibility in dealing with the exigencies of modern statecraft. There are, of course, other issues that have contributed to Sa'udi success. Oil wealth and a small and relatively homogeneous population clearly help, as do the natural geographic borders provided by the Arabian peninsula. Nonetheless, the regime does offer a good example of how religious legitimacy—whether one accepts the Sau'di interpretation of Islam or not—can be incorporated into a stable, limited geopolitical entity. Henry VIII provided another example, but his approach was very different. To be English was to be Anglican and vice-versa. That is, he formulated a religion that was coterminous with the geographic borders of his domain. The Sa'udis, on the other hand, have found a way to rely on a religion claiming universal validity for their legitimacy. It is just that Islam is not the *only* determinant of political legitimacy. One must not only be a good Muslim; one must be a good Sa'udi Muslim.

This model of national identity automatically limits the political claims made by the Sa'udis, without compromising the universality of Islam. Islam remains the basis of Sa'udi values and figures in virtually every aspect of Sa'udi statecraft. The Sa'udi model is consciously Islamic and careful to present itself as such. Sa'udi spokesmen frequently denounce nationalism and Western-style politics.[4] Yet this does not mean they intend to create a single Islamic state. The reality of plural states is accepted and the Sa'udis' call for Islamic solidarity (*tadamun*) among states. Political unity may be possible sometime in the future, but for the present, the Islamic call for justice—on a community by community basis—must take precedence.

The Sudan

The role of Islamic opposition groups in the Sudan provides an interesting contrast with the examples we have seen above. The Sudan had a long history of nationalism in the face of attempts by Egypt to control it. The religious revival and renewal that was taking place throughout the Islamic world in the eighteenth century was represented in the Sudan as well and, indeed, intensified as Muhammad 'Ali attempted to strengthen his position in Egypt vis-à-vis the central Ottoman government at the Sudan's expense. So unlike the majority of Islamic revivalist movements, the Sudan's was not directed primarily against the West. The Sudan's traditional religious elite tended to cooperate with the Ottoman authorities, leaving the independence movement to a revolutionary Islamic movement, the Mahdists. Providing a model of strength through revived Islam, the Mahdists were able to withstand Ottoman Egyptian forces and create an independent state in the 1880s. When the British succeeded the Ottomans as the foreign dominators of the Sudan in 1898, dismantling the Mahdist state, religious opposition took a decidedly pragmatic turn. Unlike their Muslim Brother counterparts in Egypt, the Sudani Mahdist leadership worked actively within the government, to keep it strong, independent, and Islamic. When the Sudan became an independent state following World War II, with a large Christian minority included within its borders, Islamic leadership recognized the expediency of maintaining a strong presence in the government.

This inevitably influenced the direction of Sudani politics. Few questioned the legitimacy of Sudani independence or the identity of Islamic Sudan (the Christian minority notwithstanding). Instead, Islamic leadership worked to intensify the Islamic identity of the state. The Mahdist leadership remained active, and were joined by a newly created branch of the Muslim Brotherhood. It grew gradually—again, as in

Egypt, on the grassroots level—and by the 1980s was popular enough to win representation in the Sudani parliament.

The career of the leader of the Sudani Muslim Brotherhood, Hasan al-Turabi, is revealing with regard to the effect of participation in the government. Al-Turabi has been involved in Sudani politics since the late 1970s, when he was chosen by then president Ja'far Numayri, as attorney general. Numayri had come to power through a military coup in 1969 and had never been a popular leader. The Mahdists and the Brotherhood had both attempted to unseat him. In addition, the Sudan had perennial problems with the Christian South. Numayri therefore hoped to strengthen both his own position and the Islamic identity of the country by including al-Turabi in his administration. As Islamic opposition continued, Numayri attempted to finesse his opponents by propogating a series of laws strictly based on the Shari'a. But the president had misread his opposition. Both the Mahdists and the Brothers were indeed Muslim; Islamic values of social well-being and solidarity formed the root and vocabulary of their rhetoric. But they were Sudanis, as well, and it was the Sudan's well-being that concerned them.

More importantly, there was no opposition between their values and nationalist values, as their cooperation with other, non-Islamic opposition groups evidenced. Sadiq al-Mahdi, great grandson of the founder of the Mahdists and former leader of the Mahdist Ummah Party, consistently called upon Sudanis to participate in the national government in order to reform it. Revolution can only cause further instability, the source of so much suffering, he said. The contemporary world of nation-states is a reality; Islamic principles of equality, justice, peaceful cooperation, and universal human solidarity must guide those states. Islamic political efforts must be directed toward that goal. Similarly, Hasan al-Turabi emphasizes reform rather than revolution. Like al-Mahdi, he advocates participation in the government. Religious leaders should be advisors to the state government, but they should not be in control of it, as was the case in the Iranian Islamic revolution.[5] What form the government should take has yot yet been determined. It is still a matter of evolution, al-Turabi says: "We are now searching for our *qibla* (direction of prayer)."[6] But whatever procedural and organizational form public life takes, it will be Islamic provided it furthers Islamic goals of peace, equality, and stability.

Thus circumstances in the Sudan made participation in the government expedient, and that very participation seems to have entrenched the legitimacy of the state. Other factors undoubtedly influenced the development of Sudani politics. It is an African state, not primarily Arab; the nature and extent of colonization there differed significantly from that in the Arab experience. However, in the present context the salient feature of Islamic oppositional politics in the Sudan is this: Because of the activists' participation in the government, discontent with the avowedly Islamic government of Numayri did not take Islam as its defining characteristic. Numayri was nonetheless ousted, in a bloodless coup, other features of his policies having been identified as unsatisfactory. Numayri was unsatisfactory for the Sudan, not for all of Islam. The change of government was a Sudani matter, not an Islamic revolution with expansionist overtones. Yet neither the legitimacy of the Sudani state nor the Islamic identity of the Sudan, at least among Muslims, is generally questioned. And interestingly, the leader of the Muslim Brotherhood in the Sudan, Hasan al-Turabi, is emerging as a leading figure is Islamic political thought, especially among members of the Muslim Brotherhood in other states.

The Muslim Brothers in Egypt

As we saw in Chapter Seven, the Muslim Brothers implicitly acknowledged nationalist goals by supporting Nasser's revolution. They called it the "blessed movement" because it had liberated Egypt. Their language was traditionally Islamic; it was, therefore, naturally devoid of nationalist rhetoric and, again implicitly, universalistic. But their energies were nonetheless directed toward nationalist goals. They insisted only that the new regime be based on Islam. But lagging development and the political reverses of Nasser's and Sadat's secularist regimes led to increasing emphasis on the call for a return to truly Islamic government. Since the last time the world knew a truly Islamic government there were no such things as multiple, geographically limited states coexisting within a single cultural milieu, the call for renewal took a decidedly reactionary form. The call to dismantle states and the equation of their very existence with godless Westernism became more distinct.

This development can hardly be considered surprising. This was a time of radical changes in sociopolitical forms, and thus in communal identities, imposed by forces very remote from the people subject to those new forms. The phenomenon of communal identity is extremely complex and dynamic. Economic circumstances may change, forcing new social configurations. The transformation of economies from agricultural to industrial, for instance, inevitably signals the demise of rural communities and increased urbanization. But rural life is fraught with cultural ramifications—levels of social identity and perceptions of security. The transition to urbanized life therefore heralds a massive cultural transformation, as former senses of security and identity fall away and are replaced with new ones. Such cultural change is a slow, plodding, and often painful process. This is the case in the present-day Middle East, as it is throughout the third world and as it was in Europe. We saw in Chapter One that the transition from Europe's medieval feudal, agricultural economy to its assertion of political self-consciousness in the Enlightenment was a fitful and war-filled process that took at least three centuries.

The popularity of the Muslim Brotherhood and its reliance on traditional perceptions of communal identity, particularly during the earliest stages of Egyptian independent statehood, were therefore only natural. The villages that comprised the majority of Egyptian society were part of an amorphous Islamic world; the village was self-sufficient, tied to the outside world almost exclusively through its religious teachers. They were generally the only representives of the larger context. The villagers were aware of themelves existing as part of a greater whole— but it rarely affected their daily lives. It was simply Islamic—Islam, their religion, the true religion, the source and repose of their highest values, confirmation that they did not exist in a vacuum and that within that greater context there was general approval, both mundane and heavenly, of their way of life. Yet on a practical and daily level, there was little outside intervention beyond periodic tax assessments.

The city, on the other hand, increasingly the center of communal life in the industrialized and industrialzing world, is a part of a state. A state is quite consciously limited by geographic and (generally) ethnographic boundaries. It may be Islamic somehow, but in a different and initially confusing way. In Albert Hourani's often quoted words:

> For rural immigrants, seeking security, employment, or wealth in the city, cut off from the ties of kinship or neighborliness which made life in the village bearable, victims of urban processes that they can neither understand nor control and living in a society of which the external signs are strange to them—for these the religious community may provide the only kind of world to which they can belong. Its spokesmen use a language which is known and appeals to moral values deeply rooted in their hearts, its rituals and ceremonies are familiar, its shrines are already known to rural visitors as places where prayer has been valid. . . . If they do not find what they need in the city, they bring it with them from the countryside.[7]

That explains why the Muslim Brotherhood was so successful in recruiting among the non-elites, those most affected by and least familiar with the rapidly changing socioeconomic order. While industrialization and, as a result, urbanization, were no doubt necessary for Egyptian development, they had not yet entered the popular consciousness, as such. The transitions experienced by developing economies are jarring and frequently take years to produce positive results. During that lag time there is little to induce people to place their faith and security in the unseen forces of change. In brief, they have developed no perceived vested interest in the new state and industrial order. The more difficult the transition, the more vociferous the call to return to the familiarity of the past. As we saw, this was just what the Muslim Brothers did during the turbulent years leading up to Sadat's assassination.

But in recent years Islamic activists in Egypt are beginning to reveal a growing assimilation into Egyptian statecraft, a growing popular perception of Egyptian identity. The Muslim Brotherhood, for instance, although it remains technically illegal, is increasingly and visibly active in Egyptian politics. Having long since abandoned revolutionary tactics, it has indeed joined the Egyptian mainstream. It has participated in the last several Egyptian elections, through government sanctioned political parties—the Wafd, the Socialist Labor Party (now independent, but originally founded in 1978 by Sadat, when he banned the Wafd and the National Unionist Party but did not want it to appear as if his own National Democratic Party were the only political option) and the Liberal Party. All these parties are strictly Egyptian; Islamic ideals remain essential but the call for Islamic political unity seems to have faded in importance.

There remain the more radical Islamic groups, such as Jihad and Tahrir al-Islami (Islamic Liberation), which criticize the Brotherhood as soft on secularism and therefore not truly Islamic. But the Brotherhood counters with condemnations of revolutionary tactics and other destabilizing activities. Echoing the approach of Hasan al-Turabi, they place Egyptian national concerns at the center of their efforts. Again, this is not to the detriment of concerns for the well-being of the greater Islamic community. It reflects instead a realization that the two goals—Egyptian stability and that of the Muslim *umma*—are not mutually exclusive. Indeed, the former is a necessary component of the latter.

As such, the Brotherhood continues to grow. In the 1987 elections, opposition parties took 108 of 448 parliamentary seats. Mona Makram-Ebeid, of the New Wafd Party, reports that this was the highest level of opposition participation since Egypt's parliamentary system began in 1924.[8] Voter turnout was still low. Makram-Ebeid attributes this to voter apathy, after twenty-five years of single-party domination, and continued widespread illiteracy. Even so, the Muslim Brotherhood, in its alliance with the Socialist Labor Party and the Liberal Party, won 17 percent of the vote or 56 seats, compared to only 10.9 percent and 35 seats for the Wafd.

Egyptian intellectuals are also beginning to evidence this growing perception of Egyptian Islamic identity. Hasan Hanafi, one of Cairo's leading intellectuals, calls for realism in Islam, which he claims is Islam's strength in the first place. The advance made by Islam over the Jewish and Christian interpretations of monotheism is that it demands God's will be implemented on earth. Individual salvation requires contribution to the establishment of social justice, and that requires pragmatism—working within the prevailing order to implement Islamic values. Arabs must stop dreaming about past victories, Hanafi says, in order to be triumphant in the present, nationalist context. And that, he says, requires participation in the political arena. There is nothing un-Islamic about national political organization, he says—contrary to the early Brotherhood position—only in the apathy that keeps Muslims from actively participating in and therefore directing national life. Egyptian Muslims must discover the strength of their religion and use it to direct and control their own government.[9]

Hasan Hanafi's work in this regard is representative of ongoing discussions among Arab intellectuals regarding the true nature of Arab society. As distinct from the popular tendency to retrench in tradition in the face of perceived "cultural imperialism" (domination by a foreign culture), the tendency among Arab intellectuals is to search for true cultural identity, trying to determine what is essential to the heritage and what were merely passing phases. Hanafi claims, just as did Fazlur Rahman, that Muslims must study their past in order to distinguish which of its components must be retained and adapted to present circumstances and which may be jettisoned, having developed in response to specific historical circumstances and therefore being no longer significant. This approach to current challenges is shared by Muhammad 'Abid al-Jabiri, who criticizes the Salafiyya approach for its inability to distinguish the essential from the superfluous in their own heritage.[10] Similarly, the Lebanese scholar Hasan Sa'b calls on Muslims to remember the dynamism of Islam, the need to understand Islamic principles of freedom and justice in order to put them into practice in any historical circumstance.[11]

Tariq al-Bishri is another Egyptian intellectual whose growing reputation reflects the tenor of contemporary Egyptian political consciousness.[12] He speaks for Egyptian nationalism and independence from foreign control as the heart of truly Islamic endeavor. Egypt has a unique national character, al-Bishri says, but its soul is Islamic. Again, the universalism of Islam is reinterpreted. It need not be expressed in political unity of the Muslim world; it is fully applicable in Egypt itself, for Islamic values are suitable to all Egyptians. Nor does Egypt's Islamic character imply religious exclusivism for al-Bishri. The Coptic

Christians are as Egyptian as anyone else, and must have equal rights. This does not undermine Egypt's Islamic character; indeed, Islam, as a religion of tolerance and social justice, demands equal rights for all citizens.

It will be recalled that these ideas are not new in Egypt. In Chapter Four we saw expressions of just such notions in the work of al-Tahtawi and others. But that was before the trials and reversals of the post–World War I period had taken their toll on Egyptian self-confidence. In the work of these scholars we see a growing awareness on the part of the Arab intellectuals of the very processes they have undergone. In the case of Egypt, al-Bishri says that process must continue. He says Egyptians must be nurtured politically, overcoming the political and class sectarianism that prevailed under Nasser and Sadat. The earlier leaders of Egyptian national consciousness failed to make their programs public and accessible to the public. As a result, he says, political consciousness overall in Egypt is lacking. For the two leading proponents of change in those early days, the Wafd and the Muslim Brothers, tended to present themselves as opponents, vying for complete loyalty among the citizenry. In lieu of open and rational debate of various issues in their programs and their appropriateness to the Egyptian context, the alternative to complete group loyalty was staunch opposition. Al-Bishri wants to transcend this apparent opposition and demonstrate that both the Wafd and the Brotherhood were and remain among the many manifestations of authentically Egyptian consciousness. Differences among the Egyptian people are to be expected—indeed, nurtured. Egypt needs both the ideological sophistication of the Wafdist, he says, and the popular allegiance of the Brotherhood models of leadership. Both are Egyptian, different aspects of the same communal identity. Egypt's problems can only be solved by Egyptians, just as the Sudan's must be solved by the Sudanese, the Syrians' by Syrians, etc. On this basis, the overall well-being of the Islamic *umma* as a whole will be advanced. Neither the latter nor the former goal is primary in importance, but the former is the only one over which Egyptians have control.

Iran

Interestingly, this tendency toward Islamic ratification of national consciousness is in evidence even in Iran. Indeed, one of the early ideologues of Islamically legitimated national politics was an Iranian intellectual, 'Ali Shari'ati (d. 1977). 'Ali Shari'ati was an Islamic reformer, immensely popular in the anti-shah movement of the late 1960s and 1970s. (His mysterious death is often attributed to the shah's secret service, SAVAK.) Shari'ati was anti-West and opposed to secularism, and believed that

Islam was a system of universal principles. He wanted Muslims to shake off Westernism and all foreign influence and reestablish a society based on *tawhid,* the unicity and supremacy of God. "All human activities and relationships, whether political, economic, literary or artistic, ought to be firmly founded on *tawhid.* It provides one, single direction and it guarantees a unified spirit for its adherents."[13] A social order based on *tawhid* is what Prophet Muhammad established during his lifetime; at his death it became the responsibility of Muslims to continue and propogate that order. Constant reference to *tawhid* is necessary, for *tawhid* "perfects the ethical conscience."[14] Islam is therefore universal in its principles; social justice based on *tawhid* is the heritage of all people. And Islam is the only religion that perfectly reflects the dual dimension of faith: Responsibility to God is the same as social responsibility, in that true faith can only be demonstrated through ethical behavior. *Nizam-i tawhid* ("the Islamic order") is the explicit challenge of Islamic revelation; the creation of a just society is the inevitable outcome of proper recognition of God.

But Shari'ati's emphasis on practical faith, faith demonstrated in social commitment, was directed specifically at Iranian youth. He believed enlightened religious leadership was required to interpret Islamic principles in terms of current social circumstances, making them applicable on a day-to-day basis. But that leadership could only be effective for an Iranian youth reawakened to their Islamic social commitment. He devoted himself, therefore, to reminding the youth that Islam is a practical culture, piety signified by nothing if not social virtue. The values are universal, but the proving ground for Iranians was Iran. Renewed in their social commitment and guided by enlightened leaders, Iran could jettison the imperialist and un-Islamic forces that had corrupted it. As a Shi'i, Shari'ati frequently spoke of Islamic social commitment in terms of the expected *mahdi:* The proper attitude toward expectation of the *mahdi* was to prepare for his return, to enable it, in fact, by working for social justice. That, no doubt, helped inform the specifically Iranian emphasis in his teaching. Yet the practical nature of his reformism, and his unquestioning acceptance of Iranian national identity within the Islamic *umma* has gained widespread popularity throughout the Islamic world.

Shari'ati's popularity in Iran itself did much to pave the way for Ayatollah Khomeini's ascent to power, particularly his emphasis on enlightened religious leadership. However, the ayatollah's emphasis on Islamic universalism went far beyond that envisioned by Shari'ati. Indeed, the ayatollah made the export of Islam a primary goal of the Iran; he did not believe a true Islamic movement could be limited to a single country. There never has been unanimity, even within Iran itself, regarding the best way to go about exporting the Islamic movement. Even the ayatollah spoke of teaching and setting good example as means of spreading Islam. However, his war with Iraq naturally took practical precedence in the people's minds. As noted in Chapter Eight, the war was always justified as a step in the process of making the world Islamic. That, coupled with the ayatollah's repeated calls for overthrowing such leaders as King Hussein of Jordan, the Sa'udis, and Hosni Mubarak of Egypt—reiterated even in his last will and testament—caused the more pacific passages in his rhetoric to recede into obscurity.[15]

But now that the ayatollah is dead, other voices are being heard, most significantly, that of the new president, Hojjatoleslam 'Ali Akbar Hashemi Rafsanjani (1934–). Rafsanjani agrees that a truly Islamic movement must include all Islamic countries. But this does not imply for him Islamic political unity, nor does he place the export of Islamic revolution at the forefront of his administration. He is known for his devotion to the Iranian nation and recognition of the need for practical measures to advance its well-being. For example, Rafsanjani supported Dr. Muhammad Mossadegh, the popularly elected prime minister overthrown by a U.S. and British sponsored coup because of his nationalization of oil and socialist inclinations. After the coup brought Muhammad Reza Shah to power, Rafsanjani worked actively in the antigovernment underground. He was imprisoned for these activities several times, and each time he was released, he resumed his activities: running schools that advocated Islamic activism and coordinating Khomeini's work while the latter was in exile in Iraq.

The ascendancy of Ayatollah Khomeini clearly demonstrates the pattern of religious reaction against the foreign domination of Iran represented by the shah. The experiment with Western lifestyle legislated by the Pahlavis—from Western dress and the prohibition of the veil for women, to Western style industrialization in a primarily and traditionally agricultural land, and Western education for an elite class increasingly isolated from its national roots—left the majority of Iranians in no better economic condition than before the nationalization of oil, yet bereft of the comfort they had previously taken in a perceived cultural integrity. They could not take control of the government or the economy and naturally sought the solace of the heart of any culture, the ground of their cherished morality—their religion.

But unlike Khomeini, Rafsanjani has survived that stage. Iranians no doubt, despite the devastion of the war with Iraq, feel a renewed sense of self-confidence, of being in control of their own destiny. With that as a basis of strength, the election of Rafsanjani indicates Iran is moving beyond reaction to genuine reform. We get an insight into Rafsanjani's character by reading his biography of the nineteenth-century reformer, Amir Kabir. Rafsanjani demonstrates in this book, published in 1967, that Iran can modernize, industrialize, and incorporate technological advances developed in the West without sacrificing the country's culture and essential character. In his election speech, Rafsanjani spoke of the same things, stressing the importance of technological training and the development of Iran's economic potential. Again, in a September 1989 speech the new president made his priorities very clear:

> We have not been able to clarify for people economic problems as befits Islam; we have differences of opinion amongst ourselves over these issues. We have not come forward with clear principles in our foreign policy. We have not yet tackled the day-to-day aspects of Islamic rule.[16]

Absent was the rhetoric of Islamic revolution; indeed, Rafsanjani is generally given credit for convincing Khomeini to end the war with Iraq. And as an advocate of centralized power, he is expected to severely curtail the activities of the Iranian troops in Lebanon. In foreign policy, Rafsanjani has always shown concern with the Palestinians, but he is also known as an advocate of normalization of relations with the regional powers, as well as with he West. As noted in Chapter Eight, Khomeini's condemnation of Salman Rushdie was largely an effort to undermine these efforts in favor of continued isolationism. But Rafsanjani's popularity and prestige were not diminished. Indeed, his election seems to represent Iran's recognition that, having rid itself of foreign domination under the shahs, it is now time to get on with things.

His job will not be easy. The forces of reaction are still present; Ayatollah Khamenei recently reiterated Ayatollah Khomeini's condemnation of Salman Rushdie as part of his ongoing effort to weaken Rafsanjani's support. And Ayatollah Khomeini's son Ahmad continues his outspoken opposition to reform. Meanwhile, some Iranians are becoming more vocal in their exasperation with the entire Islamic revolution. Violent demonstrations were recently reported in Tehran (16 February 1990), in which both Khamenei and Rafsanjani were jeered. Middle East correspondent Safa Haeri quotes eyewitness accounts that support was voiced for the late shah's son, Reza Pahlavi, and for reformist Ayatollah Montazeri.[17] The demonstrations appear to have been spontaneous, rather than part of any organized or unified opposition movement. Yet they do indicate that Iranians are ready for practical reform.

Conclusion

In 1979 Dutch scholar Rudolph Peters claimed that Muslims' "sweeping assertions about Islam recognizing the equality of all mankind and the reciprocality in inter-state relations, amount to no more than gratuitous and non-committal slogans."[18] When they come right down to it, Peters continued, Muslim activists really want a universal Islamic order in which non-Muslims as well as Muslim dissenters would be denied equality. Speaking in particular of the Muslim Brotherhood, Peters said that they reject nationalism, recognize only religious solidarity, and "their aim is to establish Islamic rule all over the earth."[19] That is why they "condemn the existing governments in the Islamic world, since, in their view, these are not really Islamic," and speak of continuous revolution. "Thus," he concudes, "they emphasize the expansionist character of jihad."[20] But as the foregoing analysis demonstrates, much has changed since 1979. No doubt the Islamic activist movement that so influenced Arab politics during the past two decades was a reaction to previous political failures. Their rejection of contemporary political developments as non-Islamic and reversion to anachronistic political models was and remains a potent source of suspicion among Arab leaders, precluding effective cooperation on regional problems. Yet just as surely, the development of states—economically and politically independent and territorially limited—has been an ongoing process in the Islamic world, as has been the effort to develop Islamic political forms suitable for them.

No doubt, a good deal of the less inflammatory Islamic rhetoric has been the result of coopted religious authorities. As we saw above, everyone from Nasser and Sadat to Hafiz al-Assad and Saddam Hussein has commissioned Islamic legitimation for his policies. But the recent trends among the Islamic activists discussed above are of a different variety. They reveal a forward step in the process of developing Islamic political consciousness congruent with modern realities.

As the quote at the opening of this chapter describes, the longer a state exists—regardless of how turbulent the existence is—the more entrenched it becomes. We saw above, for example, how even as Syria's leaders based their popular rhetoric on regaining Syria's former vast figure, the state was reinforcing its current truncated form simply by developing and maintaining the politico-economic infrastructure required to stay in power. Hafiz al-Assad's regime may not be stable. The formation of a new opposition group, the Patriotic Front for National Salvation, was recently announced. Calling for the overthrow of Assad's totalitarian regime, the front claims broad support from pro-Iraqi Ba'thists, Nasserists, democratic reformers, and even from the Muslim Brotherhood in Syria. The new group's strategy will do little to normalize relations in the region; it has announced that its headquarters will be in Baghdad.[21] Yet regardless of the outcome of the power struggle, it seems clear that the entity in question is Syria. By joining forces working to reform the state, the Islamic opposition is tacitly identifying itself with national interests. The phenomenal success of the Muslim Brothers and other Islamic activists in the recent Jordanian elections is another case in point. Just as the pan-Arab nationalists helped entrench the states of Egypt, Syria, and Iraq—even as they spoke of Arab unity—now it appears that Islamic opposition groups are following the same pattern. They may not be satisfied with their stake in the national system, but in the very process of joining it, they are strengthening it. The process takes a very long time, as we saw in the Introduction regarding European states. But eventually, political forms emerge from the familiar cultural milieu, revised somehow to fit new circumstances. Muslim intellectuals from Ibn Taymiyya to Fazlur Rahman and the current advocates of Islamic historicism have recognized the need for those revised Islamic political forms. Now developments within the Islamic states in the Middle East during the 1980s indicate that that step in the process of developing stable states is taking place. No identifiable consensus has yet emerged; there is as yet no widely accepted theory of limited Islamic state government. And indeed there are still many representatives of the reactionary, revolutionary and anti-state phase in evidence throughout the Muslim world. In Tunisia, for example, the group known as the Movement of Islamic Tendency calls for what it describes as a "realistic fundamentalism" that recognizes that "the efforts of the Islamic workers bent on bringing about the Islamic project within the context of their nation-states are bound to be wasted, so long as the vision of their thinkers and planners does not go beyond the boundaries of their own countries and their local potential."[22] However, the emerging tendency is to accept national identities and work within them for Islamic goals.

The recession of Islamic universalist rhetoric in the Arab world is therefore no accident. Just as its rise was an understandable effect of the region's political problems, its demise was equally predictable. The principle of territorial integrity has been accepted in most states—even in the extremely problematic case of Lebanon, Arab states agree that Syria's involvement in Lebanese politics is as foreign as Israel's and jointly call for Syria's withdrawal. The principle of limited political legitimacy will inevitably follow. To the extent that democracy has been implemented, indeed, accepted norms of limited political legitimacy—the essential element in regional political stability—is a *fait accompli*. And just as in the case of Europe's development of secularism, this in no way compromises the universalism of Islam. Islamic principles remain applicable for all societies. Nor does this recognition undermine Islamic unity. It simply recognizes, as Ibn Taymiyya did in the fourteenth century, that Islamic unity need not be strictly political. In fact, as the instability engendered by universalist religio-political claims has demonstrated, only by limiting the crown can the Qur'an remain universal.

Notes

Chapter One

1. Hans Kohn, *The Idea of Nationalism* (New York: Macmillan, 1961), pp. 23–24.

2. Sayyid Qutb, *Fi Zilal al-Qur'an* (Beyrouth, Cairo: Dar al-Shuruq, 1978), 8th edition, pp. 2433 and 927.

3. Imam Khomeini, *Islam and Revolution,* tr. Hamid Algar (Berkeley, CA: Mizan Press, 1981), p. 219. For similar views, see, for example, 'Ali Shari'ati, who equates secularism with humanism and considers them the root of the West's alleged atheism. See his *Marxism and Other Western Fallacies,* tr. R. Campbell (Berkeley, CA: Mizan Press, 1980), p. 19.

4. Fazlur Rahman, *Islam and Modernity* (Chicago and London: University of Chicago Press, 1982), p. 15.

5. Max L. Stackhouse, "Piety, Polity, and Policy," in *Religious Beliefs, Human Rights, and the Moral Foundation of Western Democracy* (Columbia: University of Missouri, 1986 Paine Lectures in Religion), p. 16.

6. The Roman Empire had been born and died an agricultural economy. Yet it was an urban civilization, a confederation of autonomous urban centers held together by a provincial administration whose main concern was collecting tribute. Eventually, of course, the empire became overextended. Agricultural failure sapped its economic strength. Having ignored its merchants, Rome had failed to develop the potential for credit extension or public debt. Instead, it relied solely on increased taxation. When that device failed, so, too, did Rome. It became vulnerable to foreign invasions, which ultimately led to its demise. With that, the great landowners tended to desert the urban centers and entrench themselves in the land that was the source of their security. The peasants necessarily followed suit. Classical Rome's network of towns all but disappeared, and agriculture became extremely localized. This was the origin of the feudal economic structure of Christian Rome.

7. I use the terms *pope* and *bishop of Rome* synonymously throughout this discussion. The term *pope* was used in the Eastern church from about 250. The bishop of Rome didn't start using the title until Pope Leo the Great (r. 440–461), and it wasn't until 1073 that the bishop of Rome asserted exclusive claim to the title.

8. Even classical Rome believed itself charged with a universal mission. Pliny called Rome "chosen by the providence of the gods to render even heaven itself more glorious, to unite the scattered empires of the earth, to

bestow a polish upon man's manners, to unite the discordant and uncouth dialects of the many different nations, to confer the enjoyment of discourse and of civilization upon mankind, to become, in short, the mother country of all nations of the earth" (Pliny, *The Natural History,* Bk. III, Chap. 5[6], 35, tr. John Bostock and H. T. Riley [London: Bell, 1877], cited by Kohn, *The Idea of Nationalism,* p. 67).

The Stoics gave Roman universalism a philosophical basis: "We do not dwell in separate cities or demes, each group bounded off by its own rules of justice; but we consider that all men are fellow demesmen and fellow citizens, and that life is one and the universe one" (from von Arnim, *Stoicorum veterum frag. I,* no. 262, quoted by Kohn, *The Idea of Nationalism,* p. 67). But the ultimate rationale for Rome's universal imperium was religious. That was why anyone who failed to worship the Roman gods was considered a political threat. Such was the verdict regarding Christans, for instance, and the rationale for their persecution. As Tacitus put it, "Hatred of the empire and the emperor, and uselessness from the economic standpoint—these were the standing charges against Christians, charges which the apologists were at great pains to controvert. . . . As the Christians were almost alone among religionists in being liable to this charge of enmity to the empire, they were held responsible for any great calamities that occurred" (quoted by Adolf von Harnack, *The Expansion of Christianity in the First Three Centuries,* tr. James Moffat [New York: Putnam, 1905], Vol. I, p. 342; cited by Kohn, *The Idea of Nationalism,* p. 592 n. 6).

9. Robert S. Lopez, *The Birth of Europe* (New York: M. Evans and Company, Inc., 1967), p. 15. See also Kohn, *The Idea of Nationalism,* pp. 74–75.

10. Bernard Lewis, for example, claims there is an inherent separation of church and state unique to Christianity (see his *The Political Language of Islam* [Chicago: University of Chicago Press, 1987]).

11. Kohn, *The Idea of Nationalism,* p. 82.

12. Interestingly, the lands assigned to the third grandson, Lothar—those with mixed languages such as the Italian and Provencal provinces with strong Romance characteristics, the Low Countries, Dutch and Walloon, Lorraine and Alsace, and polyglot Switzerland—did not survive intact into the modern age.

13. Unlike the majority of the population, Jews—deprived of standard citizenship rights and unlikely to swear fealty oaths sanctioned by the Christian God—were engaged in mercantile activities throughout the era. Ninth-century Arab sources marvel at their abilities, reporting that they dealt in everything from slaves to salt, from Spain and China, and operated throughout the length and breadth of the Carolingian empire.

14. This summary of medieval European history is taken largely from Donald Kagan, Steven Ozment, and Frank M. Turner, *The Western Heritage,* Vol. I (New York: Macmillan, 1983), 2d edition. For their description of the Fourth Crusade, see p. 294.

15. Kohn, *The Idea of Nationalism,* p. 82.

16. Kagan et al., *The Western Heritage,* pp. 329–30.

17. Lopez, *The Birth of Europe,* p. 150.

18. William of Ockham, *Summa Totius Logicae*, Ic, xiv, in *Ockham: Philosophical Writings*, ed. and tr. Philotheus Boehner (New York: Nelson, 1962), pp. 33–34.

19. See Marsilius of Padua's *Defensor Pacis* (1324), discussed in Kohn, *The Idea of Nationalism*, pp. 105ff.

20. Borgia Pope Alexander VI (r. 1492–1503), for instance, supported Naples when it attacked Milan. This brought the French into Italian politics, at the invitation of the Milanese leader. The French then conquered not only Naples, but Florence and the Papal States as well. Then Pope Alexander VI invited France into Italian politics yet again, this time to secure the Roman provinces for his children, Cesare and Lucrezia. Alexander assiduously courted France for this purpose, annulling the French king's marriage so he could marry Anne of Brittany and thus keep Brittany French, withdrawing papal support of northern Italian cities so France could reconquer Milan, marrying his son to a French princess, and agreeing to allow French military assistance in Romagna. Ultimately, France did reconquer Milan and in 1500 divided Naples between themselves and Spain. And the Borgias secured complete control of Romagna. Pope Alexander VI granted his son the title duke of Romagna.

21. Quoted by Kohn, *The Idea of Nationalism*, p. 128.

22. Another of the brotherhood's well-known students was Johannes Reuchlin (d. 1522). Reuchlin became famous for the controversy surrounding his teaching of Hebrew. He became the symbol of academic freedom and sound scholarship among German humanists when he was criticized by the Dominican Order of Cologne—under the inspiration of a converted Jew named Pfefferkorn, who wanted to suppress Jewish writings. The idea that Christianity had to cleanse itself of Judaism in order to right the world was still common. Fortunately, more rational voices were in the majority, as Christian self-scrutiny advanced.

23. John C. Olin, ed. and tr., *Christian Humanism and the Reformation: Desiderius Erasmus* (New York: Harper, 1965), pp. 100–101. Cited by Kagan et al., *The Western Heritage*, p. 398.

24. Kagan et al., *The Western Heritage*, p. 394.

25. In 1476 Pope Sixtus IV had officially sanctioned the extension of indulgences to the dead, via the living. By Luther's time indulgences were regularly traded for cash. The salesman, John Tetzel (d. 1519), was well known for his ability to get people to buy indulgences to relieve the suffering of their relatives. "Don't you hear the voices of your dead parents and other relatives crying out?" he is recorded to have asked. "Why do you treat us so cruelly and leave us to suffer in the flames, when it takes only a little to save us?" (see Helmar Junghaus, ed., *Die Reformation in Augenzeugen berichten* [Dusseldorf: Karl Rauch Verlag, 1967], p. 44; cited by Kagan et al., *The Western Heritage*, p. 404).

26. But Elizabeth was still left to deal with Philip's adventurism. She had, of course, incurred his and the pope's wrath by reinstating Protestantism. Pope Pius V (r. 1566–1572), in fact, excommunicated her for heresy in 1570 and encouraged Philip to conquer England. She therefore agreed to support the Netherlands against Spanish claims, to prevent Philip from using Dutch ports

to launch his attacks. When she agreed to the execution of Mary, Queen of Scots (d. 1587), the deposed Catholic leader of Scotland who was discovered plotting against the English monarch, Elizabeth ultimately did have to face the Spanish invasion. As mentioned above, Philip sent his mighty fleet, the Armada, but Elizabeth's navy defeated it so resoundingly that the Spanish military never recovered, and none of his successors again tried to press the imperial claim.

27. Kagan et al., *The Western Heritage*, p. 464.

28. Ibid., p. 428.

29. Quoted in Franklin Baumer, *Main Currents of Western Thought* (New Haven, CT: Yale University Press, 1978), 4th edition, p. 281.

30. James Harvey Robinson, ed., *Readings in European History*, Vol. 2 (Boston: Ginn and Co., 1906), pp. 275–76; cited by Kagan et al., *The Western Heritage*, p. 485.

31. Another reason Hobbes believed a kind of social contract was necessary was his observation that people are driven by "a perpetual and restless desire of power after power that eases only in death," he said (see H. W. Schneider, *Leviathan Parts I and II* [Indianapolis, IN: Bobbs-Merrill, 1958], p. 86). To prevent the universal warfare such natural inclinations would inevitably create if left unchecked, people must enter into a social contract based on the golden rule: "Do not that to another which you would not have done to yourself."

32. T. P. Peardon, ed., *The Second Treatise of Government* (Indianapolis, IN: Bobbs-Merrill, 1952), Ch. 2, Sect. 4–6, pp. 4–6; cited by Kagan et al., *The Western Heritage*, p. 526.

33. Peardon, *The Second Treatise of Government*, Ch. 13, Sect. 149, p. 84.

34. Joseph Strayer, "The Historical Experience of Nation-Building in Europe," in Karl W. Deutsch and William J. Foltz, eds., *Nation Building* (New York: Atherton Press, 1963), p. 22.

35. G. J. Holyoake, *Reasoner* (12 Dec. 1854):5. In fact, the term *secularism* was used to describe the emphasis Jewish ethics places on concerns for human welfare on earth, rather than in the afterlife. This corresponds to the term's Latin root, *saecula,* meaning measurable in time, i.e., the created world, as opposed to *aeterna,* the timeless and everlasting world of the creator.

Chapter Two

1. Fazlur Rahman, *Islam,* (Chicago and London: University of Chicago Press, 1979), 2d edition, p. 114.

2. The classic scholar on the subject, Henri Lammens, notes the difficulty of determining with precision the actual taxation practices of the early caliphs. Not only do we have to rely on the reports of later jurists who had a tendency to try to "accord contemporary practice with the sunna," but overall, he says, there was a "characteristic arbitrariness in the application of judicial principles in the Muslim state, particularly in fiscal matters" (see his *Etudes sur le regne du Calife Omaiyade Mo'awia Ier* [Beirut: Imprimeire Catholique, 1930], pp. 227ff.). Still, records are sufficient to conclude the general characteristics of

the early Islamic economic system. The main sources are Ibn 'Asakir, *al-Ta'rikh al-Kabir,* ed. 'Abd al-Qadir Badran and Ahmad 'Ubayd (Damascus: Rawdat al-Sham, 1329–1351); Ibn al-Athir, *Al-Kamil fi'l-Ta'rikh,* ed. C. J. Tornberg (Leiden: E. J. Brill, 1867–1874); Ahmad ibn Yahya al-Baladhuri, *Futuh al-Buldan,* ed. M. deGoeje (Leiden: E. J. Brill, 1866); al-Baladhuri, *Futuh al-Buldan,* tr. Philip K. Hitti as *The Origins of the Islamic State* (New York: Columbia University Press, 1916); Abu Ja'far Muhammad ibn Jarir al-Tabari, *Ta'rikh al-Rusul wa'l-Muluk,* ed. M. deGoeje et al. (Leiden: E. J. Brill, 1879–1901); Ahmad J. Abi Ya'qub al-Ya'qubi, *Ta'rikh,* ed. Th. Houtsma (Leiden: E. J. Brill, 1883). Cf. Daniel C. Dennett, Jr., *Conversion and the Poll Tax in Early Islam* (Cambridge, MA: Harvard University Press, 1950).

3. On early Islamic commercial economy, see the classic works by Martin Hartmann (*Der Islamische Orient,* Bk. II: *Die Arabische Frage* [Leipzig: R. Haupt, 1909], pp. 445ff.) and Henri Lammens, S. J. (*La Mecque a la veille de l'hegire* [Beirut: Imprimeire Catholique, 1924], esp. pp. 135ff.) and the works of contemporary scholar Maxime Rodinson (*Islam and Capitalism,* tr. Brian Pearce [Austin: University of Texas Press, 1973] and *Marxism and the Muslim World,* tr. Jean Matthews [New York and London: Monthly Review Press, 1981]).

4. This is not to say there were not abuses in the system. See discussion, for instance, in Bandali al-Jawzi, *Min Ta'rikh al-Harakat al-Fikriyya fi'l-Islam* (Beirut: n.p., 1928), Chap. 2.

5. Marshall G. S. Hodgson, *The Venture of Islam: Conscience and History in a World Civilization,* Vol. II (Chicago and London: University of Chicago Press, 1974), p. 3.

6. Ibid., p. 81. Hodgson, whose work forms the basis of this summary, believes the nomadic pastoralists were therefore "probably the most decisive component in weakening the agrarian power" (ibid.).

7. On the issue and its effects on the future development of Sunni and Shi'i intellectual traditions, see Chapter Eight in this book.

8. Hodgson, *The Venture of Islam,* Vol. I, p. 485.

9. Ibid., p. 486.

10. For a discussion of the crusades from the Arab standpoint, see Francesco Gabrieli, *Arab Historians of the Crusades* (Berkeley and Los Angeles: University of California Press, 1984). Salah al-Din's career is discussed by Stanley Lane-Poole in *Saladin and the Fall of the Kingdom of Jerusalem* (Beirut: Khayats, 1964).

11. See Jawzi, *Min Ta'rikh,* Chap. 4. For a discussion of Isma'ilism, see S. M. Stern, *Studies in Early Ismailism* (Leiden: E. J. Brill, 1983).

12. Jawzi, *Min Ta'rikh,* p. 126.

13. Ibid., p. 130.

14. Ibn al-Athir, *Al-Kamil fi'l-Ta'rikh,* Vol. XII, pp. 137–38. Cited by Victor E. Makari, *Ibn Taymiyyah's Ethics: The Social Factor* (Chico, CA: Scholars Press, 1983), p. 10.

15. Joseph Schacht, *An Introduction to Islamic Law* (Oxford: Clarendon Press, 1982), pp. 70–71.

16. Quoted from Ibn Khaldun, *Al-Muqaddimah,* by Muhammad Yusuf Musa, *Ibn Taymiyyah* (Cairo: Al-Mu'assasah al-Misriyyah al-'Ammah li'l-Ta'lif wa'l-Tiba'ah wa'l-Nashr, 1962), pp. 46–47.

17. Cited by Makari, *Ibn Taymiyyah's Ethics,* from Ibn al-Athir's *Khutat al-Maqrizi,* Vol. 2, pp. 358–60.

18. For a discussion of the religious tone of Islamic revolutionary movements, see Jawzi's *Min Ta'rikh,* esp. Chap. 3.

19. Ibn Taymiyya was not the first or only *faqih* to reject *taqlid.* Dawud ibn Khalaf (d. 884), the founder of the literalist Zahiri school of *fiqh,* had done so, and Ibn Tumart (d. 1130), founder of the Almohad movement, had based his claim to independent leadership in North Africa on the doctrine of *ijtihad.* But Ibn Taymiyya was the first member of the official *madhahib* to reject the accepted doctrine of *taqlid.*

20. Ibn Taymiyya, *Raf' al-Malam 'an al-A'immah al-A'lam,* ed. M. H. al-Faqqi (Cairo: Matba'at al-Sunnah al-Muihammadiyyah, 1958), p. 9.

21. Taqiyy al-Din Ahmad Ibn Taymiyya, *Majmu'at Al-Fatawa al-Kubra,* Vol. I (Cairo: Dar al-Kutub al-Hadithah, 1966), p. 484. Cf. Makari, *Ibn Taymiyyah's Ethics,* p. 98.

22. Taqiyy al-Din Ahmad Ibn Taymiyya, *Majmu'at al-Rasa'il wa al-Masa'il,* Vol. V (Cairo: Matba'at al-Manar, 1922–1930), p. 22.

23. See Henri Laoust, *Essai sur les Doctrines Sociales et Politique de Taki-d-Din b. Taimiya* (Le Caire: Institut Francais D'Archaeologie Orientale, 1939), pp. 253ff.

24. Taqiyy al-Din Ahmad Ibn Taymiyya, *Majmu'at al-Fatawa al-Kubra,* Vol. IV (Cairo: Dar al-Kutub al-Hadithah, 1966), p. 219.

25. See Taqiyy al-Din Ahmad Ibn Taymiyya, *Kitab Majmu'at Fatawa Shaikh al-Islam Taqiyy al-Din b. Taymiyya al-Harrani,* Vol. IV (Cairo: Kurdistan al-'Ilmiyya, 1326–1329), "Kitab al-Ikhtiyarat al'Ilmiyya," p. 189; and *Majmu'at al-Rasa'il wa'l-Masa'il,* Vol. I, p. 229. Cited by Laoust, *Essai,* p. 266.

26. Taqiyy al-Din Ahmad Ibn Taymiyya, *Al-Hisbah fi al-Islam* (Damascus: Dar al-Bayan, 1967), p. 4.

27. Interestingly, the same belief is attributed to Thomas Hobbes (see Chapter One in this book). The condemnation of rebellion was well entrenched in Islamic law by the time of Ibn Taymiyya. Al-Mawardi (d. 1058) had declared that even a usurper must be obeyed. As he put it, the caliph must be obeyed "even if one of his vassals seizes control of him and usurps the executive power while formally recognizing his authority." See discussion by Gerhard Endress, *An Introduction to Islam,* tr. Carole Hillenbrand (New York: Columbia University Press, 1988), p. 72.

28. Laoust, *Essai,* p. 252.

29. Quoted by Laoust, *Essai,* p. 255, from Taqiyy al-Din Ahmad Ibn Taymiyya, *Majmu'at al-Rasa'il al-Kubra,* Vol. I (Cairo: n.p., 1323), pp. 307–08.

30. The term *unicity* is used instead of *unity* to connote not only lack of plurality, but of uniqueness and comprehensiveness as well. See Taqiyy al-Din Ahmad Ibn Taymiyya's *Risala Kubrusiyya* (Cairo: Al-Mu'aiyad, 1319), pp. 2–3, as cited by Laoust, *Essai,* p. 17.

31. Cited by Makari, *Ibn Taymiyyah's Ethics,* p. 136, from Ibn Taymiyya, *Al-Siyasah al-Shari'iyyah fi' Islah al-Ra'i' wa'l-Raiyyah,* ed. Muhammad al-Mubarak (Beirut: Dar al-Kutub al-'Arabiyyah, 1966), p. 7.

32. Ibn Taymiyya, *Al-Siyasah al-Shari'iyyah,* p. 17; cf. Makari, *Ibn Taymiyyah's Ethics,* p. 136.

33. For a discussion of these views, see Laoust, *Essai,* pp. 280ff.

34. See Taqiyy al-Din Ahmad Ibn Taymiyya, *Minhaj al-Sunnah al-Nabawiyyah fi Naqd Kalam al-Shi'ah wa'l-Qadariyyah,* Vol. II, ed. Muhammad Rashad Salim (Cairo: Maktabat Dar al-'Urubah, 1962), pp. 112–13; cited by Laoust, *Essai,* p. 281.

35. See Laoust's discussion of this issue in *Essai,* pp. 282ff.

36. See Laoust, *Essai,* p. 282.

37. Ibn Taymiyya, *Minhaj al-Sunnah,* Vol. I, pp. 111–15.

38. Ibn Taymiyya, *Al-Fatawa al-Kubra,* Vol. III (Cairo: Dar al-Kutub al-Hadithah, 1966), pp. 350ff.; cited by Laoust, *Essai,* p. 287.

39. It should be noted that the importance of spiritual unity in the Islamic world did not indicate to Ibn Taymiyya the equality of all races, even among Muslims. Although the basis of Islamic unity lay in doctrine and social will, Ibn Taymiyya consistently maintained the superiority of Arabism.

40. Hodgson, *The Venture of Islam,* Vol. II, p. 471.

Chapter Three

1. Roger Owen, *The Middle East in the World Economy, 1800–1914* (London and New York: Methuen, 1981), pp. 12–13.

2. See, for example, Halil Inalcik, "The Emergence of the Ottomans," in *The Cambridge History of Islam,* Vol. IA, ed. P. M. Holt, Ann K. S. Lambton, and Bernard Lewis (Cambridge: Cambridge University Press, 1970), from which this summary is taken.

3. Ibid., p. 295.

4. From F. Babinger, "Mehmed II der Eroberer und Italien," in *Byzantion,* 21 (1951):140; cited by Inalcik, "The Rise of the Ottoman Empire," in *The Cambridge History of Islam,* Vol. IA, ed. P. M. Holt, Ann K. S. Lambton, and Bernard Lewis (Cambridge: Cambridge University Press, 1970), p. 297.

5. See, for example, M. Dols, "The Second Plague and Its Recurrence in the Middle East," in *Journal of Social and Economic History of the Orient,* Vol. 22, No. 2 (May 1979); I. M. Lapidus, *Muslim Cities in the Later Middle Ages* (Cambridge, MA: Harvard University Press, 1967), pp. 39–40 (cited by Owen, *The Middle East in the World Economy,* p. 295 n. 10).

6. By contrast, areas such as Mount Lebanon in Syria and Basra in Iraq, where Ottoman control remained tenuous, seem to be exceptions to this trend. See Owen's *The Middle East in the World Economy* for a summary of historical research on economic conditions during the Ottoman period.

7. Halil Inalcik, "The Heyday and Decline of the Ottoman Empire," in *The Cambridge History of Islam,* Vol IA, p. 344.

8. Peter Gran, *Islamic Roots of Capitalism. Egypt, 1760–1840* (Austin, TX, and London: University of Texas Press, 1979), p. xvii; Owen, *The Middle East in the World Economy,* p. 4.

9. Owen, *The Middle East in the World Economy,* pp. 4–5.

10. For a characterization of the third world, see Alasdair Drysdale and Gerald H. Blake, *The Middle East and North Africa: A Political Geography* (New York and Oxford: Oxford University Press, 1985), p. 22.

11. See, for example, A. Raymond, "Quartiers et mouvements populaires au Caire au XVIIIe siècle," in *Political and Social Change,* ed. P. M. Holt (London, 1968); G. Baer, "Popular Revolt in Ottoman Cairo," in *Der Islam,* Vol. 54, No. 2 (1977); R. W. Olson, "The Esnaf and the Patrona Halil Rebellion of 1730: A Realignment of Ottoman Politics?" in *Journal of the Economic and Social History of the Orient,* Vol. 17, No. 3 (Sept. 1974); and "Jews, Janissaries, Esnaf and the Revolt of 1740 in Istanbul. Social Upheaval and Political Realignment in the Ottoman Empire," in *Journal of the Economic and Social History of the Orient,* Vol. 20, No. 2 (May 1977). Cited by Owen, *The Middle East in the World Economy,* p. 23 n. 114.

12. See Owen, *The Middle East in the World Economy,* p. 13, for a discussion of Egyptian elites' competition.

13. Scholars traditionally attribute France's invasion of Egypt to French competition with imperial England. See, for example, Philip K. Hitti, *The History of the Arabs,* (New York: St. Martin's, 1970), 10th edition, p. 722; and Marshall G. S. Hodgson, *The Venture of Islam: Conscience and History in a World Civilization,* Vol. III (Chicago and London: University of Chicago Press, 1974), p. 216. However, the economic advantages offered by an Egyptian colony were clearly operative as well in France's strategic considerations. See Gran's discussion in *Islamic Roots of Capitalism,* pp. 28ff.

14. 'Abd al-Rahman al-Jabarti, *'Aja'ib al-Athar fi'l-Tarajim wa'l-Akhbar,* Vol. III (Cairo: n.p., 1322/1904–1905), pp. 4–5; cited by Albert Hourani, *Arabic Thought in the Liberal Age: 1789–1939* (London, Oxford, New York: Oxford University Press, 1970), p. 50.

15. See Stanford Shaw, *The Financial and Administrative Organization of and Development of Ottoman Egypt, 1517–1798* (Princeton, NJ: Princeton University Press, 1962), p. 194. Cited by Gran, *Islamic Roots of Capitalism,* p. 14.

16. This was not the first time in Islamic history such a massacre had occurred. For a similar event in 'Abbasid annals, see Ahmad G. Abi Ya'qub al-Ya'qubi, *Ta'rikh,* Vol. II, ed. Th. Houtsma (Leiden: E. J. Brill, 1883), pp. 425–26. Cf. Abu al-Hasan 'Ali Mas'udi, *Kitab al-Tanbih wa'l-Ishraf,* Vol. VI, ed. M. deGoeje (Leiden: E. J. Brill, 1893–1894), p. 76; Ibn al-Athir, *Al-Kamil fi'l-Ta'rikh,* Vol. V, ed. C. J. Tornberg (Leiden: E. J. Brill, 1867–1874), pp. 329–30.

17. Some scholars believe Ibrahim's change of policy was forced on him by his father, who, having been challenged by the sultan in Syria, decided to raise enough money to equip a modern army and navy in that region to assure his position there. Ibrahim is considered to have been an enlightened leader

who offered the first modern reforms in the Arab world. See, for example, George Antonius, *The Arab Awakening* (New York: Capricorn Books, 1965), pp. 23ff.

18. This sentiment would be echoed by Lord Palmerston in 1933, when he said, "Turkey is as good an occupier of the road to India as an active Arab sovereign would be." Cited by Antonius, *The Arab Awakening*, p. 31.

19. Hitti, *History of the Arabs*, p. 734.

20. For a discussion of these trends, see Hans Kohn, *The Idea of Nationalism* (New York: Macmillan, 1961).

21. From an unpublished manuscript cited by Kohn, *The Idea of Nationalism*, p. 181.

22. James Heyworth-Dunne, *Introduction to the History of Education in Modern Egypt* (London: Luzac and Company, 1939), p. 110; cited by Hourani, *Arabic Thought*, p. 54.

23. See Gran, *Islamic Roots of Capitalism*, especially Chap. 2.

24. The first Arabic press was established in Syria at Aleppo in 1702 by Christians; the first Turkish press, in the 1720s. But printing in Arabic or Turkish was forbidden until the eighteenth century, largely due to the influence of the *'ulama'*. Basing themselves on the central Islamic belief in the inimitability of the Qur'an, from which followed the belief that the Qur'an could not even be translated into other languages and still be sacred, they taught that the Qur'an printed by a machine would no longer be authentic. See Bernard Lewis, *The Emergence of Modern Turkey* (New York: Oxford University Press, 1968), 2d edition, pp. 41 and 50.

25. See, for instance, Hourani, *Arabic Thought*, p. 41; and Gran, *Islamic Roots of Capitalism*, pp. 159–61. In both analyses it is pointed out that Ibn Khaldun was becoming popular among the Turks as well as the Arabs, indicating that the phenomenon of growing historical awareness, or critical self-awareness, was widespread during the decline of the Ottoman caliphate.

26. See Ibn Khaldun, *Ibn Khaldun's Muqaddimah*, tr. Franz Rosenthal (New York: Bollingen Series, Princeton University Press, 1967), 2d edition.

27. See citations from 'Abd al-Rahman al-Jabarti's *'Aja'ib al-Athar fi'l-Tarajim wa'l-Akhbar* by Hourani, *Arabic Thought*, p. 51; and from al-Jabarti, *'Aja'ib al-Athar* by Gran, *Islamic Roots of Capitalism*, p. 72.

28. Unless otherwise indicated, "Syria" is used in its traditional sense, i.e., to include the areas that are now called Syria, Lebanon, Palestine, and Jordan. This has been the meaning of "Syria" since Rome divided it into four districts: Hims (from south of Antioch to north of Tripoli), Dimashq ("Damascus," from north of Tripoli to south of Tyre), al-Urdunn ("Jordan," including Galilee to the Syrian desert), and Filastin ("Palestine," the land south of the Esdraelon Plain, including Nablus all the way to Rafah).

29. Published in Rome from 1719–1728 under the title *Bibliotheca Orientalis*.

Chapter Four

1. Hans Kohn, *A History of Nationalism in the East* (New York: Harcourt, Brace and Co., 1929), p. 14.

2. Bassam Tibi discusses this issue in his *Arab Nationalism: A Critical Enquiry,* ed. and tr. Marion Farouk-Sluglett and Peter Sluglett (New York: St. Martin's, 1981), noting in particular the German efforts to distinguish themselves from the French.

3. See, for example, *Nafir Suriya,* 3 (15 Oct. 1860) and 4 (25 Oct. 1860), as cited by Albert Hourani, *Arabic Thought in the Liberal Age: 1789–1939* (London, Oxford, New York: Oxford University Press, 1970), p. 101.

4. See *Nafir Suriya,* 7 (19 Nov. 1860) and 10 (22 Feb. 1861); cf. Hourani, *Arabic Thought,* p. 102.

5. Bandali al-Jawzi, *Min Ta'rikh al-Harakat al-Fikriyya fi'l-Islam* (Beirut: n.p., 1928), Chap. 10.

6. Max L. Stackhouse, "Piety, Polity, and Policy," in *Religious Beliefs, Human Rights, and the Moral Foundation of Western Democracy* (University of Missouri–Columbia, 1986 Paine Lectures in Religion), p. 16.

7. For a discussion of this period, see Philip K. Hitti, *History of the Arabs* (New York: St. Martin's, 1979), 10th edition, p. 735.

8. Hitti, *History of the Arabs,* p. 735.

9. Al-Tahtawi's diary is called *Takhlis al-Ibriz ila Talkhis Bariz (The Extraction of Gold from the Paris Report).* See Tibi, *Arab Nationalism,* p. 59.

10. Translated by Hazem Zaki Nuseibeh, *The Ideas of Arab Nationalism* (Ithaca, NY: Cornell University Press, 1956), p. 117.

11. Quoted from Al-Tahtawi, *Takhlis al-Ibriz,* in Tibi, *Arab Nationalism,* p. 59.

12. Tibi, *Arab Nationalism,* p. 60.

13. Cited by Hourani, *Arabic Thought,* p. 79. Cf. Ernest C. Dawn, *From Ottomanism to Arabism: Essays on the Origins of Arab Nationalism* (Urbana, Chicago, London: University of Illinois Press, 1973), p. 124.

14. Rifa'a Badawi Rafi' al-Tahtawi, *Manahij al-Albab al-Misriya fi Mabahij al-Adab al-'Asriya* (Cairo, 1912), 3d edition, p. 7; tr. by Hourani, *Arabic Thought,* p. 77.

15. Rifa'a Badawi Rafi' al-Tahtawi, *Al-Murshid al-Amin li'l-Banat wa'l-Banin* (Cairo, 1289/1872–1873), p. 124, cited by Hourani, *Arabic Thought,* p. 77.

16. See Yusuf Sufayr, ed., *Majali al-Ghurar li Kuttab al-Qarn al-Tasi' 'Ashar* (Beirut, 1906), p. 100; cited by Hisham Sharabi, *Arab Intellectuals and the West: The Formative Years, 1875–1914* (Baltimore and London: Johns Hopkins University Press, 1970), p. 57.

17. See, for example, al-Tahtawi, *Manahij al-Albab,* p. 373; and 'Abdul-Rahman al-Kawakibi, *Taba'i' al-Istibdad wa Masari' al-Isti'bad* (Cairo, n.d.), p. 79; cited by Sharabi, *Arab Intellectuals,* pp. 27 and 98.

18. Quoted by Sharabi, *Arab Intellectuals,* p. 98.

19. Jamal al-Din al-Afghani, *Al-Radd 'ala al-Dhahriyyin,* tr. M. 'Abduh, (Cairo, 1955), 2d edition. French translation by D. M. Goichon, *La Refutation des materialistes* (Paris: P. Geuthner, 1942).

20. Muhammad Rashid Rida, *Ta'rikh al-Ustadh al-Imam al-Shaykh Muhammad 'Abduh,* Vol. I (Cairo, 1931), p. 320; cited by Sharabi, *Arab Intellectuals,* p. 28.

21. Rashid Rida, *Ta'rikh al-Ustadh,* Vol. I, p. 328; cf. Sharabi, *Arab Nationalism,* p. 48.

22. D. M. Goichon, *La Refutation,* pp. 177ff.

23. Because of his criticism of foreign control and agitation for reform, al-Afghani had been forced to leave both Persia and Egypt. After a forced confinement in India, he went to Paris, where he was joined by 'Abduh.

24. Jamal al-Din al-Afghani, "Philosophie de l'union nationale basée sur le race et l'unité linguistique," *Orient,* 6 (1958):123ff.; cited by Hourani, *Arabic Thought,* p. 118; cf. Tibi, *Arab Nationalism,* p. 142.

25. See, for example, *al-'Urwa al-Wuthqa,* Vol. II, no. 42 and 110 (Beirut, 1328/1910).

26. Hourani, *Arabic Thought,* p. 115.

27. Quoted by Hourani, ibid., p. 118.

28. Quoted by Tibi, *Arab Nationalism,* p. 140, from al-Afghani, *Al-A'mal al-Kamila,* ed. M. 'Ammara (Cairo, 1968), p. 345.

29. See Edward Granville Browne, *The Persian Revolution of 1905–1909* (London: The University Press, 1910), p. 7; cited by Hourani, *Arabic Thought,* p. 118.

30. Quoted by Sharabi, *Arab Intellectuals,* p. 32, from Muhammad al-Makhzumi, *Khatirat Jamal al-Din al-Afghani al-Husayni* (Beirut: al-Matba'ah al-'ilmiyya li'l-Yusuf Sadir, 1931), pp. 153–54.

31. "Laws vary as the conditions of nations vary" (quoted by Hourani, *Arabic Thought,* p. 137).

32. Rashid Rida, *Ta'rikh al-Ustadh,* Vol. I, p. 11.

33. Muhammad 'Abduh, *Risalat al-Tawhid* (Cairo, 1361/1942–1943), p. 19; cited by Hourani, *Arabic Thought,* p. 150.

34. Quoted by Hourani, *Arabic Thought,* p. 157, from Sir Wilfred Blunt, *Secret History of the British Occupation of Egypt* (London: Martin Secker, 1922), p. 191.

35. Rashid Rida, *Ta'rikh al-Ustadh,* Vol. I, p. 11; cited by Hourani, *Arabic Thought,* p. 141.

36. Muhammad 'Abduh, *Al-Islam wa'l-Nasraniyya* (Cairo, 1367/1947–1948), p. 84.

37. Rashid Rida, *Ta'rikh al-Ustadh,* Vol. II, p. 15; cited by Hourani, *Arabic Thought,* p. 156.

38. Hourani, *Arabic Thought,* p. 156; cf. Rashid Rida, *Ta'rikh al-Ustadh,* Vol. I, p. 647.

39. George Antonius, *The Arab Awakening* (New York: Capricorn Books, 1965), p. 55.

40. See, for instance, Tibi, *Arab Nationalism,* p. 146; Hazem Zaki Nuseibeh, *The Ideas of Arab Nationalism* (Ithaca, NY: Cornell University Press, 1959), 2d edition, p. 129; cf. Ernest C. Dawn, *From Ottomanism to Arabism: Essays on the Origins of Arab Nationalism* (Urbana, Chicago, London: University of Illinois Press, 1973), pp. 139–40.

41. Al-Kawakibi's writings are collected in two works: *Umm al-Qura* (Aleppo, 1959); and *Taba'i' al-Istibdad wa Masari' al-Isti'bad* (Cairo, n.d.). Cf. Tibi, *Arab Nationalism,* p. 145.

42. Qasim Amin, *Al-Mar'a al-Jadida* (Cairo, 1901), pp. 29 and 152; cited by Hourani, *Arabic Thought,* p. 167.

43. Qasim Amin, *Al-Mar'a,* p. 176; Hourani, *Arabic Thought,* p. 168.

44. Husayn al-Marsafi, *Risalat al-Kalim al-Thaman* (Beirut: Dar al-Tali'ah, 1982).

45. *Al-Watan* was written by 'Abd Allah al-Nadim, spokesman of 'Urabi's group, and stresses the importance of equality of all Egyptians for the sake of national strength through unity. It specifically excludes Europeans and—more significantly—Syrians as non-Egyptians. See 'Abd Allah al-Nadim, *Sulafat al-Nadim,* Vol. II (Cairo, 1897–1901).

46. Hourani, *Arabic Thought,* p. 170.

47. Ahmad Lutfi al-Sayyid, *Safahat Matwiyya,* Vol. I (Cairo, 1946), p. 118; Hourani, *Arabic Thought,* p. 172.

48. Ahmad Lutfi al-Sayyid, *Ta'ammulat* (Cairo, 1946), p. 68; Hourani, *Arabic Thought,* p. 178.

49. 'Abd al-Rahman al-Rafi'i, *Mustafa Kamil* (Cairo, 1950), p. 108; tr. by Hourani, *Arabic Thought,* p. 206.

50. Hourani, *Arabic Thought,* p. 202. Bassam Tibi interprets this as superficial Islam in *Arab Nationalism,* pp. 154–55.

51. Hourani, *Arabic Thought,* p. 205.

52. 'Abd al-Qadir al-Mugharibi, *Al-Bayyinat,* Vol. I (Cairo, 1344), pp. 5–6; cited by Sharabi, *Arab Intellectuals,* p. 34.

53. Antonius, *The Arab Awakening,* p. 104.

54. This section is taken mainly from Antonius's description of the various societies, their membership, and their development and demands, which remains the classic source for this material (ibid., pp. 108ff.). See also Tibi, *Arab Nationalism,* pp. 82–84.

55. For membership of the Arab societies, see Dawn, *From Ottomanism to Arabism,* pp. 152–55. For a discussion of the social and educational distinctions among the Arab nationalist leaders, see ibid., pp. 164–74. On Christian membership in the societies, see ibid., pp. 143–47.

Chapter Five

1. Alasdair Drysdale and Gerald H. Blake, *The Middle East and North Africa: A Political Geography* (New York and Oxford: Oxford University Press, 1985), p. 63.

2. The classic telling of the story of the Arab Revolt is George Antonius's *The Arab Awakening* (New York: Capricorn Books, 1965), on which this account is largely based.

3. Iraq was always a distinct region in the Arab world and was administered as such by the Ottomans. This very distinction tended to emphasize Iraq's uniqueness, as did the British claim to it, vis-à-vis French claims to Syria. William L. Cleveland describes it as "the awkward amalgamation of under-developed provinces that became Iraq" (*Islam Against the West* [Austin: University of Texas Press, 1985], p. 46). The Arab nationalists themselves will call

Syria and Iraq "two brother regions" in the 1920 Syrian General Congress (see Ernest C. Dawn, *From Ottomanism to Arabism: Essays on the Origins of Arab Nationalism* [Urbana, Chicago, London: University of Illinois Press, 1973], p. 151).

4. Antonius, *The Arab Awakening*, p. 168. For a discussion of the conflicting interpretations of the McMahon-Hussein Correspondence, see Dawn, *From Ottomanism to Arabism*, pp. 99–121. Regarding Hussein's rejection of the caliphate, see ibid., pp. 40–45, 81–83, 116–19.

5. Antonius, *The Arab Awakening*, pp. 170, 203.

6. The original text of the British communiqué was in Arabic. This translation is by Antonius, *The Arab Awakening*, p. 432.

7. Ibid., pp. 266–67.

8. See, for example, Maxime Rodinson, *Israel: A Colonial-Settler State?* (New York: Monad Press, 1973). See also Tamara Sonn, "The Arab-Israeli Conflict," in *Movements and Issues in World Religions: A Sourcebook and Analysis of Developments Since 1945 (Religion, Ideology, and Politics)*, ed. Charles W. H. Fu and Gerhard E. Spiegler (New York, Westport, CN, and London: Greenwood Press, 1985), pp. 1–38.

9. For a discussion of spiritual Zionism, see M. Perlmann, "Chapters of Arab-Jewish Diplomacy, 1918–1922," in *Jewish Social Studies*, Vol. 6, No. 2 (April 1944):123–24.

10. See, for example, "Memorandum of Edwin Montagu on the Anti-Semitism of the Present (British) Government—Submitted to the British Cabinet, August 1917" (Great Britain, Public Record Office, Cab. 24/24, Aug. 23, 1917); cited in "Edwin Montagu and Zionism," in *From Haven to Conquest: Readings in Zionism and the Palestine Problem Until 1948*, ed. Walid Khalidi (Washington: Institute for Palestine Studies, 1971), pp. 143–52.

11. See *Al-Qibla* (Mecca), 183 (23 March 1918), cited by Antonius, *The Arab Awakening*, p. 269.

12. Text of "Declaration to the Seven," given in full in Antonius, *The Arab Awakening*, Appendix D, pp. 433–34.

13. Translated by Antonius, *The Arab Awakening*, pp. 435–36.

14. Ibid., p. 287.

15. Ibid., pp. 440–41.

16. "The American King Crane Commission of Inquiry, 1919," in Khalidi, *From Haven to Conquest*, pp. 215–18.

17. A. Chouraqui, *A Man Alone, the Life of Theodor Herzl* (Jerusalem: Keter Books, 1970), p. 256. See also Alexandre Bein, *Introduction au Sionisme* (Jerusalem: Rubin Mass, 1946), p. 139; cited by Rodinson, *Israel: A Colonial-Settler State?* pp. 58–59.

18. Bassam Tibi claims, in fact, that the Nationalist Party had been established by Britain in an effort to counter the extreme nationalist efforts of Mustafa Kamil's National Party. See Bassam Tibi, *Arab Nationalism: A Critical Enquiry*, ed. and tr. Marion Farouk-Sluglett and Peter Sluglett (New York: St. Martin's, 1981), p. 155.

19. This, despite the fact that Britain included the Sudan in their Anglo-Egyptian condominium, established in 1899. See Drysdale and Blake, *The Middle East and North Africa,* pp. 54, 69, 95–97, 252–53.

20. See 'Abbas Mahmud al-'Aqqad, *Sa'd Zaghlul* (Cairo, 1936), p. 195. Cited by Albert Hourani, *Arabic Thought in the Liberal Age: 1798–1939* (London, Oxford, New York: Oxford University Press, 1970), p. 218. Zaghlul himself denied that the Wafd was a party, but called it "a delegation empowered by the nation and expressing its will about a matter which it has assigned to us: this matter is complete independence, and we strive to this end alone" (Sa'd Zaghlul, *Majmu'at Khutab* [Cairo, 1924], p. 27; translated by Hourani, *Arabic Thought,* p. 221). However, the Wafd did become a political party after Egyptian independence and, in its current state, is generally called the New Wafd Party.

21. Hourani, *Arabic Thought,* p. 214. Some of Zaghlul's detractors doubted his Islamic sincerity. Hourani quotes his biographer, 'Abbas Mahmud al-'Aqqad, as saying Zaghlul was only interested in the Qur'an for the quotations it could supply to persuade his Islamic audience (*Arabic Thought,* p. 217).

22. Cited by Hourani, *Arabic Thought,* p. 215, from Sa'd Zaghlul, *Athar al-Za'im,* Vol. I, ed. Muhammad Ibrahim al-Jaziri (Cairo, 1927), p. 54.

23. Cited by Hourani, *Arabic Thought,* p. 185, from 'Ali 'Abd al-Raziq, *Al-Islam wa Usul al-Hukm* (Cairo, 1925), pp. 18, 24; French translation by L. Bercher, "L'Islam et les bases du pouvoir," in *Revue des etudes islamiques,* 7 (1933):374ff.

24. Cited by Hourani, *Arabic Thought,* p. 191, from Muhammad Bakhit al-Muti'i, *Haqiqat al-Islam wa Usul al-Hukm* (Cairo, 1926), p. 30.

25. Cited by Hourani, *Arabic Thought,* p. 299.

26. Compare Muhammad Rashid Rida, *Al-Manar wa'l-Azhar* (Cairo, 1353/1934–1935), p. 179, for example, with Muhammad Rashid Rida, *Al-Sunna wa'l-Shi'a* (Cairo, 1947), p. 79; or Muhammad Rashid Rida, *Al-Wahhabiyyun wa'l-Hijaz* (Cairo, 1344/1925–1926).

27. Farah Antun, *Ibn Rushd wa-Falsafatuhu,* pp. 151ff; cf. Hourani, *Arabic · Thought,* p. 256.

28. Rashid Rida, *Al-Manar,* 12 (1909–1910):823, 832; cited by Hourani, *Arabic Thought,* p. 302.

29. Rashid Rida, *Al-Manar,* 23 (1920):254; Hourani, *Arabic Thought,* p. 304. Malcolm Kerr assesses Rashid Rida, saying he "symbolizes in some ways the political failure of the whole Islamic modernist movement. Without any particular shifts in doctrine his position evolved, under pressure of circumstances, from that of liberal reformer to radical fundamentalist to orthodox conservative" (*Islamic Reform: The Political and Legal Theories of Muhammad 'Abduh and Rashid Rida* [Berkeley and Los Angeles: University of California Press, 1966], pp. 15–16).

Chapter Six

1. Qustantin [Constantine] Zurayq, *Ma'na al-Nakba Mujaddan* (Beirut: Dar al-'Ilm li'l-Malayin, August 1967), p. 29. Although Zurayq's analysis actually

concerns developments following the 1967 "Six-Day" War, the reference to the attraction of socialist thought, both economic and political, is pertinent to the period between the First and Second World Wars. Translated by Tareq Y. Ismael, *The Arab Left* (Syracuse, NY: Syracuse University Press, 1976), p. 12.

2. From Edward W. Said, Ibrahim Abu-Lughod, Janet L. Abu-Lughod, Muhammad Hallaj, and Elia Zureik, "A Profile of the Palestinian People," in *Blaming the Victims: Spurious Scholarship and the Palestinian Question,* ed. Edward W. Said and Christopher Hitchens (London and New York: Verso, 1988), pp. 242–43.

3. Shakib Arslan, *Rashid Rida aw Ikha' Arba'in Sana* (Cairo, 1937), pp. 600ff; cited by Albert Hourani, *Arabic Thought in the Liberal Age: 1789–1939* (London, Oxford, New York: Oxford University Press, 1970), p. 305.

4. Nuri al-Sa'id, *Arab Independence and Unity* (Baghdad, 1943), p. 11; cf. Hourani, *Arabic Thought,* p. 294. This, in fact, did occur in 1945, although it did not transcend the differences among the states represented.

5. For a brief discussion of Sati' al-Husri's life and works, see Hourani, *Arabic Thought,* pp. 311–16.

6. See Bassam Tibi, *Arab Nationalism: A Critical Enquiry,* ed. and tr. Marion Farouk-Sluglett and Peter Sluglett (New York: St. Martin's, 1971), pp. 90–172.

7. 'Abd al-Rahman al-Bazzaz, *Al-Islam wa'l-Qawmiyya al-'Arabiyya* (Baghdad, 1952). English translation by S. G. Haim, "Islam and Arab Nationalism," in *Welt des Islams,* 3 (1954):201–18.

8. See Qustantin Zurayq, *Ma'na al-Nakba* (Beirut, 1948), English translation by R. Bayly Winder, *The Meaning of the Disaster* (Beirut: Khayyat's College Book Cooperative, 1956); Qustantin Zurayq, *Nahnu wa'l-Ta'rikh* (Beirut: Dar al-'Ilm li'l-Malayin, 1963); Qustantin Zurayq, *Al-Wa'y al-Qaymi* (Beirut: n.p., 1939); and Qustantin Zurayq, *Ayyu Ghad?* (Beirut: Dar al-'Ilm li'l-Malayin, 1956).

9. Alasdair Drysdale and Gerald H. Blake, *The Middle East and North Africa: A Political Geography* (New York and Oxford: Oxford University Press, 1985), pp. 71–72.

10. See Shibli Shumayyil, *Falsafat al-Nushu' wa'l-Irtiqa'* (Cairo, 1910); and Shibli Shumayyil, *Majmu'a* (Cairo, n.d.).

11. 'Abd al-Rahman al-Bazzaz, *Hathihi Qawmiyyatuna* (Cairo, 1964), p. 66. Cited by Ismael, *The Arab Left,* p. 8.

12. Quoted from Fahmi Jad'an, *Usus al-Taqadum 'inda Mufakkir al-Islam fi'l-Alam al-'Arabi al-Hadith* (Beirut: al-Mu'asasat al-'Arabiyya li'l-Dirasat wa'l-Nashir, 1979), p. 509, by Tareq Y. Ismael and Jacqueline S. Ismael, *Government and Politics in Islam* (New York: St. Martin's, 1985), p. 47.

13. Tareq Y. Ismael, *The Middle East in World Politics* (Syracuse, NY: Syracuse University Press, 1974), p. 216.

14. The development of communist parties in the Arab world will not be discussed here, as they have never played more than a minor role in the region. Their history is long (having begun soon after the Bolshevik Revolution) and complex (related to Soviet policies with regard to the Soviet Muslim population, as well as other foreign policy considerations in the Soviet Union). For a recent

work on the subject, see Joel Beinin and Zachary Lockman, *Workers on the Nile: Nationalism, Communism, Islam, and the Egyptian Working Class, 1882–1954* (Princeton, NJ: Princeton University Press, 1988); see also Selma Botman, *The Rise of Egyptian Communism: 1939–70* (Syracuse, NY: Syracuse University Press, 1988); cf. Mahmood Ibrahim, *Merchant Capital and Islam* (Austin: University of Texas Press, 1989).

15. From Shibli al-Aysami, *Hizb al-Ba'th al-'Arabi al-Ishtiraki: 1–Marhalat al-Arab'inat al-Ta'sisyah, 1940–49* (Beirut: Dar al-Tali'ah, 1974), pp. 27–28, summarized by Ismael, *The Arab Left*, p. 20, from which this account is largely drawn. Ismael relies heavily on primary sources such as *Nidal al-Ba'th*, Vol. 1 (Beirut: Dar al-Tali'ah, 1972), 3d edition; *Nidal Hizb al-Ba'th al-'Arabi al-Ishtiraki 'abra Mu'tamaratihi al-Qawmiyyah: 1947–1964* (Beirut: Dar al-Tali'ah, 1972), 2d edition; Michel Aflaq and Salahaldin al-Bitar, *al-Qawmiyyah al-'Arabiyyah wa Mawqifuha min al-Shuyu'iyyah* (Damascus, n.d.); and Michel Aflaq, *Fi Sabil al-Ba'th* (Beirut: Dar al-Tali'ah, 1963), 2d edition.

16. All quotations from the constitution of the Ba'th Party, 1947, are translated by Ismael, *The Arab Left*, pp. 126–37.

17. Antun Sa'ada, *Nushu' al-Uman* (Damascus, 1951), 2d edition. This summary of Sa'ada's views is derived largely from L. Z. Yamak, *The Syrian Social Nationalist Party, an Analysis* (Cambridge, MA: Harvard University Press, 1969); K. H. Karpat, ed., *Political and Social Thought in the Contemporary Middle East* (London: Pall Mall Publishers, 1968), pp. 72–79 and 87–98; and Hourani, *Arabic Thought*, pp. 317–18. See also Tibi, *Arab Nationalism*, pp. 165–72; and Daniel Pipes, "Radical Politics and the Syrian Social Nationalist Party," in *International Journal of Middle East Studies*, Vol. 20, No. 3 (August 1988):303–24.

18. Quoted by Tibi, *Arab Nationalism*, p. 157, from Sati' al-Husri, *Ara' wa Ahadith fi'l-Qawmiyyat al-'Arabiyya* (Beirut, 1964), 4th edition, p. 7.

19. From *The Charter*, submitted by Jamal 'Abd al-Nasser May 21, 1962, to the National Congress of Popular Forces (Cairo: Information Department), pp. 27–28. Cited by Ismael, *The Arab Left*, pp. 86–87.

20. Munif al-Razzaz, *Al-Tajruba al-Mura* (Beirut: Dar Ghandur, 1967), p. 87; cited by Ismael, *The Arab Left*, p. 29.

21. Cited by Pipes, "Radical Politics,"p. 317, from Eric Rouleau, "The Syrian Enigma: What Is the Ba'th?" New Left Review, Vol. 45 (1967):63.

22. Yahya M. Sadowski, "Patronage and the Ba'th: Corruption and Control in Contemporary Syria," *Arab Studies Quarterly*, Vol. 9, No. 4 (Fall 1987):442–61, from which this summary of Assad's rise to power is taken.

23. Ibid., pp. 444–45.

24. Hanna Batatu, "Some Observations on the Social Roots of Syria's Ruling Military Group and the Causes for Its Dominance," *Middle East Journal*, Vol. 35 (Summer 1982):331–44.

25. R. Hrair Dekmejian, *Islam in Revolution: Fundamentalism in the Arab World* (Syracuse, NY: Syracuse University Press, 1985), p. 110.

26. Reported in *Middle East International*, Vol. 285 (10 Oct. 1986):11.

27. Reported in *World Press Reports*, Vol. 33, No. 12 (Dec. 1986):41.

28. This brief description of the rise and fall of the Arab Nationalist Movement is taken from Ismael, *The Arab Left,* pp. 63–70.

29. Ibid., p. 68.

Chapter Seven

1. Malcolm H. Kerr, *Islamic Reform: The Political and Legal Theories of Muhammad 'Abduh and Rashid Rida* (Berkeley and Los Angeles: University of California Press, 1966), p. 2.

2. Indeed, as one version of the story goes, Transjordan was created with Hashemite approval as a sort of consolation prize for the Arabs, so bitterly betrayed by Britain. See Alasdair Drysdale and Gerald H. Blake, *The Middle East and North Africa: A Political Geography* (New York and Oxford: Oxford University Press, 1985), pp. 63–64. In fact, the story was a bit more complicated than that. See Faisal's own account as recorded by George Antonius, *The Arab Awakening* (New York: Capricorn Books, 1965), pp. 316–18, where it is clear the (Trans)Jordanian state was accepted by the Hashemites (April 1, 1921) as a step toward ending the mandates and asserting Arab claims over all the liberated territory.

3. Richard P. Mitchell, *The Society of the Muslim Brothers,* Princeton University Ph.D. dissertation, 1960, p. 524. This work was published under the title *The Society of the Muslim Brothers* (London: Oxford University Press, 1969) and is the standard work on the origin and development of the Society of Muslim Brothers. References herein are to the former text.

4. Quoted by Mitchell in an interview with an unnamed Muslim Brother (*The Society,* p. 430). It is possible to distinguish three different terms used in Brotherhood writings, each of which may be translated as "the nation": *umma, watan,* and *qawm.* The term *umma* almost always refers to the overall Islamic community, irrespective of political distinctions. The early modernists introduced the term *watan* as they tried to induce a counterpart of Montesquieu's "love of country." Mitchell points out that the term *qawm* can be distinguished from *watan* in that the former actually refers to the people, whereas the latter refers to the land (*The Society,* p. 432). In the present context, however, when the terms are used in their adjectival forms, both *wataniyya* and *qawmiyya* can be translated adequately as nationalism.

5. Mitchell, *The Society,* p. 19.

6. Quoted in ibid. from *Risalat Da'watuna fi Tawr Jadid,* pp. 11-12; and *Risalat al-Shabab,* p. 14. Mitchell's references, quoted here, are to the official *rasa'il* (plural of *risalah,* "epistle"), various undated editions published in Cairo and collected in Hasan al-Banna, *Al-Mu'thurat,* ed. Radwan Muhammad Radwan (Cairo: 1952).

7. Mitchell, *The Society,* p. 383.

8. Ibid., p. 364.

9. Ibid., p. 431.

10. Ibid., p. 432.

11. Ibid.

12. Rashid Rida's views on this subject are summarized by Albert Hourani, *Arabic Thought in the Liberal Age: 1798–1939* (London, Oxford, New York: Oxford University Press, 1970), pp. 227–34. On the issue of national strength, Hourani cites Shakib Arslan, *Limatha Ta'akhkhar al-Muslimun?* (Cairo, 1358/1939–1940), p. 87.

13. Hourani, *Arabic Thought,* p. 229.

14. Mitchell, *The Society,* p. 379.

15. Ibid., p. 375.

16. Ibid., p. 373.

17. Ibid., p. 374.

18. Ibid., p. 384. Elsewhere: "If the French Revolution decreed the rights of man and declared for freedom, equality, and brotherhood, and if the Russian Revolution brought closer the classes and social justice for people, the great Islamic revolution decreed all of that thirteen hundred years before. It did not confine itself to philosophical theories but rather spread these principles through daily life, and added to them [the notions of] divinity in mankind, and the [possibility of the] perfectibility of his virtues and [the fulfillment] of his spiritual tendencies" (ibid., p. 385).

19. Ibid., p. 390.

20. Ibid., p. 405.

21. Ibid., p. 347.

22. Ibid., p. 401.

23. Ibid., p. 347.

24. Ibid., p. 354.

25. Ibid., p. 433.

26. Ibid., p. 435.

27. Paraphrased in ibid., p. 349. Ibn Taymiyya had expressed the same sentiments, as well (see Chapter Two n. 39 in this book).

28. Ibid., p. 432.

29. Ibid., p. 175.

30. When al-Banna first began to attract a wide following, he had described his motivation vaguely as a desire to serve humanity: "I believe that the best people are those who . . . achieve their happiness by making others happy and in counselling them" (ibid., p. 19). Later, as the society grew in strength in Cairo and some of his followers agitated for more direct action, al-Banna had warned "the anxious and hasty" and reminded them of the need for patience: "When the time comes for action, we will be ready" (ibid., p. 33). By 1937, apparently, the time had come. King Faruq had been crowned, and all of Egypt's hopes were high. The Society of Muslim Brothers joined in the celebration, pledging their allegiance to King Faruq on the Qur'an and the Sunna. Even this was not enough for some of the disaffected Egyptians, who looked to al-Banna to lead them in revolution against the British-controlled regime. As early as 1939, therefore, some left the group to form a more militant organization, the Society of Our Lord Muhammad's Youth, bent on forcibly restructuring Egyptian society.

31. Anwar al-Sadat, *Sahafat* (Cairo: Dar al-Tahrir li'l-Tab wa'l-Nashr, 1954), pp. 33–48; cited by Mitchell, *The Society,* p. 48.

32. The Muslim Brother who made contact with Nasser was Mahmud Labib, as reported by Mitchell, *The Society,* p. 150.

33. Mitchell (*The Society,* p. 61) relies for his treatment of postwar Egypt on Charles Issawi, *Egypt at Mid-Century: An Economic Survey* (London: Oxford University Press, 1954), pp. 262–63.

34. The population of the Zionist state was to be approximately half Jewish and half Arab (500,000 each), while the Arab state was to have about 725,000 Arabs and 20,000 Jews. As Drysdale and Blake report, "The plan was deeply flawed. . . . No map could have heightened each side's sense of vulnerability more successfully. Both territories were fragmented and had highly irregular, interdigitated shapes and long sinuous boundaries" (*The Middle East and North Africa,* p. 279).

35. Although the date of the creation of the paramilitary Secret Apparatus (*al-nizam al-khass* or, more frequently, *al-jihaz al-sirri*) is a matter of controversy, Mitchell (*The Society,* p. 55) makes a solid case for its establishment in 1942 or 1943.

36. Mitchell, *The Society,* p. 106.

37. Mitchell relates in *The Society* (p. 106) that several investigations were carried out, all pointing to the Egyptian police and palace. The official trials were not held until after the revolution of 1952.

38. Mitchell, *The Society,* p. 125.

39. Ibid., p. 154.

40. Ibid., p. 171.

41. The RCC did not know about the negotiations at the time; they were themselves still trying to determine the extent of Brotherhood power in May, when an RCC representative approached al-Hudaybi regarding the Brotherhood's preparedness should hostilities break out in the Canal zone. The Brotherhood general guide's equivocal answer heightened suspicions regarding the society's commitment to the RCC's government. For a discussion of the charges levelled against al-Hudaybi and the Society of Muslim Brothers by the RCC and the Brothers' defense, as well as the British version of the meeting, see Mitchell, *The Society,* pp. 172–74.

42. Mitchell (*The Society,* p. 577) reports that there were allegations the entire event was staged by the government as an excuse to finally eliminate the Society of Muslim Brothers.

43. R. Hrair Dekmejian, *Islam in Revolution: Fundamentalism in the Arab World* (Syracuse, NY: Syracuse University Press, 1985), p. 85.

44. By then Nasser's union with Syria had fallen apart, his troops were embroiled in the Yemeni civil war, and his economic reforms were showing little success. These issues were the subject of growing criticism of the regime, particularly by communists. Nasser knew the Brotherhood would openly criticize him again, but he apparently believed their vehement anticommunist stance would be an effective counterweight to his secularist opponents.

45. See, for example, Hasan Hanafi, "Wa Kanat al-Naksah Nuqtah Tahawwul," in *Al-Watan* (20 Nov. 1982), as cited by Dekmejian, *Islam in Revolution,* p. 215 n. 10.

46. Quoted by Tareq Y. Ismael, ed., *The Middle East in World Politics: A Study in Contemporary International Relations* (Syracuse, NY: Syracuse University Press, 1974), p. 141. Indeed, it was the United States' misunderstanding of Nasser's nonalignment policy that led to the 1956 Arab-Israeli War: "The United States misconstrued Nasser's nonalignment policy and withdrew its offer to aid in the construction of the vital High Dam at Aswan. Egypt responded by nationalizing the Anglo-French Suez Canal Company, hoping to use canal tolls to finance the dam's construction. This caused much anxiety to Britain and France, who decided to seize the canal and topple Nasser. Israel quickly recognized an opportunity to address some of its own concerns by launching a strike against Egypt" (Drysdale and Blake, *The Middle East and North Africa,* p. 287).

47. See 'Abd al-Halim Mahmud, *Fatawa 'an al-Shuyu'iyya* (Cairo: Dar al-Ma'arif, 1976), called by Fouad Ajami "a very shallow book" because of its obvious effort to sanction whatever policies Sadat chose to implement (see Fouad Ajami, "In the Pharaoh's Shadow: Religion and Authority in Egypt," in *Islam in the Political Process,* ed. James P. Piscatori [Cambridge: Cambridge University Press, 1983], pp. 12–35). See also 'Ali 'Abd al-Azim, *Mashaikhat al-Azhar min Inshaihi hata Alan,* Part 2 (Cairo: Al-Ha'y al-Amma li Shu'un al-Matabi', 1979), pp. 307–17, for which reference I am most grateful to Frank Mullaney, Sociology Department, Harvard University. Mullaney pointed out that Sh. 'Abd al-Halim Mahmud died five months before the Camp David accords were signed. His successor, 'Abd al-Rahman Bisar, provided the official blessing for the accords.

48. "The [state appointed leadership of the] *'ulama'* of al-Azhar believe that the Egyptian-Israeli treaty is in harmony with Islamic law. It was concluded from a position of strength after . . . the *jihad* and the victory realized by Egypt on the tenth of Ramadan of the year 1393 (6 October 1973)" (quoted by Ajami, "In the Pharaoh's Shadow," p. 16, from a fatwa published in the official Egyptian newspaper *al-Ahram,* 10 May 1979).

49. Quoted from 'Asim al-Dasuqi, *Mujtama' 'Ulama' al-Azhar, 1895–1961* (Cairo, 1980), p. 57, by Ajami, "In the Pharaoh's Shadow," p. 18. See also Afaf Lutfi al-Sayyid Marsot, "The Ulama of Cairo in the Eighteenth and Nineteenth Centuries," in *Scholars, Saints, and Sufis: Muslim Institutions Since 1500,* ed. Nikki R. Keddie (Berkeley and Los Angeles: University of California Press, 1972).

50. The shaykh's statement was carried in Cairo's daily newspaper *al-Ahram,* 16 July 1977.

51. See Philippe Rochot, *La grande fievre du monde Musulman* (Paris: Sycamore, 1981), pp. 143–45; cf. Dekmejian, *Islam in Revolution,* pp. 88, 215.

52. See Johannes J. G. Jansen, *The Neglected Duty: The Creed of Sadat's Assassins and Islamic Resurgence in the Middle East* (New York: Macmillan, 1986), pp. 91–120.

53. For a discussion of the dispute regarding the affiliation of the assassins of Sadat, see Jansen, *The Neglected Duty,* pp. 13–14. Jansen disputes the claim

made by many that Sadat's assassins were members of *al-Takfir wa'l-Hijra,* citing criticism of that group in the assassins' testimony.

54. For a translation and discussion of the statement left by Sadat's assassins, see Jansen, *The Neglected Duty,* pp. 159–234; cf. Gilles Kepel, *Le prophete et pharaon: Les mouvements islamistes dan l'Egypte contemporaine* (Paris: La decouverte, 1984).

55. See Umar F. 'Abd Allah, *The Islamic Struggle in Syria* (Berkeley, CA: Mizan Press, 1983); and Dekmejian, *Islam in Revolution,* pp. 112–25.

56. See Patrick Seale, *The Struggle for Syria* (London: Oxford University Press, 1965), p. 180, as cited by Michael C. Hudson, "The Islamic Factor in Syrian and Iraqi Politics," in *Islam in the Political Process,* ed. James P. Piscatori (Cambridge: Cambridge University Press, 1983), p. 96; see also Nikolaos van Dam, *The Struggle for Power in Syria* (New York: St. Martin's, 1979).

57. See Olivier Carré and Gerard Michaud, *Les Frères Muslims (1928–1982)* (Paris: Editions Gallimard, 1983); and Hanna Batatu, "Syria's Muslim Brethren," *MERIP Reports,* No. 110 (Nov. 1982):12–20.

58. Quoted by Hudson, "The Islamic Factor," p. 84, from the Higher Command of the Islamic Revolution in Syria, "Declaration and Program of the Islamic Revolution in Syria" (Damascus, 9 Nov. 1980), p. 8.

59. See Yahya Sadowski, "Patronage and the Ba'th: Corruption and Control in Contemporary Syria," *Arab Studies Quarterly,* Vol. 9, No. 4 (Fall 1987):451–52.

60. Reported by Hudson, "The Islamic Factor," p. 96.

61. See the study on Iraq by Hanna Batatu, *The Old Social Classes and the Revolutionary Movements of Iraq* (Princeton, NJ: Princeton University Press, 1978).

62. In the Shi'i model, the Islamic state would be under the guidance of Islamic legists (*fuqaha'*), interpreting the will of the infallible imam. For a detailed discussion of the Shi'i notion of leadership, see Abdulaziz Abbulhussein Sachedina, *The Just Ruler (al-Sultan al-'Adil) in Shi'ite Islam: The Comprehensive Authority of the Jurist in Imamite Jurisprudence* (New York and Oxford: Oxford University Press, 1988). See also Emmanuel Sivan, "Sunni Radicalism in the Middle East and the Iranian Revolution," *International Journal of Middle East Studies,* Vol. 21, No. 1 (Feb. 1989):1–30. For the theories of the Da'wa Party, see the Islamic Da'wa Party, "The Form of Islamic Government and Wilayat al-Faqih" (Bethesda, MD: The Islamic Revival Movement, 1981).

63. Dekmejian, *Islam in Revolution,* p. 59. I disagree with the use of the adjective *fundamentalist* to describe the Islamic activist groups. Fundamentalism refers to the tendency to take scripture literally, even as a source of scientific and historical truth, as well as religious. The Islamic groups are more properly called "integralist," referring to movements that advocate a return to the time when religious and political institutions were united. This tendency is represented in Christianity, for instance, in the Opus Dei movement in Roman Catholicism, currently popular among arch-conservative anticommunists in Europe and the United States and enjoying papal support.

64. Reported in *Inquiry* Vol. 2, No. 9 (Sept. 1985):63.

Chapter Eight

1. Malcolm H. Kerr, *Islamic Reform: The Political and Legal Theories of Muhammad 'Abduh and Rashid Rida* (Berkeley and Los Angeles: University of California Press, 1966), p. 3.

2. Lisa Anderson, "Religion and State in Libya: The Politics of Identity," *The Annals of the American Academy of Political and Social Science*, Vol. 483 (Jan. 1986):61–72.

3. Ibid., p. 68.

4. Quoted in ibid., p. 70, from interviews published in *Thus Spoke Colonel Moammar Kazzafi* (Beirut: Dar al-Awda, 1974) and *Time* (9 April 1979), by Anderson, p. 70.

5. Reported in *Insight* (3 Nov. 1986):38.

6. Anderson, "Religion and State in Libya," p. 72.

7. For a detailed discussion of the boundary disputes between Iran and Iraq, see Alasdair Drysdale and Gerald H. Blake, *The Middle East and North Africa: A Political Geography* (New York and Oxford: Oxford University Press, 1985), pp. 85–86.

8. Safa Haeri, "The Ayatollah's Motive," *Middle East International* 345 (3 March 1989):11.

9. Nadim Jaber, "Challenge to the Saudis," *Middle East International* 345 (3 March 1989):11.

10. It should be noted that the ayatollah's response to apostasy is not shared by all Muslims. The great Pakistani scholar Fazlur Rahman claimed that apostasy is not a punishable crime for two reasons. First, the Qur'an explicitly states that "there is no compulsion" in matters of religion. If people are not allowed freedom of choice there can be no merit in proper choice. Furthermore, the Qur'an states that God will not forgive "those people who believed then disbelieved, then again believed, and once more disbelieved and then became entrenched in their disbelief" (4:137). In Islam there is no concept of purgatory, i.e., the need to purge one's soul, if one has accepted the punishment for a crime prescribed by Islamic law. Once the required retribution is made (punishment), forgiveness is granted. Rahman interprets this to mean that Islamic law only pertains to professed Muslims. If someone rejects Islam, he takes himself out of its legal system. In other words, if punishment cannot ultimately yield forgiveness, it should not apply (see Fazlur Rahman, "The Law of Rebellion in Islam," in *Islam in the Modern World,* ed. Jill Raitt [University of Missouri–Columbia, 1983 Paine Lectures in Religion], p. 2).

11. See R. Hrair Dekmejian's compilation of the names of ninety Islamic organizations in *Islam and Revolution: Fundamentalism in the Arab World* (Syracuse, NY: Syracuse University Press, 1985), Appendix I.

12. See, for instance, Sir Sayyid Ahmad Khan, *Review on Dr. Hunter's Indian Musulmans: Are They Bound in Conscience to Rebel Against the Queen?* (Benares: Medical Hall Press, 1872); Syed Ameer Ali, *A Critical Examination*

of the Life and Teachings of Mohammed (London: Williams and Norgate, 1873); and Muhammad 'Abduh, *al-Islam wa'l-Nasraniyya* (Cairo, 1367/1847–1848).

13. Rudolph Peters (*Islam and Colonialism: The Doctrine of Jihad in Modern History* (The Hague: Mouton Publishers, 1979), p. 195 n. 58) cited Rashid Rida's "al-Jihad fi'l-Islam" in *al-Manar* 15 (1912):35.

14. Hasan al-Banna, "Risalat al-Jihad," in *Majmu'at Rasa'il al-Imam al-Shahid Hasan al-Banna'* (Beirut: Dar al-Nur, n.d.), p. 58; cited by Peters, *Islam and Colonialism,* p. 193 n. 39.

15. Sayyid Qutb, *Fi Zilal al-Qur'an* (Beirut: Dar al-Shuruq, 1977), Vol. 10, p. 117; cited by Muhammad Tawfiq Barakat, Sayyid Qutb (Beirut: Dar al-Da'wa, n.d.), p. 64.

16. Sayyid Qutb, *Fi'l-Ta'rikh: Fikrah wa Minhaj* (Beirut: Dar al-Shuruq, 1974), pp. 18–19.

17. Ibid., pp. 310–11.

18. See Michael Yousef, *Revolt Against Modernity: Muslim Zealots and the West* (Leiden: E. J. Brill, 1985), p. 177.

19. Abu'l-A'la Mawdudi, *Al-Jihad fi Sabil Allah* (Beirut: Dar al-Fikr, n.d.), pp. 27–28.

20. Ibid., pp. 12–13.

21. Ibid., p. 13.

22. Imam Khomeini, "The Form of Islamic Government," in *Islam and Revolution,* tr. Hamid Algar (Berkeley, CA: Mizan Press, 1981), p. 116; and Imam Khomeini, "Program for the Establishment of an Islamic Government," in *Islam and Revolution,* p. 132.

23. Imam Khomeini, "Legal Rulings," in *Islam and Revolution,* p. 438.

24. Ibid., p. 440; cf. p. 331.

25. This shift of the Arab League's focus away from the plight of the Palestinians no doubt accounts for the origin of the *intifadeh*—the uprising within the Occupied Territories representing the Palestinians' frustration with Arab leaders' failure to rescue them and their consequent attempt to take matters into their own hands. It is no coincidence that the uprising began less than a month after the Amman summit.

26. Reported by Michael Jansen, "Desecration of the Hajj," *Middle East International* 306 (Aug. 1987):4.

27. Reported by Tom Porteous, "Khomeini's Sympathizers," *Middle East International* 306 (Aug. 1987):8.

28. Robert W. Carlyle and A. J. Carlyle, *A History of Medieval Political Theory in the West,* Vol. 5 (London: Blackwood, 1928), p. 208; cited by Joseph R. Strayer, "The Historical Experience of Nation-Building in Europe," in *Nation Building,* ed. Karl W. Deutsch and William J. Foltz (New York: Atherton Press, 1963), p. 31.

Chapter Nine

1. Alasdair Drysdale and Gerald H. Blake, *The Middle East and North Africa: A Political Geography* (New York and Oxford: Oxford University Press, 1985), p. 104.

2. Fazlur Rahman, *Islam and Modernity: Transformation of an Intellectual Tradition* (Chicago and London: University of Chicago Press, 1982), p. 86.

3. This summary of Sa'udi history is taken from James P. Piscatori, "Ideological Politics in Sa'udi Arabia," in *Islam in the Political Process,* ed. and comp. James P. Piscatori (Cambridge: Cambridge University Press, 1983), pp. 56–72.

4. James P. Piscatori, *Islam in a World of Nation-States* (Cambridge: Cambridge University Press, 1986), pp. 110, 83.

5. Hasan al-Turabi, "The Islamic State," in *Voices of Resurgent Islam,* ed. John L. Esposito (New York: Oxford University Press, 1983), p. 248.

6. Richard P. Mitchell, "The Islamic Movement: Its Current Condition and Future Prospects," in *The Islamic Impulse,* ed. Barbara Freyer Stowasser (London and Sydney: Croom Helm/Washington, DC: Center for Contemporary Arab Studies, 1987), p. 79.

7. Albert Hourani, "Conclusion," in James P. Piscatori, ed., *Islam in the Political Process* (Cambridge: Cambridge University Press, 1983), p. 227.

8. Mona Makram-Ebeid, "Political Opposition in Egypt: Democratic Myth or Reality?" in *The Middle East Journal,* Vol. 43, No. 3(Summer 1989):432.

9. Hasan Hanafi, "The Relevance of the Islamic Alternative in Egypt," Arab Studies Quarterly," Vol. 4, Nos. 1 and 2 (Spring 1982):61–74. Other important works by Hasan Hanafi include *Al-Turath wa'l-Tajdid: Mawqifuna min al-Turath al-Qadim* (Beirut: Dar al-Tanwir, 1981); and *Dirasat Islamiyya* (Beirut: Dar al-Tanwir, 1982). For an interesting discussion of Hanafi's work, see Issa J. Boullata, *Trends and Issues in Contemporary Arab Thought* (Albany: State University of New York Press, 1990), pp. 40–45.

10. See Muhammad 'Abid al-Jabiri, *Al-Khitab al-'Arabi al-Mu'asir: Dirasa Tahliliyya Naqdiyya* (Beirut: Dar al-Tali'a, 1982); cited by Boullata, *Trends and Issues,* p. 47.

11. Hasan Sa'b, *Al-Islam Tujah Tahadiyyat al-Haya al-'Asriyya* (Beirut: Dar al-Adab, 1965) and Hasan Sa'b, *Tahdith al-'Aql al-'Arabi: Dirasat hawl al-Thawra al-Thaqafiyya al-Lazima li'l-Taqaddumal-Arabi fi'l-'Asr al-Hadith* (Beirut: Dar al-'Ilm li'l-Malayin, 1972), pp. 86–88; cited by Boullata, *Trends and Issues,* p. 72.

12. See Leonard Binder, *Islamic Liberalism: A Critique of Development Ideologies* (Chicago and London: The University of Chicago Press, 1988), esp. Chapter 7.

13. 'Ali Shari'ati, *Islam Shinasi* (Meshad: n.p., 1347/1978), pp. 75–76. Abdulaziz Sachedina, tr., "Ali Shari'ati: Ideologue of the Iranian Revolution" in *Voices of Islamic Resurgence,* ed. John L. Esposito (New York: Oxford University Press, 1983), p. 200.

14. Ibid., pp. 83–87; English tr., p. 201.

15. See *Imam Khomeini's Last Will and Testament,* Embassy of the Democratic and Popular Republic of Algeria: Interests Section of the Islamic Republic of Iran, 1989.

16. Reported by Scheharazade Daneshku, *Middle East International,* 357 (25 Aug. 1989):17.

17. Safa Haeri, "Iran: Behind the Football Riots," *Middle East International,* 370 (2 March 1990):15.

18. Rudolph Peters, *Islam and Colonialism: The Doctrine of Jihad in Modern History* (The Hague, Paris: Mouton Publishers, 1979), p. 140. See also James P. Piscatori, *Islam in a World of Nation-States* (Cambridge: Cambridge Univerity Press, 1986), p. 42.

19. Peters, *Islam and Colonialism,* p. 164.

20. Ibid.

21. Safa Haeri, "Syria: Set to Topple Assad," *Middle East International,* 370 (2 March 1990):13.

22. Quoted from "The Movement of the Islamic Tendency in Tunisia: The Facts," prepared by the Islamic Society of North America and North African Students for Freedom of Action, 1377 K Street, Washington, DC 20005 (Sept. 1987), p. 99.

About the Book and Author

The struggle for political legitimacy in many Middle Eastern countries today poses a dilemma for ruling elites. In order to maintain authority, leaders often must capitulate to Islamic universalist dogma, which may conflict with their own views of the state as well as threaten the legitimacy of other leaders in the region who are attempting to establish a secular, national basis for government.

Tracing the roots of this dilemma in Middle Eastern history and Islamic philosophy, Dr. Sonn compares the contemporary Middle Eastern period to Europe's "Age of Religious Wars" that preceded the emergence of the Western secular state. She describes how a process similar to the organic development of the secular state in Europe was interrupted in the Middle East by oppressive Western colonialism, which eventually led to the Muslim rejection of nationalism and all things "Western" and to the reassertion of Islam as the sole source of political legitimacy. The author shows how the philosophy of Islamic traditionalism opposes the two fundamentals of stable national political systems— a geographical limitation of authority and an institutionalized process for regular changes in leadership. Dr. Sonn bases her argument on an insightful examination of Middle Eastern history, from the formation and disintegration of the Ottoman Empire in the late nineteenth century to the present, and caps it with a detailed look at a possible solution to the dilemma: the teachings of modern scholars who advocate a new "Islamic realism" incorporating a limited definition of national identity and interests while retaining Islamic social goals.

Tamara Sonn is director of the International Studies Program at St. John Fisher College, Rochester, New York. She is the author of numerous articles on Islamic political thought.

Index

255